P9-DNA-381

Praise for I'll BE WATCHING YOU

"This tale skillfully balances a victim's story against that of an arrogant killer as it reveals a deviant mind intent on topping the world's most dangerous criminals. Phelps has an unrelenting sense for detail that affirms his place, book by book, as one of our most engaging crime journalists."

—Dr. Katherine Ramsland, author of *The Human Predator*

Praise for MURDER IN THE HEARTLAND

"Drawing on interviews with law officers and relatives, *Murder in the Heartland* will interest anyone who has followed the Stinnett case. The author has done significant research and—demonstrating how modern forensics and the Internet played critical, even unexpected roles in the investigation—his facile writing pulls the reader along."

—*St. Louis Post-Dispatch*

"Phelps uses a unique combination of investigative skills and narrative insight to give readers an exclusive, insider's look into the events surrounding this incredible, high-profile American tragedy. . . . He has written a compassionate, riveting true crime masterpiece."

—Anne Bremner, op-ed columnist and legal analyst on Court TV, MSNBC, *Nancy Grace*, FOX News Channel, *The O'Reilly Factor,* CNN, *Good Morning America,* and *The Early Show*

"When unimaginable horror strikes, it is certain to cause monstrous sufferings, regardless of its locale. In *Murder in the Heartland*, M. Williams Phelps expertly reminds us that when the darkest form of evil invades the quiet and safe outposts of rural America, the tragedy is greatly magnified. Get ready for some sleepless nights."

—Carlton Stowers, Edgar Award–winning author of *Careless Whispers, Scream at the Sky,* and *To the Last Breath*

"This is the most disturbing and moving look at murder in rural America since Capote's *In Cold Blood*."

—Gregg Olsen, *New York Times* bestselling author of *Abandoned Prayers*

"A crisp, no-nonsense account . . . masterful."

—*Bucks County Courier Times*

"An unflinching investigation . . . Phelps explores this tragedy with courage, insight, and compassion."

—*Lima News* (Lima, OH)

Praise for SLEEP IN HEAVENLY PEACE

"An exceptional book by an exceptional true crime writer. In *Sleep in Heavenly Peace*, M. William Phelps exposes long-hidden secrets and reveals disquieting truths. Page by page, Phelps skillfully probes the disturbed mind of a mother guilty of the ultimate betrayal."

—Kathryn Casey, author of *She Wanted It All* and *A Warrant to Kill*

Praise for EVERY MOVE YOU MAKE

"An insightful and fast-paced examination of the inner workings of a good cop and his bad informant culminating in an unforgettable truth-is-stranger-than-fiction climax."

—Michael M. Baden, M.D., author of *Unnatural Death*

"M. William Phelps is the rising star of the nonfiction crime genre, and his true tales of murderers and mayhem are scary-as-hell thrill rides into the dark heart of the inhuman condition."

—Douglas Clegg, author of *The Lady of Serpents*

Praise for LETHAL GUARDIAN

"An intense roller-coaster of a crime story. Phelps' book *Lethal Guardian* is at once complex, with a plethora of twists and turns worthy of any great detective mystery, and yet so well-laid out, so crisply written with such detail to character and place that it reads more like a novel than your standard non-fiction crime book."

—*New York Times* bestselling author Steve Jackson

Praise for PERFECT POISON

"*Perfect Poison* is a horrific tale of nurse Kristen Gilbert's insatiable desire to kill the most helpless of victims—her own patients. A stunner from beginning to end, Phelps renders the story expertly, with flawless research and an explosive narrative. Phelps unravels the devastating case against nurse Kristen Gilbert and shockingly reveals that unimaginable evil sometimes comes in pretty packages."

—Gregg Olsen, bestselling author of *Abandoned Prayers, Mockingbird,* and *If Loving You Is Wrong*

"M. William Phelps's *Perfect Poison* is true crime at its best—compelling, gripping, an edge-of-the-seat thriller. All the way through, Phelps packs wallops of delight with his skillful ability to narrate a suspenseful story and his encyclopedic knowledge of police procedures. *Perfect Poison* is the perfect antidote for a dreary night!"

—Harvey Rachlin, author of *The Making of a Detective* and *The Making of a Cop*

"A compelling account of terror that only comes when the author dedicates himself to unmasking the psychopath with facts, insight, and the other proven methods of journalistic leg work."

—Lowell Cauffiel, bestselling author of *House of Secrets*

"A blood-curdling page turner and a meticulously researched study of the inner recesses of the mind of a psychopathic narcissist."

—Sam Vaknin, author of *Malignant Self Love—Narcissism Revisited*

Also by M. William Phelps

I'll Be Watching You

Perfect Poison

Lethal Guardian

Every Move You Make

Sleep in Heavenly Peace

Murder in the Heartland

Because You Loved Me

If Looks Could Kill

Deadly Secrets

Published by Kensington Publishing Corporation

CRUEL DEATH

M. WILLIAM PHELPS

P

PINNACLE BOOKS
Kensington Publishing Corp.
http://www.kensingtonbooks.com

Some names have been changed to protect the privacy of individuals connected to this story.

PINNACLE BOOKS are published by

Kensington Publishing Corp.
119 West 40th Street
New York, NY 10018

Copyright © 2009 by M. William Phelps

All rights reserved. No part of this book may be reproduced in any form or by any means without the prior written consent of the Publisher, excepting brief quotes used in reviews.

If you purchased this book without a cover you should be aware that this book is stolen property. It was reported as "unsold and destroyed" to the Publisher and neither the Author nor the Publisher has received any payment for this "stripped book."

All Kensington Titles, Imprints, and Distributed Lines are available at special quantity discounts for bulk purchases for sales promotions, premiums, fund-raising, and educational or institutional use. Special book excerpts or customized printings can also be created to fit specific needs. For details, write or phone the office of the Kensington special sales manager: Kensington Publishing Corp., 119 West 40th Street, New York, NY 10018, attn: Special Sales Department, Phone: 1-800-221-2647.

Pinnacle and the P logo Reg. U.S. Pat. & TM Off.

ISBN-13: 978-0-7860-1932-8
ISBN-10: 0-7860-1932-8

First Printing: July 2009

10 9 8 7 6 5 4 3 2 1

Printed in the United States of America

For Peter Miller, the roaring literary lion.

Acknowledgments

Thank you . . .

Deborah Dawkins, Donna Dudek, Amanda Evans, and everyone else at Jupiter Entertainment. Deb, Donna, and Amanda were extremely helpful to me during the early stages of considering this case for a book, introducing me to the right people, and pointing me in the right direction.

The Ocean City Police Department (OCPD) as a whole was incredibly obliging. Several detectives opened up their lives and made this book truly what it is. I can never thank them enough for their time, input, expertise, and commitment. Scott Bernal and Brett Case were always willing to answer my questions, even when those answers did not suit their own needs; and that, to me, shows immense integrity and honesty. Scott Bernal inspired me in ways I could never explain. He is one of the most candid, passionate, dedicated lawmen I have ever met. Finally, great appreciation to OCPD chief Bernadette DiPino for allowing her detectives to speak with me about this case.

Kensington editor Mike Shohl and copy editor Stephanie Finnegan.

I dedicated this book to my agent, Peter Miller, president of PMA Literary & Film Management. Peter has been championing my career for years, and any success I achieve would not be possible (or worth much to me) without his guidance and friendship. Likewise, without the help of Peter's assistant, Adrienne Rosado—well, I would be far less efficient.

Of course, none of this would be possible without my editor, Michaela Hamilton, who has been by my side for all ten books, or my family.

Law without a foundation in morality becomes injustice.

—Joseph Cardinal Ratzinger (Pope Benedict XVI),
The Spirit of the Liturgy

Author's Note

Throughout my years of writing true crime, I've always drifted away from the more gruesome cases. Granted, every murder is an act of evil; every untimely death a tragedy. But I have not waded in terribly bloody waters, if you will excuse my frankness. I have generally written about those murders we tend not to cringe at—those deaths that have been quick and rather painless.

That being said, as I began this book, I knew it would involve a certain amount of horror I had not yet covered: the brutal dismemberment of two human beings. What I *didn't* know was that this act of savagery by the killers was only the tip of the iceberg. What I would uncover while researching and writing this book—some of which has not been yet reported—affected me in ways I had never experienced, in all my years reporting on murder. There were times when I had to leave the book alone for a day or two to catch my breath and think about things. Now and then, as you write these books day in and day out, you can get caught up to a point where some of what you're doing doesn't seem real. Sure, I used dozens of interviews, thousands of pages of court records, trial transcripts, photographs, police reports, military reports, depositions, interviews with the perpetrators, and scores of other documents to write this book. A process of which becomes, at times, like putting together the pieces of a puzzle. But here, within this case, the way the victims were treated before, during, and after death was so profoundly evil and cruel—there are not enough adjectives in the English language to describe the treatment these people received—that as I wrote about it, a part of me began to drift into a despair

I had not experienced while writing true crime. It made for an incredibly bumpy experience—emotionally. There were days when I had to put this project aside—due to the graphic nature of what I had uncovered—and work on something else. There were also days when I thought I could not go back to it.

In the end, though, I am glad I did.

There are sections of this book family members of the victims should not read—parts of this case that were never made public. For some time, I weighed whether to include all of my findings in the text. I have left things out of this book that were not important to the story, the dynamic of understanding these crimes, or the psyche of the murderers. I wish certain things in this case did not happen and I didn't have to report them. As a reporter, however, I believe that what I have included is imperative to the greater scope of these crimes; it allows us to take a deeper look into the most evil part of the human soul in order to recognize what some people are truly capable of.

My goal is always to tell the most complete, unreported story I can. In addition, it is a story that needs telling. If one person reads this book and understands that the strangers we meet at clubs and bars and out in society at various places and stages of our lives every day might not be who they claim to be, it was well worth the effort.

Part 1

Memories Are Like Raindrops

1

Ebb & Flow

It was midmorning, May 29, 2002, when Ocean City Police Department (OCPD) detective Scott Bernal took a call from Fairfax City, Virginia, police officer Mike Boone. Fairfax City was a good three-and-a-half-hour hike from Ocean City on a good day, without traffic. Although the OCPD routinely received calls from various police departments for different reasons, Detective Bernal sensed right away that this call had a different smell to it. Something, his gut instinct told him, was amiss.

"We have a woman whose coworkers are reporting [her] missing," Boone said. "This woman never misses a meeting, apparently. She had a meeting scheduled with fifteen coworkers for yesterday at ten. She didn't show up or call."

"She came here?" Bernal asked, meaning Ocean City.

"Yeah, with her boyfriend. I called his employer. He hasn't returned to work, either—and should have on the same day."

Bernal took down a description of the couple's vehicle.

It was a red or maroon Acura with the recognizable license tag that few would have a tough time forgetting: GENEY C.

"Where are they staying?"

Boone said, "Atlantis Condominium."

"Let me check it out."

Bernal finished up what he was doing at the station house in midtown Ocean City and took off down the strip to check out the Atlantis.

There is a repetitive, soothing, and rhythmic flow to the steadiness and cyclical nature of ocean waves. No matter how high or low the tide, waves begin from an unknown, initial source out in the middle of the sea and ripple into shorelines around the world at a continuous, melodic pace, speeding up and slowing down. One can sit for hours and become mesmerized by their sheer beauty and elegance, while getting lost in the meditative genuineness, sound, feel, and even smell of simple seawater lapping against beach sand. Perhaps a gull or two squeaking in the remote background adds to the ambiance. But ask those who live for it, and you'll hear about an unexplainable grace assigned to the ocean that they all crave: the one place where your troubles seem to melt into the salty foam left over along the shoreline after the baptismal power of the water fades into the wet sand.

How healing.

How omnipotent.

How uncomplicated.

Ocean City, Maryland, is one of those places along the East Coast where one can indulge in such summer splendor and magnificence. For some, though, mainly the younger crowd, Ocean City is more of "Party Town, USA," where you can let your hair down when the sun sets, violently crack crab legs with wooden mallets, and party at any one of the scores of nightclubs and seaside bars located along "the strip," or as Random McNally deems it, "the Coastal Highway." In fact, the one day of the year that almost every bar owner, resort keeper, hotel manager, and seasonal worker waits for is the Friday before Memorial Day. This is the day when summer unofficially begins, and tourists and beachgoers and partiers and graduates start filing into town: to spend money, sun themselves, dance, drink, eat, and hang out poolside. Interestingly, between Labor Day (September) and Memorial Day (May), Ocean City is home to about twenty-five thousand people. Just a normal community of working-class folks, who love living by the sea. Yet between those two summer holidays, the number of people fluctuates from 250,00 to 500,000, depending on weekend weather.

Thus, the summer season becomes the time of the year in Ocean City that perhaps only one group of professionals in the region do *not* look forward to: the OCPD, which itself doubles in size during this same period.

2

Intuition

OCPD detective Scott Bernal did not always see himself as a cop in Ocean City, Maryland. The Brooklyn-born, Queens-bred transplant had followed family down into what he calls "good old boy" country, where it's not at all that easy to fit in. Still, at about six feet, 220 solid pounds, the stocky detective with the unmatched New "Yawk" accent had weathered the licks his adversaries had tossed at him, putting together a solid record as a hungry detective looking to serve the community. It was that veteran, seasoned experience prowling Ocean City's streets and solving cases for all those years that led Bernal to believe that something had happened to the missing female from Fairfax City. Not necessarily her boyfriend, but for the woman—Bernal sensed something was out of place.

As Bernal pulled onto 103rd Street, 10300 Coastal Highway, and saw the maroon Acura with GENEY C on the license plate just sitting there by itself in the parking lot of the Atlantis Condominium complex, he had a sinking feeling about the situation. It was the way the car was parked. Bernal could tell it hadn't been driven for quite a while. Beyond that, every parking space in the front of the building was empty—except for the last space, where that maroon Acura was just sitting. There was nothing all that peculiar about it. It was just the car's presence, Bernal said later. It spoke to him. That same uneasy feeling you get sometimes when you walk into your home and you just *know* someone has been inside.

As Bernal got out and checked around the outside of the vehicle, he could tell it hadn't been moved. The tires alone had sediment and leaves and sand on all sides.

What's going on here? Bernal considered.

So he called in for another officer to accompany him into the condo itself. He didn't want to enter the room alone. He needed someone with him, just in case he ran into a situation.

Born exactly one week and nineteen years apart, nearly two decades of life and experience had separated thirty-two-year-old Joshua Ford and his fifty-one-year-old live-in girlfriend, Martha Margene "Geney" Crutchley. Yet, that division of time did little to diminish the love and respect they shared for each other. Joshua and Geney liked to have fun, but at the same time they were committed to their devotion to each other. Photographs of them depict what appears to be an old married couple lapping up the wonder years of their lives together, planting trees and making faces into the camera lens, raking leaves in the yard of the spacious Fairfax City home they shared, or just sitting, holding each other in supple grace that a park bench brings, happy in the delicate way love had entered and then *changed* their lives.

Joshua and Geney met at a Christmas party in Boston in 1999, but they had lived together since April 2001 in a modest home in a suburban Virginia hamlet located just on the outside boundary of the Beltway in Washington, DC. Joshua had been torn by love once already; he had a six-year-old son he adored, born from a first marriage, and an ex-wife who spoke nothing but good things about him. They liked each other still, Joshua and his ex-wife. It was just that their marriage, a high-school romance, wasn't in the cards, and they understood love's way. Still, Joshua's "whole world," a family friend later told a newspaper reporter, "spun around" his son, and his ex-wife allowed him to see the child anytime he wanted.

For Joshua, a mortgage banker, and Geney, an insurance executive accountant working with a company in Chantilly, Virginia, there was never a second thought when it came to dropping everything, leaving the fast-paced pool of economics they swam in all week, and, on a Friday after work, heading off to the beach. Living near such an abundance of ocean real estate, the hardest part about planning a weekend getaway was choosing the spot. In some respects, the move to Virginia for Joshua, away from most of his family in Boston, had been a reprieve. Just last year, in October 2001, a terrible tragedy had struck the Ford family. Joshua's brother, Mark Ford, got a call from law enforcement that his twenty-three-year-old daughter, Kelly, who had been missing for eighty days after leaving a Massachusetts rehabilitation center, and never being heard from again, had been found. Her headless body, buried in a shallow grave along the Cape Cod shoreline, was discovered by a passerby. Her heart had been cut out. Police had no suspects in the murder, but suspected the murder to be the work of a serial killer. Mark Ford and his wife Deb, like Joshua and the rest of the family, had been left to wonder what animal would do such a thing to an otherwise beautiful, helpless, innocent young woman with so much life ahead of her. But the Ford family went on in the face of such heartbreak. Lived life. Loved one another. Carried on best they could.

It was Saturday, May 25, 2002, just four days before Detective Scott Bernal took that call about Geney, when Joshua and Geney decided to take their first weekend trip of the new summer season to Ocean City, a 175-mile journey due east of their Virginia home. It was a long trip, but then Memorial Day weekend was the first blowout of the summer year, and, like many, they had an extra day off. Both had been expected back at work on Tuesday, May 28. In fact, Geney had that planned meeting, which Officer Mike Boone had mentioned to Bernal, scheduled with her staff at ten o'clock that morning. Geney and Joshua had planned a relaxing weekend together. They could party a little, sun themselves, eat some great seafood, then hit the road late on Monday afternoon after all the holiday weekend traffic had somewhat dissipated.

As Bernal waited for a fellow officer before going into Geney's room, he spoke to a manager on duty. It appeared that Joshua had rented the room at the Atlantis, a twenty-story high-rise located directly on the beach at 103rd Street, smack in the middle of the "strip," with the Atlantic Ocean on one side and postcard bay views on the other. In walking distance from the Atlantis was the Coastal Highway, where any number of nightclubs and bars and seafood and steak house restaurants were dotting the strip. It was the perfect location to celebrate summer.

Mini golf.

Batting cages.

Moped, bicycle, and boogie board rentals.

T-shirt factory outlets.

Taffy stores.

The popular restaurant chain Hooters was down the block, as was the glorious Rainbow Condominiums, with the Seacrets nightspot a five-minute, two-mile ride, or half hour walk south. Traveling throughout the resort town, however, was not going to be a problem: just a small fare allows you to ride the bus anywhere you want to go. And if you were planning on drinking, the bus was a smart move. DUI and other alcohol-related arrests made up a large percentage of summer citations and court appearances.

When OCPD officer Brian Brown showed up at the Atlantis, Bernal and Brown were let into the unit Geney and Joshua had rented. Bernal knew that Joshua and Geney should have left Ocean City already. There was no reason, so late in the week, that they should have been still hanging around town. Then there was Geney's car. Just sitting there by itself in the visitor's parking space, alone.

"Strange," Bernal said as they made their way up to the room. "Something doesn't sound right."

Normally, Bernal would have handed this case off to a patrol officer and moved on to more pressing things. But something, he later said, had brought him to the Atlantis and tugged at him. What it was that dragged him down there would become evident in the days and weeks to come; but for now, Bernal was going with it.

Bernal walked into the room with Brown and found all of Joshua and Geney's personal belongings still where they had left them. They weren't packed up or even collected in any sort of natural order. It appeared, in fact, as though Joshua had been working. There was a computer and some documents scattered about a table. Geney's camera was there on the counter. All their clothes. It was as if Geney and Joshua had gone out and not returned—or had been plucked out of the room somehow.

Bernal spied a purse on one of the beds and walked over to it. Without touching it, he saw an ID of Geney sitting on top. There was a half-smoked cigar in an ashtray on the coffee table. Next to that was what appeared to be a small amount of marijuana.

Walking throughout the unit, Bernal spotted something that, to him, spoke volumes. There were two wineglasses on the table. The liquid levels in the glasses were different. Next to those wineglasses were two other glasses, which also had wine in them.

"Four people," Bernal said to himself. "Huh?"

Either they had visitors, or had met up with someone here in town.

Then Bernal checked the bathrooms. All of Geney and Joshua's toiletries were there: toothbrushes, shampoos, shaving things.

Bad sign.

Bernal flipped open his cell phone and called his captain, who was at home for the night already. "Listen," he said, "something's not right over here. We need to make this a crime scene immediately."

"Why, what's up?"

"Well, look, four glasses of wine, all their things are still there."

Bernal had also uncovered a receipt on a table. It listed all of the groceries Geney and Joshua had purchased on Saturday, May 25. He checked the refrigerator and cabinets. All of the items were still there, unopened, unused. No one had obviously been in the unit since Saturday.

"Don't worry about it," Bernal later said his captain

had told him during that call. "We'll go by there tomorrow and check it out."

"OK," Bernal said. "Will do." Then he sat for a moment after talking to his captain and thought about it. *They're dead.* "I never came out and said it," Bernal recalled, "but as a cop you just get a *feeling*—and I had this strong sense tugging at me while walking through that condo that these people, or one of them, were dead."

"Brian," Bernal said to the officer with him, "get some yellow crime-scene tape and secure this unit." Bernal found the manager and security detail for the condo. "No one goes in or out of that room," he told the manager. He was closing it off and—going over his boss's head—making it a crime scene.

"No problem, sir."

Bernal then called into the OCPD to get a tow truck out to impound Geney's car for safekeeping. When he returned to the OCPD a while later, he called the Delaware State Police (DSP), Maryland State Police (MSP), and "other police agencies," he said, "in two additional states. I also called the [medical examiner's] office in Delaware and Maryland. Then the deputy medical examiner. I called family members and friends. . . ."

But no one had heard from Geney and Joshua, and no agency had any record of two unidentified individuals being hurt or killed or arrested.

Like the morning mist along the coastline and famous Ocean City Boardwalk, Martha "Geney" Crutchley and Joshua Ford had seemingly disappeared into the magnificent Maryland sunset.

3

Backtracking

On May 25, 2002, three days before Detective Scott Bernal was actively pursuing the missing persons case of Geney Crutchley, Geney was in the Atlantis condo bathroom getting ready to go out, when Joshua Ford called his brother, Mark.

"How 'bout those Celtics?" Joshua beamed.

The team had come from behind earlier that night and pulled one out.

"Yeah, can you believe they did it!" Mark said. It was good to hear Joshua's voice. He sounded relaxed. Happy to be with Geney at the beach. The guy worked hard. He deserved a break.

"Unbelievable win," Joshua said excitedly.

"You havin' a good time?" Mark asked, knowing the answer. As brothers, they were close.

"Yeah," Joshua said, "it's great here."

After moving to Boston from Iowa, a 1989 graduate of Kennedy High School in Cedar Rapids, Joshua was schooled, you could say, in "Southie," a popular section of Boston known for its rough streets and ties to James "Whitey" Bulger and his gang of crooks and thieves. An avid sports fan, Joshua was forever analyzing the Boston Celtics' performance. Any Southie transplant was a Celtic, Rex Sox, and Bruin fan; if not, you'd get your arse handed to you for talking down about any of the teams.

Mark was exhausted. He had worked a twelve-hour shift that day and just wanted to plop himself down on the couch, zone out with the remote control and some television, and then fall asleep. He could speak to Joshua anytime.

"I'm tired. . . . Call me back," Mark told his brother.

Joshua understood. "I'll talk to you soon. Get some rest."

Outside their condo, Joshua and Geney waited for the bus. It was dusk. A beautiful picture, really. The sun rose on one side of the strip and set on the other. On clear nights, like this one, it projected a reddish orange glow throughout the town that spoke of God's wholesome grace. Standing, staring out at the scene, one couldn't help but notice or deny there was some sort of Maker out there pushing celestial buttons, turning out these magical landscape settings.

Getting on the bus, Joshua and Geney sat in the front. They'd be drinking tonight, so why chance it and drive? Moreover, buses weren't any problem for Joshua. During college, Joshua wanted to be by his best friend's side, so he followed him to historic Norfolk State University, in Virginia, which has been a traditionally black college. In fact, riding the bus on campus, Joshua's mother, Doris, later told the (Salisbury, Maryland) *Daily Times* that Joshua was the only white person. The first time, Joshua didn't even have a seat, so he sat on the floor. "By the end of the trip," Doris told *Daily Times* reporter Anita Ferguson, "they all knew his name."

It took about two minutes to travel a few blocks south, down to 11200 Coastal Highway, outside the Rainbow Condominium, where the bus always stopped to pick up people heading farther south. As the tired brakes of the bus squealed, Joshua and Geney looked up to see a young couple standing, waiting there, at the stop.

"Exact change," the driver said when the couple stepped up onto the bus landing by the driver's seat. The man was tall and handsome. He looked drunk. The woman was petite, and stumbling around a bit herself.

They didn't look happy.

"What do you have on you?" the man asked the woman with him. He was a good foot taller. He had short cropped black hair, nearly a buzz cut. Solid build. He had either worked out regularly, or was in some line of work that had kept him in shape.

A black belt in karate, a solid, firmly built Joshua sat and watched the couple get on the bus and begin a conversation with the driver. As they stood, the man seemed impatient. Come to find out, he and his wife had just left Hooters, directly across the street. They'd had two pitchers of beer and two plates of hot wings. Drinking throughout much of the day, popping pills, hanging out in the sun, the beers and drugs had finally gotten to them. Both were seemingly wasted.

"All I have is a five-dollar bill," the man slurred to the bus driver.

"Exact change, sorry—"

"Does anybody have change for a five?" the man yelled to the audience on the bus, obviously hoping someone would come forward. He sounded groggy.

Joshua sat, listening to what was going on. There was a part of Joshua Ford that wanted to help everyone. He couldn't hide from it or keep it contained. It was who he was as a human being. He had been involved in Salvation

Army youth programs, worked with kids in his karate classes throughout the years, and had no trouble reaching out a helping hand to strangers. It was an innate unselfishness. What could the man do? He couldn't help himself from helping others.

"Are you two going to Seacrets?" Joshua spoke up and asked. Really, who on the bus *wasn't* going to Seacrets? It was only the most popular nightspot on this part of the strip.

The man looked at his wife.

She shrugged.

"Yeah," the man said.

"Sit down . . . ," Josh started to say, "I'll get it." He handed the driver the money for the bus fare.

"I'll buy you a drink when we get to the bar," the man said.

The man and woman sat down in an empty seat next to Geney and Joshua. Geney looked over and smiled. Geney had such a dominant beam about her. It was genuine and infectious. She wasn't smiling at the stranger to be nice; she was content. She meant it from her heart. Her man was helping out a couple of strangers. Truthfully, it was Joshua that Geney was so happy about. How lucky they were to have each other.

"Erika," the small stranger said, introducing herself to Geney. "That's my husband, Beej . . . BJ. Benjamin."

It was Erika with a *K*.

"I'm Geney. This is Josh."

4

Moving Forward

Not having any luck locating Joshua or Geney, on the following morning, May 30, Detective Scott Bernal arrived to work early. This was a major shock not only to Bernal, but many of his colleagues.

One of the reasons Bernal was in earlier than normal was to see if his supervisor, Detective Richard Moreck, would take a ride over to the Atlantis with him and come to the same conclusion about Geney and Joshua.

Something had gnawed at Bernal all night long. Pulled at him as he poured himself a cup of coffee and drove into work. There was an inner voice telling him to keep the pressure up on the case and follow his instincts. It would end up costing Bernal his job in the end, and a lot of internal problems, but there was a force, he later explained, bigger than the case or anyone involved, driving it forward. There was little he could do to stop it. He didn't want his feelings to sound strange, abnormally paranormal, celestial, or crystal ball–like, but there was a sense, an aura, something larger than life, bigger than him or anyone else working the case, surrounding the things he and the other detectives were doing early on, which made every move seem like the right thing to do.

A colleague of Bernal's agreed with this. "It was bigger than us."

At his desk early, Bernal prepared a missing persons flyer. He had a photograph of Geney and Joshua, which the City of Fairfax Police Department (FPD) had e-mailed him. In the photo, Geney and Joshua were sitting in a restaurant, smiling into the camera. They looked happy. Pleased to be in each other's company. The flyer said the OCPD had "seized" the couple's condominium unit. By this point, detectives had searched the room more thoroughly. Bernal's boss, Detective Moreck, had located a second receipt on one of the tables inside the room and immediately called for the OCPD's forensic team to respond.

The receipt was from the Greene Turtle, a local sports bar. The receipt was dated May 25, 9:25 P.M., which put Geney and Joshua in town on that night; the grocery receipt Bernal had found was from earlier on that same night. Whatever happened, possibly took place shortly after they left the Greene Turtle. But they were definitely active on that night, Bernal now considered.

Bernal and Moreck took a ride over to the Greene Turtle with the photograph and several copies of the flyer.

"I don't recognize them," said the daytime manager, handing Bernal the flyer back. "But they were here at night." The receipt, the manager confirmed, put them in the lounge area of the restaurant. "We have surveillance cameras all over the place. We probably have them on tape."

Bernal got the night manager on the telephone, who said he remembered the couple based on what they had eaten. He also said, "We have a videotape of the inside of the restaurant, including the entrance."

Bernal and Moreck watched part of the video for the night and verified that Geney and Joshua had been in the restaurant. There they were, casually eating, drinking, and watching the Celtics game, like a thousand or more other couples that would pass through town throughout the summer season. They were having a good time. Just being plain old Americans on vacation.

"Thanks," Bernal said. "We'll be in touch."

Bernal hung a missing persons flyer on the front door of the bar and went back to the OCPD with Moreck.

At some point throughout the morning, Bernal had heard about Mark Ford's daughter, Joshua's niece, being the victim of a brutal unsolved murder. Bernal sat with a colleague, Detective Brett Case, a mountain of a man at six feet eight inches, about 250 pounds. Case, who had played football for the Maine Black Bears, was heading into his second decade as an OCPD cop. Case was something of a popular cop around the department, the kind of guy everyone liked and everyone went to for advice on all levels.

Case had heard of the missing couple over the past few days and also thought something didn't sound right, so he started conversing with Bernal, banging around ideas and theories. Now, with the information of Mark Ford's daughter being the victim of such an atrocious crime, Case and Bernal began to speculate that maybe things weren't what they seemed. Maybe Joshua wasn't the poster boy for traditional American values that he seemed to be. They had spoken to several of Geney's friends and Joshua's family members by now and had gotten a fairly good portrait of both Geney and Joshua. They were good, hardworking people. Joshua didn't have a blemish to his record. Heck, even his ex-wife had said great things about the guy.

"What about Joshua?" Bernal asked. They were in Bernal's office.

"I know," Case answered, shaking his head. It pained them, of course, to think it was possible. To think that Joshua had done something to Geney, especially after talking with friends and relatives and hearing how much they loved each other. That tape from the Greene Turtle proved they were close that night. Not at all at odds.

But Case and Bernal had been on the job long enough to know that people snapped. People could turn at the drop of a hat. A seemingly "nice guy" could be a vicious killer, and nobody would ever know it. Still, Case and Bernal were also smart enough to know that there was no reason to go broadcasting their theory to the families or the media.

But truth be told, Joshua Ford needed to be looked at more closely.

"I spoke to the families and friends," Bernal told Case. "I've learned some 'things' about Geney and Joshua and what they were getting into."

"Well, let's keep it to ourselves," Case said, "and continue looking."

5

New York
Born and Bred

Detective Scott Bernal spoke with what can only be described as a hybrid of a Queens, New "Yawk," accent flavored with a slight seasoning of living on the cusp of the South for the past fifteen years. For Bernal, it was the marine uniform he had seen a soldier wearing one day that spawned a burning desire to don it himself.

"It was a challenge," Bernal recalled of that time in high school when the bug of the military bit him. "I like challenges. That's all me."

Bernal was the first to admit that he was a streetwise, undisciplined kid from the streets of New York when he entered the U.S. Marines. Fighting and gangs were just a way of dealing with life on the streets of Queens. He'd punch and kick his way to school, trying to protect that dollar he kept in the bottom of his Chuck Taylor high-top Converse sneakers, which were often torn from his feet and stolen along with his lunch money. He dabbled in petty crimes. And then something happened.

It was 1977. Bernal and his family moved, from the city to, of all places, Germantown, upstate. Germantown Central High School. It was a culture shock. On his first day, he wore a Black Sabbath T-shirt. His new English teacher took one look at the shirt and sarcastically said, "Black Sabbath? What is that? The gang you were in?"

At first, Bernal thought she was kidding.

She wasn't.

It was tough adjusting from city life to the country. There was a little girl who used to live in the house the Bernals had purchased who started hanging around (she had moved behind the Bernal house). One day, she ran up to Bernal and his brother, Kevin, crying and screaming. "The Rochas are coming. . . . The Rochas are coming to get me." The girl was maybe eight years old. Kevin and Scott thought there was some sort of gang after the girl. Not knowing how many there were, Scott and Kevin went outside to confront and possibly fight them.

It turned out that the "Rochas" were nothing more than three dark-haired Italian sisters who walked from uptown to downtown to cause mischief. In the end, the Rochas were the biggest gang Germantown had to offer. Deanna, Geney, and Theresa Rocha turned out to be some of the best friends Scott and Kevin ever had.

Life changed for Bernal once he got inside the confines of the military. It took only a few days, he later said, and the marines broke the cocky, tough-guy attitude he had gone in with. "In a few days, all I was saying was 'Sir, yes, sir!'"

Bernal graduated from the marines on the corps' birthday celebration, November 10, 1981. Not only did he excel in the military, but he graduated honor man, a distinction he had never known to be achieved by any other military person he had met before. Upon graduation, Bernal traveled the world. Back in the States during the mid-1980s, having served the Marine Corps as a military policeman (MP) throughout much of his career, it wasn't such a tough decision for him when it came to choosing a more focused career path.

"I cannot say enough about my brother, Kevin, who was also in the Marine Corps," Bernal reflected, "as far as being an example to follow. . . . If it wasn't for [having] him to follow, I'd be dead or in jail. I credit him for me going into the Marine Corps, and then later for becoming a cop."

As Bernal began to learn more about Geney and Joshua, talking about the case with colleagues, more bizarre scenarios became possible, but not very probable. When you're a cop investigating a missing persons case involving adults, no theory is out of your wheelhouse. No end result too far-fetched to consider. For one, it was entirely plausible from a cop's viewpoint, as Bernal and his partner and colleague, Brett Case, had discussed at length, that Joshua had done something to Geney and then had taken off somewhere by himself—on the run, so to speak. Maybe there had been an accident and Joshua had panicked and booked to New Jersey or Georgia or Florida.

It all had to be checked out.

"This theory was nothing that we were sticking to or focusing exclusively on," Bernal said later (and Brett Case agreed), "but it was a possibility and it had to be looked into."

The OCPD began distributing missing persons flyers

to area businesses and police departments, hoping that some sort of information would send them in a direction. Any direction. Bernal faxed the flyer to several police departments in the local area of the OCPD, hoping to get some sort of hit or lead.

An anonymous tip.

Anything.

"Because right now, nothing is happening," Bernal said.

This was all about change, however, in a dramatic unfolding of events that no one could have predicted or ever seen coming.

"Divine intervention," Case said. Bernal nodded his head, agreeing. "Someone bigger than ourselves was helping us with this investigation. We *all* believed that."

"The things that happened," Bernal added, "should not have happened the way they did."

Every case for detectives has some sort of shit luck associated with it. But this missing persons case, Bernal and Case insisted, wasn't about luck.

"It was about someone upstairs," Case said, looking above, "helping us along the way, pointing things out to us."

The Criminal Investigation Division (CID) of the OCPD, as a working police force, had gone through some remarkable changes over the years. Two detectives, good guys who were great cops, Case and Bernal later said, had up and quit one day. Not because the job got to be too much. Or they had gotten better jobs somewhere else.

None of that had made a difference in these decisions.

Both had, in fact, been *called* into a new vocation, literally: the seminary.

Both detectives had left the department to become priests.

6

Third Wheel

During the summer of 1999, Virginia Beach, Virginia, was an exciting place to be for a kid born outside Roaring Spring, Pennsylvania, a small, working-class community of people who grew up in town and never left. By contrast, Virginia Beach was bright, cheerful, contemporary, full of kids and military families from all over the country. Tourists mingled about, looking for good times, while college kids frolicked on the beaches, drinking beers and playing volleyball; and what was mainly a blue-collar community of military families, looking to make a go of it in life, hummed along in the background.

During the summer of that year, twenty-one-year-old Erika Grace was in Virginia Beach, about 150 miles from her dorm at the University of Mary Washington in Fredericksburg, Virginia, sunning herself, having some fun in the sand with friends. Erika was all about looking her best, even if the image she had of herself—which she rarely shared—was flawed, corrupted, or disrupted in any way by her own issues of self-worth and lack of personal confidence. Whatever Erika did—be it basketball or her own business or her studies—was never good enough for her own needs; she always felt she could do better, do more and be more successful.

As a kid in Roaring Spring, Erika Grace was well-liked and thought of as someone who had been given things others were never going to get, said an old friend. One might expect that Erika, as an only child, had every opportunity handed to her, or maybe she was the "light" of her parents' eyes. Sure, the Graces had the big brick house, or "mansion," as Erika herself would later call it, with the plush green golf course grass, the nice cars in the driveway, and all the latest gadgets and "things" to keep up with the Joneses; but according to Erika years after she left college, "I always felt like the third wheel." It was her parents' attitude toward her, Erika explained to a government agent, that was hard to deal with. Erika's dad, Mitch Grace, was authoritative and intense where Erika's basketball potential was concerned, Erika suggested. Others placed Mitch in the caring and coddling mold—a father who gave his only daughter whatever she wanted, whenever she wanted it. Owning a business afforded Mitch the opportunity to tell people what to do. Erika's mother, Cookie, was the trophy wife in a certain way. She was pretty, like her daughter. Cookie could shop all day, if she chose, but instead wanted to be by Mitch's side. There was a bond between her parents so tightly wound, Erika later explained, that as the years passed, Erika felt she could never wiggle her way in between them. It was something that bothered Erika immensely, she said, and as she grew up, that confusion blossomed into full-blown resentment.

"My father lived for my mom," Erika later told a government agent interviewing her. "They had a close relationship." That connection was so strong, Erika went on to note, it "could not break."

During Erika's teen years, Mitch uprooted his family and moved them from Roaring Spring to Hollidaysburg, where he built what is a ten-room, two-story redbrick home with a swimming pool in the back and an indoor basketball court in the garage—all for three people. Erika wanted more playing time on the basketball court in school and on her AAU pickup team, and wasn't getting it in Roaring Spring. So instead of fighting with the coaches (which Mitch often did), he moved the family to a town where he knew Erika could get all the playing time she wanted.

"The other parents were always getting mad," said one of Erika's former teammates, "because she always had the most playing time. It wasn't fair."

In Hollidaysburg, things were much different. Mitch coached her team and stood, every night, on the balcony above the home basketball court as Erika shot free throws and practiced layups. He hired a coach to teach her moves that others were blown away by. Erika would work and work and work, Mitch later said, until she got the move exactly how her private coach had wanted it. Later, in letters to a friend, Erika called this private coach her "soul mate," saying that there was no other person in the world who understood her like this guy did.

On many nights, Mitch would spend hours rebounding for Erika as she pitched shot after shot. The Graces wanted Erika to enter college under a full scholarship. Erika had the talent to run any top college basketball program in the country from the point guard position. But, unfortunately, she didn't have the one thing Mitch couldn't buy her with all the money he had: the height.

Growing up, watching what many later described as a "fairy-tale marriage" unfold before her, Erika herself later claimed that it set forth a model she believed she needed to mimic as she set out into the world looking for a man. Later, Erika said that she hoped "her own marriage would be" like her parents' had been. That was her representation. She held on to that image: a fantasy that her life needed to follow along the same path as her parents, or she was doomed to fail.

Erika was the first one to admit that her "parents, grandparents and aunt had a lot of money. I was a 'material girl.'"

"Her family," a former friend later speculated, "was upper-class, very well-off. She had the all-American life. Good parents who adored her and were involved in her life. They took care of her."

Mitch was a "very nice" guy, said another family friend. "Awesome, really. Both of her parents were. Her mother was more strict than he was, which caused some problems in the family."

In what many described as a materialistic, privileged existence, Erika Grace had grown accustomed throughout her youth and early adult life to these circumstances. Before she ended up at the University of Mary Washington, Erika was thought to be a "gifted" basketball player in high school and with the AAU teams she played for. But once she got out into the world of collegiate athletics, out of that small-town bubble of rural Pennsylvania, she was more or less slightly above average, rather than outstanding. That was why, most likely, Erika Grace got into Mary Washington on only a partial scholarship, and her life, shortly after entering college, began a slow descent.

7

Star Athlete

Kristin Heinbaugh grew up in Hollidaysburg, Pennsylvania, and ended up, like a lot of her friends, staying in town after high school.

"It's home," she said later. "I like it here. What can I say?"

Located in Blair County, Hollidaysburg is approximately seven miles south of Altoona, a much larger and more populated city. Not much has changed in Hollidaysburg since a census had been kept, beginning in 1910. In fact, the town had grown from 3,734 residents at the turn of the century to only 5,368 in 2000, which was not that big of a difference in the scope of what amounted to almost one hundred years. With coal, iron ore, and ganister secreted in the earth surrounding Hollidaysburg, it's not the natural material the earth yields that many associate with the town. Situated on the outer perimeter of town is an area known as Ant Hill Woods, which is famous for its colonies of ants.

For a few years Kristin and Erika were on opposing

basketball teams, each going to different high schools. Like Erika, Kristin had a knack and passion for basketball. A few area coaches, however, including Mitch Grace, "rounded up," Kristin said, the best players in the region to form an AAU pickup team. The team traveled and played in Pittsburgh and tournaments all over the United States, eventually ending up at the nationals in Utah one year. As they traveled together and became closer, Kristin got to know Erika fairly well. She saw a different side of her—that part of a child only her friends get to see. The one most kids keep hidden.

Erika didn't have the height, so she stuck to point guard position. She had a great jump shot when it was on, but for the most part, point guard was not a position that suited Erika's personality.

"She was never aggressive," Kristin remembered. "No, she was, I guess you could say, always more passive." Point guards generally run the show, flipping up fingers, calling out play numbers, and charging at opponents.

Not Erika.

"She kind of kept herself around the three-point line, which was her best shot."

More than that, though, Erika Grace was always very thin, fragile, and petite. Just a tiny thing. If there was a rush for a loose ball, Erika might go for it, but she hardly ever came up out of the tussle with the ball. That size would later hamper her ambitions—or maybe Mitch's ambitions—of Erika being an all-American women's college basketball star playing for a Big East or Pac-10 team.

Off the court, Erika was shy. Not so much around her close friends, but whenever a stranger came to pass or a boy came near, Erika backed away. Furthermore, she wasn't one to ever instigate a conversation with someone she didn't know, or even introduce herself.

During her high-school years in the mid 1990s, Erika

was not a socially active teenager, as most of her friends were. At parties, for example, Erika was the girl in the corner by herself: shy and standoffish. She had boyfriends, sure. But not many. When there was booze around, Erika was afraid to indulge. The first one, in other words, to step up and say, "We shouldn't be doing that."

There was one afternoon in high school when a friend tapped Erika on the back, trying to get her attention. She was standing by her locker. The bell had rung. It was that frantic three minutes in the hallway before the next bell and you were reprimanded for being late to class.

Erika turned. "What?"

"Can we copy your homework?" the friend asked. Erika was the smart one of the bunch. She never had much trouble with the curriculum. Getting honor grades seemed effortless.

"No," Erika said. She was adamantly against anyone looking at her work and using it. She had done the labor of the homework. She had stayed up late and paid the price. She couldn't stand lazy classmates.

"Come on, Erika."

"No!"

And that was it.

But when Erika went to class, her friends, if they needed her homework to cover themselves, broke into her locker instead and took it, anyway. Realizing this, Erika, of course, could do nothing.

And this is how Erika Grace's life would continue: she'd say no to things, get into a tug-of-war, and then eventually give in to them or do nothing to stop them from happening.

Back then, Erika had kinky brunette hair. Hundreds of coils of naturally tightly wound hair that other girls might have paid lots of money to have done at a salon.

She was attractive in a simple, unadorned, librarian type of way. As far as confidence, Erika knew she was good on the basketball court and displayed poise and attitude. When it came to school and socializing, though, she was intimidated. Because of this, she was always "hard on herself," a friend later claimed.

"I think maybe because of how hard her parents were on her. They were supportive, definitely supportive, but Erika, as an only child, was always pushed *very* hard."

As far as following the kids into bad behavior, "I could tell," another friend recalled, "that she really only drank [alcohol] in high school to fit in. When we went on trips . . . and would sneak alcohol into our rooms, she wouldn't participate."

Levelheaded Erika.

Afraid of the consequences.

Scared of how one mistake might affect her future.

But more than anything else, afraid to let down the two most important people in her life—her parents—and of not living up to the standards expected of her. In many ways, Erika Grace was a parent's dream child. Born in the image of goodness and wholesomeness, with a father who could give her anything she wanted. Erika yearned to impress her parents. She desired to be the person they had taught her to be: caring and honest, hardworking, and able to take care of herself.

"I'm surprised she wasn't voted most likely to succeed, in high school," Kristin Heinbaugh said.

As Mitch Grace put it later, a hard-work ethic was in the Grace bloodline; Mitch didn't expect any more from his daughter than she could give, on or off the basketball court.

"I was a construction foreman at age twenty," Mitch

told this author, "job superintendent at twenty-one, and started my own business at twenty-two."

Regarding the notion of being hard on Erika and pushing her, Mitch believed he was just being a dad.

"Have you ever worked for anyone in an authority position who was *not* authoritative? . . . I learned to be a take-charge-type person. I am not a good follower. I would not be a good assistant coach. So, yes, I was probably too bossy about basketball issues [with Erika], because, without realizing it then, if I would just ask, 'Do you want to play in this or that?' I now feel she wanted to, but if I mentioned it, she probably felt that I *wanted* her to. . . ."

In addition, whatever Mitch did in life, he put his heart and soul into, whether digging a trench on the job, coaching a basketball team, or supporting his family. For this, some later said, Mitch had gone too far with Erika and was too intense with his pushing basketball on her.

On the other hand, hindsight, Mitch said, was always going to give people what they believed to be a clearer picture of any situation. If nothing had ever happened to Erika, no one, in other words, would have ever accused Mitch of going overboard with his raising her to be an overachiever.

"Intense? If there is anything worth doing," Mitch recalled, "it's worth doing to the best of your ability. . . . I always felt Erika could do anything she worked hard enough to do. I loved basketball too much and still do. I love coaching, which I quit [in 2002] because I did not feel I could do it to my best [ability]. I loved watching her play. I never missed a game. . . . I guess, looking back . . . you realize the big things you worried about every day in life were *nothing*. They were so little and really unimportant . . . . I know for a fact that when people are in a situation . . . people will look back and say a lot about you, things that are only highlighted because of this [new] situation, and meant nothing before. Most people will not speak up to say something good, but their memory gets great about adversity."

8

The Ghost Husband

They'd lost touch since high school, but one day in 2001, Kristin Heinbaugh was at the local Altoona mall when she ran into Erika, her mother, Cookie, and Erika's new man, Benjamin Sifrit. Erika and BJ had met during the spring of 1999, in Fredericksburg, Virginia, at a bar. They exchanged names, but it went nowhere.

It was BJ; he wasn't interested. He had been focused for most of his adult life on his career as a U.S. Navy SEAL and, upon meeting Erika, had a vision of what he wanted to do in life—which did not include a wife.

A few months later, in late July, however, BJ and Erika ran into each other again at a SEAL party and began a more "steady relationship," as BJ later called it. Two weeks after that, Erika and BJ were in Ocean City, New Jersey, where they met up with Mitch and Cookie for the first time. Erika looked happy in the photographs she took of the trip, as did BJ, who was smiling and cuddling Erika close to him. They were already talking about getting married, but they weren't sharing the news with anyone.

"Hey, how you been, Erika?" Kristin asked, walking over, noticing Erika and Cookie just browsing in the mall. The guy with Erika, Kristin noticed, looked strangely uninvolved with the chance meeting. He was looking around, surely indifferent to the conversation. Erika smiled. Kristin could tell she thought it was great to see an old friend. A touch of what her old life used to be like was there in front of her and it gave Erika a jolt or even a sense of comfort. Since leaving college and hooking up with BJ, Erika had been running on empty; becoming, some later said, in just over a few weeks after meeting him, dangerously obsessed with the guy to the point where she was going out of her mind.

"What have you been doing with your life, Erika?" Kristin asked. Erika didn't look so good. Skinnier than she had ever been. Quite gaunt and tired.

As they started talking, BJ drifted away from the group without saying anything. It was odd to Kristin that he never stuck out his hand to introduce himself, or even acknowledged that he was with Erika.

A ghost, essentially.

It was uncomfortable. BJ had "no desire," Kristin later recalled, "to meet." It was weird, too. He was so into *not* wanting to be noticed that his behavior actually stood out. Unlike a bored husband whose wife is off rummaging through clearance racks inside a department store, BJ walked away without saying a word, but making it known that he wasn't interested in socializing. It made Kristin feel as though she didn't matter to the guy. Uneasy. Like maybe she had done something wrong.

"He could have cared less," she remembered.

Erika was the type of person who her friends thought would have wanted a glorious, over-the-top wedding, seeing that she was daddy's girl, and her daddy had lots of money to make the day as special as she wanted. Mitch even later told the author that he had always dreamed of walking his girl down the aisle and giving her the wedding of her dreams. On top of that, one would think Erika would want both her parents, along with her large family (some of whom had lots of money) and friends, to see her get hitched.

Instead, Erika ran off to Las Vegas and married BJ at the Silver Bell Wedding Chapel in Clark County. The Reverend David King, a retired minister, oversaw the five-minute ceremony. When they returned, Erika transferred all her classes to Virginia Beach, Virginia, and moved off campus and into where BJ was stationed with the SEALs in North Carolina. Soon after that, the navy sent BJ to Arkansas until January 2000, so they hadn't really lived together until later. When they did start actually living together, BJ began to notice that the woman he had married on a whim, essentially, was not the woman he was now living with.

In his absence, another person had emerged.

"She worried," BJ later said in court. "She had obsessive compulsive disorders and anxiety problems."

And it started to drive him crazy.

Later, when friends looked at the guy she had actually chosen, they couldn't believe it. Erika was not into the "rough and tough" guys, said a friend. Back in high school, she was more of the type to go after the nerdy guys who fit with her more conservative nature. A man like BJ—gruff, strong, quiet, intense, and into all things military, obviously not cut from the same cloth—was a strange choice for a mate.

But then again, as Kristin Heinbaugh stood and spoke to Erika in the mall that afternoon, it hit her that she really didn't know Erika anymore. She hadn't hung out with her for years. People change. Sometimes for the better.

Sometimes for the worse.

Erika was a woman now. She was no longer that basketball star kid everyone talked about and Kristin had played with.

"Married," Erika said to Kristin that day in the mall after Kristin asked what she had been up to.

Erika stuck out her hand to show off the wedding band. Kristin couldn't believe it. How come she hadn't heard about the wedding? No notice in the newspaper?

Surprised, Kristin asked, "Married?"

"Yeah, on a dare," Erika responded, laughing, watching BJ out of the corner of her eye as he sauntered around the mall by himself.

"He dared you to run away and get married?"

"Yes."

"Where'd you two meet?"

"At a party."

As strange as all this may have sounded to Kristin, Erika had gone as far as to bring BJ home once after they had gotten married, but she did not tell her parents what she had gone and done. It was only the second time Mitch and Cookie had ever met BJ. It wasn't until months later that Erika made the announcement. Shortly afterward, Mitch and Cookie put up the money to buy Erika her own business: a one-stop shop for all things associated with creating a scrapbook. The store, located in that same Altoona mall where she ran into Kristin that day, opened April 2001. There was talk about Erika opening the store in Fredericksburg, Virginia, where she and BJ first lived after getting married (and Erika had gone to college). But after spending some time in the area and scoping it out, Erika and BJ found other scrapbooking stores already up and running.

"So they came back here," Mitch explained to this author, "and found no other store . . . here and decided to open. [It was] nice to have her close [to] home, certainly."

Regarding a later assumption that Mitch fronted the money to Erika in order to keep her close to him and Cookie, so he could keep an eye on her, he said, "[It's] possible that I influenced that decision."

It wasn't a conscious decision on his part, in other words, or some sort of devious plan to keep his grown daughter near home, Mitch insisted. It was more of, "What father wouldn't want his children near him?"

For BJ, it was a move he needed to make for Erika's sake, he later explained. After being discharged from the navy under serious charges, and a slew of rather odd circumstances that he and Erika had found themselves in with the navy, Mitch financed a "two-month trip" for him and Erika to South America—a trip Erika later admitted to police that had been fueled by her growing addiction, at the time, to Xanax and Valium, which she and BJ had bought by the drawerful down in South America and smuggled back home. When they returned in late 2000 from that trip, Erika demanded they move to Altoona and, moreover, open a business together, so she could be with BJ 24/7.

BJ wanted to get a job outside the home, he claimed.

"But if I was to leave the house eight hours a day," he said later, "either somewhere where she couldn't be close by, she would have panic attacks." The only thing that would solve the problem, BJ explained, was if they worked together every day.

They decided to call the store Memory Laine. It was a play on Erika's middle name, Elaine, for which one of her nicknames, Lainey, had been designed around (the other being Gracey).

Memory Laine was perfect. The two of them together all day in the store. What could be better? Husband and wife and their own business.

BJ later said that it was Mitch who financed the entire store: "I had no money."

There was a day after BJ and Erika had moved into their own apartment just outside Altoona and began running Memory Laine when Mitch asked BJ to go hunting with him. A boys' weekend in the woods, with campfires and beers and guns. "Testosterone City." Male bonding. They needed to get to know each other. They hadn't really talked much. And Erika was so crazy about this guy she had married after knowing him for only a few weeks, Mitch wanted to get to know him. Kind of accept BJ into the family.

BJ was thrilled. Growing up in Iowa as a young boy, he had hunted with his father in the Midwest. Pennsylvania had some of the best big-game hunting in the region. BJ had already gotten all his gun permits squared away in the state. There was nothing stopping him.

"No," Erika said (according to BJ). She was firm.

"What? Why not?" he asked. "It's your father."

"I don't want you away from me for that long."

"A few days, Erika," BJ said. "That's all."

"No, no, no." She was hysterical. Panicking. Crying and yelling.

"So I never went," BJ said later.

If you ask Mitch Grace about this particular event, he recalls the proposed hunting trip a bit differently.

"I really did not hunt much," he said later. "They (Erika and BJ) were only here one year . . . and he was sick the whole week before [hunting season] and could not go to work."

As they started living together, Erika and BJ began to learn of each other's little quirks and habits. Living outside Altoona was the first time, really, that they had stayed in the same home, together, for an extended period of time. Throughout their first few years of being married, before BJ had gotten himself tossed out of the navy, he was always traveling with the SEALs and training in some far-off place. Now they were together.

BJ soon suggested that Erika get a gun. A Smith & Wesson .357 Magnum. It was versatile, easy to load and use, BJ explained. Erika generally kept it in an ankle or waistband holster, maybe in her purse. Maybe she'd put it in the crook of her back down into the crack of her ass, but the point was, BJ said, she always had the gun on her.

Beyond the gun, it was jewelry, many later said, that excited Erika more than anything else. She was "obsessed" with not only the Coach handbag she kept most of her jewelry in, but diamonds were what she wanted. This was something, no doubt, she had learned from her mom, who was also a jewelry fanatic, according to several sources. So much so, Detective Scott Bernal told the author, "that when we went into the Graces' home to talk to them, there were these glass jewelry cases all over, like the ones you'd see in a jewelry store."

Then there was Erika's closet full of Hooters clothing and memorabilia, which Erika obsessed over.

"She had quite a collection," BJ remarked. "She probably had over one hundred, maybe over two hundred, [Hooters clothing items]."

Erika had a fetish, no doubt about it, which included a proclivity for anything with the Hooters trademark symbol on it. And it would be that desire to acquire as much Hooters merchandise as she could, and likely boredom on BJ's part after being expelled from his life-long dream of being a SEAL, that would soon send Erika and BJ out on the town at night to indulge in what had become their new hobby after moving outside Altoona.

Burglary.

It was such a high for BJ to break into a store and steal, Erika later told Detective Scott Bernal, that he generally got an erection from it and masturbated afterward.

"He just didn't want to have sex with me after a while," she said. "Maybe once a month. But this [stealing] began to get him off."

Part II

Snakes, Crocodiles, Drugs, Murder

9

Pill Snorter

It was near noon when Erika and BJ Sifrit left for Ocean City, Maryland, on Saturday, May 25, 2002, from their apartment outside Altoona, Pennsylvania. Erika had just finished a nail-grooming appointment at the local salon, and she and BJ took off in their Jeep Cherokee immediately after. It was a bit odd that Erika and BJ had a Jeep Cherokee—because they also drove an Audi. Cookie and Mitch Grace drove an Audi and a Jeep Cherokee. As much as Erika had said later that she despised her parents' storybook marriage and close friendship, she was certainly doing her best to mimic every little nuance of it.

That Saturday had been a summerlike morning. From the moment the sun rose, it was hot and sticky. As Erika strolled out of the nail salon into the waiting Jeep, she caught a glare from the sun against her already heavily tanned face. She and BJ were ready now to head southeast, toward Ocean City.

To drink.

And drug.

And do whatever else had given them that thrill both had been chasing lately by breaking into Hooters restaurants and retail stores of all types—a thrill, however, that the burglaries just weren't satisfying anymore.

Erika had some Xanax and Valium on her. She still had several hundred pills left over from a gross of about three hundred that she said she had purchased in South America. It was a good thing. Erika was into snorting Xanax these days. Just popping a few pills with a beer wasn't doing it anymore.

"We bought them in Chile," Erika later told Scott Bernal. "They were like ninety for a dollar. . . . My doctor at home had gotten word from my mother that my husband and his . . . friends had taken all of what my doctor prescribed me, so he refused to prescribe me anymore."

She'd packed the pills in her Coach purse before they left the apartment that morning. Erika was crazy about her purse, not to mention the jewelry inside it that she had collected and usually kept with her wherever she went. Jewelry and the finer things in life had made the difference to Erika: Some said she relished in gloating over what others couldn't afford. She got off on the fact that she had it and others didn't.

"Stop and get some beer," Erika told BJ as they headed out of town on the freeway.

"Yeah," BJ said excitedly. BJ was drinking more these days. Any chance he could, really. Stuffing that dream of his deeper down into an abyss of alcohol and criminal behavior.

They stopped at a gas station about halfway between Pennsylvania and Ocean City, and Erika picked up a twelve-pack of Bud Light. They could get more when they arrived in Ocean City.

Bottoms up!

As BJ drove, Erika popped two Xanax and washed them down with a slug of her Bud Light.

After the long ride down Route 1, part of which went alongside the Delaware coastline, in through Rehoboth Beach and onto the Ocean City strip, BJ parked the Jeep, then hauled their baggage up to the top-floor penthouse, room 1101, inside the Rainbow Condominiums. He would have made Erika do it, she later claimed, as he generally made her do most of the heavy lifting around the apartment back home, but he was excited to get up in the room and party, and so he helped.

The room was spectacular. A friend of Mitch's owned the building. Mitch and his company had done some of the construction work. Anytime Mitch (or Erika and BJ) needed the room, Mitch picked up the phone.

When they got into the room, BJ filled the fridge with more beer, broke out Erika's Xanax, and crushed it up on the glass table, just beyond the kitchen. Erika, kneeling over her husband with a rolled-up twenty-dollar bill in hand, started the party all over again.

BJ didn't want any. He was more of a joint-and-beer man.

The view from the penthouse's balcony was magnificent: something out of a magazine.

Coastline for miles.

Sand.

Surf.

The infamous Ocean City Boardwalk.

What more could they ask for? What a life. BJ smiled at his wife. When he was feeling good, BJ and Erika got along well. One could say with certainty that Erika was frightened of BJ on some levels. On others, Erika was the yin to BJ's yang.

"Dynamite" was how one source described BJ, "but Erika was the wick."

"Without her, he would have been fine. And without him, she would have been fine," said another source close to the case. "Together, though, watch out. Something happened when they were together."

Indeed, Erika and BJ were like a virus, feeding off each other's weaknesses, while using each other's strengths to manipulate situations to get what they wanted. Staying at the Rainbow, which was then one of the higher-quality condominiums on the Ocean City strip, turned out to be one of those perks BJ had enjoyed in marrying Erika.

At one time, Mitch Grace had a large company. He'd started the small construction business a few decades ago and it had grown into a massive workforce of over 150 employees through its first incarnation, but then "averaged about seventy-five for about ten years," Mitch said later, "and now [2007] with our need for finances at its worst, I am hoping to get back up to fifteen [employees] in the spring [of 2008]."

Mitch's company had built the likes of high-rises and hotels and office buildings up and down the East Coast.

No sooner had BJ unpacked and chopped a few lines of Xanax for Erika to snort, when she said, "I want to go to Hooters, Beej."

BJ smiled.

Erika collected Hooters waitress tank tops (which customers couldn't buy) like baseball cards.

"I had some of them with me," she said later, "and I wanted to go there and see if they would trade me. I didn't have one from Ocean City yet, so the first place we went was to Hooters."

At Hooters, BJ and Erika had two pitchers of beer and some hot wings.

"Hey," Erika said to one of the waitresses, "where can a girl go for a good time around here?"

The waitress thought about it. "Seacrets."

BJ and Erika looked at each other. Smiled. Seacrets it was.

So they drove the Jeep back to the Rainbow and boarded the bus out front, where they ran into Joshua and Geney, who paid their fare, and headed off together to the hottest nightspot on the strip, Seacrets.

10

Everyone Has Secrets

The line to get into Seacrets was out the door and around the corner. After one of them in Erika and BJ's party—which included Geney and Joshua, and now another couple they met on the bus ride over—walked up and asked, the bouncer said it would be an hour, at the least, before they got in.

"I would much rather have just gone to a hole-in-the-wall," Erika explained later. "But we were obligated to buy them (Geney and Joshua) a drink."

It was that deal BJ had made on the bus: pay our fare and we'll buy the first round.

Funny, they had burgled scores of restaurants and retail stores by this point in their marriage, but Erika said later that they were "obligated" and maybe even afraid to burn this couple out of a few bucks.

So they stood in line and waited.

Erika became quickly irritated and impatient. As she later put it, "I was losing my high." She had snorted some

Xanax before leaving Hooters, but now Erika was worried that if she didn't get into the bar soon, that high she had worked so hard to maintain throughout the evening would be lost. On top of that, the Xanax "intensified the alcohol," she explained. "It just gives you a different high."

And she was craving it.

Erika had started taking the Xanax after BJ had "an affair on me," she claimed. "And then I started having depression, anxiety attacks, panic, symptoms of obsessive-compulsive [disorder], so my psychiatrist prescribed me Xanax. . . ." She insisted that it was BJ who suggested she snort and take them with booze. He was the one who introduced her to a more intense and a more animated high than simply popping them with a few beers.

One of the other couples standing in line waiting to get into Seacrets besides Joshua and Geney, a couple who had gotten off the bus with them, had taken a walk to a local liquor store and had come back with a six-pack of pony beers.

"You want one?" the guy asked Erika, BJ, Geney, and Joshua.

Erika spoke up, "Yeah, thanks."

No one else was interested.

"No problem," the guy said.

"Hey, you want to go with me over there," Erika said to the guy, pointing. She made a gesture with her hand to her nose, giving the impression that she wanted to duck out of line and snort some drugs.

"No," the man said.

"Come on," Erika insisted.

"No!"

So Erika grabbed him by the crook of his arm, latched her arm around his, and pulled the man away from the line.

"I'm going around the corner over there," she shouted

as Joshua, Geney, and BJ waited, watching her leave. Erika was pointing again to an area near the beach. No one would see her. It was dark out by now. She could zip in between a few cars or the Dumpster and blast a few lines of Xanax with her new friend by her side.

"I'll be back," she said, and took off with the new guy.

To BJ, it didn't matter. ("I liked to let her do what she wanted. It didn't bother me," he said later.)

Erika saw it differently. Ever since BJ had cheated on her in October 1999, not even a year into their marriage, she had gone off the deep end when it pertained to doing what she wanted. Erika had found e-mails between BJ and his lover, which explicitly detailed the relationship. She followed him. She had heard him on the telephone talking to the woman, who lived in Arkansas. It was a one-night stand BJ had while on SEAL maneuvers, but turned into a six-week Internet romance when he returned home. Erika said the woman started calling and e-mailing her, which sent her into a "diagnosed serious depression." She couldn't even get out of bed at times. Yet, even with all that evidence against him, Erika said, BJ would "not admit to it, because he has no sense of guilt or remorse."

Erika walked around the corner of the building, found an out-of-the-way space where no one would see her, and snorted some Xanax.

There we go . . . there it is . . . back to normal.

When she returned about fifteen minutes later, she was ready for a drink. She'd gotten that original buzz back and was feeling good. Geney, Joshua, BJ, and the newly met woman were still in line, but a lot closer to the door.

The woman whose male friend had left with Erika leaned over to BJ and asked him, "Doesn't that bother you that your wife walked off with another guy like that?"

BJ didn't have much to say.

Erika was getting restless again and said to the guy she had strolled off with, "Hey, she's cute," referring to the woman he was with. "She's *really* cute."

"This is my friend," he said.

"She's nice . . . cutie!" Erika said again.

As the woman listened to Erika, she felt that she was making a pass at her. It was "uncomfortable," the woman said later, and would continue to be throughout the night as Erika continued making strange remarks to the woman. There was one time when Erika began rubbing the woman's arm slowly, petting her sexily, saying, "Let's go into the bathroom . . . me and you."

The woman refused.

"Come on," Erika demanded.

"No."

Later, police would learn that Erika had dabbled in homosexuality, but it had always been in the context of her marriage. She claimed that BJ wanted to bring another female into the bedroom. He had gotten bored with their sex life, apparently. The deal was, however, that BJ could touch Erika; the other female could touch Erika; and BJ couldn't touch the other female.

11

Don't Shoot

After waiting for an hour in line, they were finally inside the club: dancing, drinking, drugging, and just living it up—the way that Erika had grown accustomed to over the past year.

Joshua had given BJ bus fare and BJ had responded kindly, per his promise, by buying Geney and Joshua a drink. Inside the club, lights flashed and pulsated in strobes all around them, the music of a DJ blared so loud you could barely hear the person next to you. Erika was nervous, cagey, and out of it, she claimed, after doing a shot of her favorite liquor, vodka. Watching her, Geney noticed how "out of it" Erika seemed. BJ and Erika were young; Geney certainly must have registered that. Both Erika and BJ were twenty-four years old. Hell, they were just kids, really. But still, there was something going on with Erika, Geney noticed. Throughout the night, Erika had been consumed with the idea of losing her high— or, rather, maintaining it. Even though she had snorted some additional Xanax outside while waiting in line, and more when she got into the club, Erika was preoccupied with keeping the party going. It wasn't enough to do shots and beers.

She needed more.

She demanded more.

As the night progressed, at some point, Erika ordered more shots for everyone. This one must have been the tipping point, because Erika said later that she "blacked out" for a time after downing this second shot of vodka, but then she recalled BJ slapping her on the arm somewhere near midnight.

"How cool is that, girl, you got in here with your piece?" BJ said in a slur of words. "Some security they have here," he said, laughing.

Geney was standing nearby. She had a quizzical look about her: *What's he talking about?* she wondered.

BJ was referring to Erika making it past security with her .357 Magnum revolver—a gun Erika rarely left home without. There were four security guards at the door with wands.

Erika had made it past them all.

Indeed, there it was, tucked in her waistband, as if she were Annie Oakley. The way Erika talked it up, she was "Bonnie" to BJ's "Clyde"—two names, in fact, Erika explained to Joshua and Geney, they had given to their pythons, one of which was back at the Rainbow right now. They had cobras, too. Even a crocodile. BJ had named the cobra Hitler, after one of his and Erika's idols. In private, BJ had made no secret to Erika of the fact that he was a racist, according to what Erika later said. Erika would later refer to BJ as a control freak who had become mentally and physically abusive over the short span of their marriage. But tonight they were partners, living up to that "Bonnie and Clyde" image. Erika had laughed as she explained to Geney and Joshua how they had acquired the nickname.

Erika smiled at BJ's announcement. Actually, it was more at the way in which he demeaned the security guards by suggesting that a woman like Erika could get a loaded weapon into a popular, packed nightclub.

"Yeah," Erika said, stammering. "Imagine that."

And yet, it was probably that innocent appearance of being so small and delicate that had allowed Erika to get the gun into the club to begin with.

Either way, Geney walked over to Erika. Geney was concerned. Worried about the gun. Geney liked to party. After all, she and Joshua were on a short vacation. But what type of people had they met?

Guns. Snakes. Crocodiles. Xanax. Hitler.

That's one hell of a combination.

"Why would you have guns? Why would you need guns?" Geney asked Erika (who spoke in detail about this conversation later on to Detective Scott Bernal). Geney was referring to BJ's gun, too.

Erika laughed, screaming over the loud music. "I've only had mine for a few months. It was a gift from BJ."

Later, Erika was asked if it was customary for her and BJ to carry guns.

"Yes, I always carried my Smith and Wesson in my red Coach bag. I'm addicted to Coach! I even carry my pills and jewelry in a little Coach pouch inside my Coach bag." BJ, she added, went for the more rugged, manly look, and carried his gun inside his waistband, or wore it on his side in a leather shoulder holster. But on the night they met Geney and Joshua, Erika said, she did have her .357 in the club. Being around BJ and his SEAL friends so often, Erika continued, had made her immune to the sight of weapons. "With me, it's like, like, if I sat around with ten SEALs drinking in some bar, they all had weapons, and there's ten pistols laying on the table. That's just the way it is, you know—I got used to it."

Joshua stepped in as Geney was asking Erika about the guns. He could tell Geney was getting worried.

"It's no big deal, Geney," Joshua said. "Don't worry about it."

They had a third weapon also.

"But that was in the Jeep," Erika said later. "It never leaves the console of the Jeep."

12

Natural Born Lovers

The Erika Sifrit of 2002 hanging out in Ocean City with her dishonorably discharged husband was quite a different person from the Altoona girl and basketball star back in the days before she met BJ. It was as if BJ had brought out all of Erika's repressed nature and hidden evil desires. The intercourse between their personalities was charged with a doomed disaster. It was almost as if BJ knew there was a dirty girl in there somewhere that he could exploit and raise whenever he wanted her to come out. BJ loved it, of course. It fed his enormous ego. Yet, it also added to an underlying will he had developed, probably during his Navy SEAL training, to make the people around him believe he was this quietly tamed machine of power—that because he had made it through what some claimed to be the most rigorous military training on record, having graduated from the SEALs at the top of his class as honor man, BJ was somehow a different human being: stronger, able to conduct himself one way—and be totally planning something different in another.

A chameleon. Sneaky. A pragmatist.

Erika would later write to friends and detail her view of the marriage during this period. She said that her "final weakness," when all was said and done, was that she *loved BJ more than life,* she penned.

He was her entire being.

Her lifeline.

Her inspiration.

Motivation.

There were times during the marriage, Erika went on to note, when they seemed to be at their best, working together as a fine-tuned machine. It was as if they had been living out some sort of fantasy.

One of their favorite films, Erika said, was *Natural Born Killers.*

There was one time when Erika looked at BJ, and in a phrase that now sounded more clichéd than sincere or even sinister, said, "I would die for you, Beej."

13

Hot Tub

Erika spent twenty minutes in the bathroom with Joshua inside Seacrets at some point that night. It was near the time the bar was about to turn on the lights and motion for everyone to get the hell out. Part of what would become known later to police was that Erika was famous for making dirty promises to the men she and BJ met at bars—that is, if they wanted to continue to party with a couple after the bar closed. Some detectives from the OCPD assumed Erika had made one of these same graphically sexual promises to Joshua when they were in the restroom together for that twenty-minute span. In one instance later that same week, Erika told a man that she and BJ met at a bar and were hanging out with, "Come back to our condo and I'll let you do me in the ass. I like it. My husband wants to watch."

BJ kept Geney busy while Erika was gone with Joshua. There's no doubt that Erika asked Joshua if he and Geney "wanted to come back to our penthouse and hang out?"

The Rainbow.

Erika said she and BJ wanted to continue the party. It would be fun.

A dip in the hot tub.

Drinks.

Drugs.

According to Erika, Joshua mentioned something about having "some really good" marijuana back in his Atlantis room and he wanted to pick it up and bring it over to the Rainbow. On top of that, Geney and Joshua needed to pick up their bathing suits if they were all going for a romp in the hot tub.

"Sure," Erika said, referring to stopping by the Atlantis. "Beej loves to smoke. I don't. I hate it."

So after Joshua and Erika emerged from the restroom, Erika later said, they grabbed BJ and Geney and decided to take the bus back to the Atlantis.

"My husband really jumped at the opportunity [to smoke weed], because I don't smoke," Erika later explained to Detective Bernal. "He loves to smoke it, because I don't. . . ."

After getting off the bus, Erika, BJ, Joshua, and Geney went up to Geney and Joshua's room at the Atlantis. After Joshua got his and Geney's things together (his weed was in an Altoids tin canister), they walked along the beach back to the Rainbow, which was just a few city blocks away.

14

Stranded

According to BJ, only Erika, Geney, and Joshua got off the bus. He decided to take the bus back to the Rainbow and meet them there.

"I'm going back to the condo," BJ said.

"We'll meet you there, then," Erika replied.

When BJ got to the Rainbow, he realized that he couldn't get in. Erika had the keys.

"Shit."

So, BJ said later, he waited by the door for a while.

"But it was uncomfortable."

Sick of sitting on the concrete floor by the door waiting for Erika, he went downstairs and passed out in the Jeep Cherokee, which, he said, was unlocked.

15

The 130 Ways to Torture a Person

One of the main reasons Erika was so bold—so offensively oversexual and fearless when she and BJ went out on the town to drink or steal or just cause mischief a teenager would be proud of—centered around a feeling she had that he was paying very little attention to her anymore. It wasn't even that they didn't have sex anymore. It was that BJ, according to Erika, was more concerned with putting his wife down and demeaning her than he was with handing out compliments.

"I'm not a shy person," Erika explained to Detective Scott Bernal. Her lawyer and the state's attorney Joel Todd were also present during this same interview. "I talk to people at bars. I sit down beside someone at a bar, ask them how they're doing . . . because I do not get that sort of attention from my husband. He's not turned on by me. I'm not what gets him excited."

Erika was embarrassed by the discussion. It was hard, she claimed, to talk about such intimate things with strangers.

"No, just tell," her lawyer encouraged.

Erika stopped talking, looked over at her lawyer, and grimaced, whispering, "You know . . . you know—"

"No, it's OK to tell them," her lawyer said.

"We hardly ever have sex," Erika said after a slight hesitation. "When we were first married, we did, but then it really slowed off to the point that I don't even think we had sex while we were on vacation (in Ocean City)."

It was once or twice a month, Erika said, *if* she was lucky—and *if* she pleaded and pleaded with BJ for it.

"I would practically have to beg."

The problem wasn't her, however, she went on to explain. BJ had even told her one day what it was that was going on with him.

According to Erika, BJ told her, "Sex is not what excites me. It's not what gets me off. If you want me to have sex with you, then fine. I'll take the time out of my day, if that's what I have to do to make you happy."

She was curious, of course, as was the state's attorney and Bernal. The questions then became: What excited BJ? What was it that stimulated this failed SEAL, who had been trained to kill with his bare hands and to get out of just about any situation he found himself in?

Erika said BJ had turned into the type of person who "swerved to hit animals on the road, instead of not to hit them."

He was perpetually chasing a thrill.

Bernal asked Erika what else.

"BJ is the kind of person that, when he's bored, he makes lists of, like, one hundred thirty ways to torture someone."

Pen and paper.

Detective Bernal asked Erika for an example.

She spoke of BJ's mistress, the woman from Arkansas that he'd had an affair with. To prove that this woman indeed had had an affair with BJ (he would not admit to it) and that she had no idea he was married, the woman had called Erika and told her intimate details about BJ that only someone who had slept with him would have known. The mistress also said BJ had a separate cell phone set aside just for her.

Erika found out this was true.

But he still would not admit to the affair.

"So what does BJ do?" Erika told Bernal, shaking her head in disbelief. "He gets on the computer. He sends her an e-mail and it says—again, forgive my language—'Hey, bitch, you better tell my wife I never fucked you. . . .'" Erika went on to say that BJ promised the mistress that if she didn't call Erika and tell her it was all a lie, he would drive down to Arkansas and "amputate your bastard kids with a butcher—with a butter knife" and then "board up the windows and doors" and torch her house down. He signed the e-mail, "Your worst enemy, BJ."

That e-mail, according to a naval investigation report I was able to obtain, was the beginning of the end for BJ Sifrit and his relationship with the military, along with several incidents involving cars, foul language, and threats.

Erika talked about what truly turned BJ on: getting chased by the police. He would actually instigate pursuits with cops. BJ drove a hot rod, a bright orange (with black stripes) 1972 Chevelle, all decked out. It was a fast car, a muscle car. He was your typical gearhead. There was one time, Erika recalled, when she and BJ were cruising down the main strip in Virginia Beach, Pacific Avenue.

"It's like a strip," she explained, "where you cruise, like, twenty miles an hour."

BJ spotted some cops hanging around a 7-Eleven convenience store. He pulled up. Revved the engine. Then pulled the car up in front of the cruiser and took off like a racing flag had been waved, burning rubber, leaving a trail of smoke behind him.

"He did that purposely?" Bernal asked when Erika was finished telling the story.

"I'd say weekly."

"Why do you think?"

"Because that's what got him off: to outrun police."

There was another instance—the episode that solidified BJ's ousting from the navy—shortly after Erika's father bought her a new Audi. Erika and BJ had met up with two of his friends, who had spent the day drinking at a bar. They were afraid of getting popped for a DUI and getting expelled from the navy, so BJ offered to follow them back to the base.

"They were swerving and Beej sees a cop, so he's afraid they're going to get pulled over, plus he wants the rush," Erika said. Not to mention that he was living up to his true SEAL reputation of protecting your fellow men at any cost.

BJ got into the left lane of a two-lane, thirty-five-mile-an-hour road. His plan was to make himself noticed by the cop—BJ was heading straight into oncoming traffic.

"All the cars coming toward us," Erika explained, "are going into the trees and bushes and onto the other side of the road." By this point, BJ was pushing the Audi to speeds of 125, 130, Erika insisted.

The cop was close behind.

Erika was screaming, "Slow down . . . Beej," tightly gripping the dashboard. "Stop, you're going to kill us."

Then she peed in her pants.

And grabbed the keys out of the ignition, which slowed the car instantly, thus propelling her head against the dashboard.

BJ was convicted in a Norfolk, Virginia, courtroom on

a variety of charges. But, because he was a SEAL, some later asserted, he was given a slap: community service.

This was one of the only times, Erika remembered, that BJ had ever gotten caught.

Erika finished this portion of her interview with a story that spoke to BJ's bigotry and staunch hatred toward any other race besides his own. They'd be driving around, Erika explained, and BJ would say, "Hey, let's go shoot us a nigger."

"What?"

"No one will ever know."

"What are you talking about?"

"You've *got* to kill someone," BJ told his wife, "where there's no motive."

BJ was saying that it was the toughest murder for investigators to solve because there was really no reason for the person to have been killed.

"Let's go down to the ghetto," he continued saying to Erika, "and shoot us a nigger. It'll be really fun."

"No! I want to go home. Let's go home."

Erika admitted that there was a time when she and BJ liked to snort cocaine. It was approximately the end of the year 2001, when she and BJ went out one night to buy come coke. They were in Altoona. BJ found some woman, Erika explained, and made the buy.

When they got back to the apartment and set up the lines, BJ was the first to snort.

The coke burned his nose something terrible. Made him cough and choke.

It was Ajax. They had been ripped off.

BJ couldn't let it go, Erika said. He had to do something about it.

BJ left the house. Went to the "cement store," Erika said, "and bought a big . . . five-gallon" bucket of acid.

In order to see if the acid would indeed melt away the

drug dealer's body after he killed her, BJ took one of the rats they fed to their snakes. He placed the rat, alive and kicking, inside the acid bath. There was a smile on BJ's face, Erika said.

A day later, the rat was just about completely gone.

16

Control Freaks

Erika called home one night in 1999 after she met BJ. She wanted to speak to her dad. According to Mitch, Erika explained that she and BJ were *thinking* about getting married.

"Erika," Mitch explained, "why would you ever do that? You've known him for what, a few weeks? Why would you even *consider* doing that, honey?" Mitch was perplexed. This wasn't the daughter he knew. "If you're that intent on getting married, live with him for a while and find out who he is."

Mitch's astute point was centered on the notion that you not only have to love someone to get married, you also have to *like* the person. You don't marry someone because you have fallen in love with him. People fall in love every day. And people also fall out of love every day.

That old cliché has some wisdom to it: get to know each other first.

"No, I won't do that. I won't live with someone without

marrying him," Erika said sharply, subtly using religion as an available crutch to go through with something she obviously had already done.

And that was the end of the discussion. Mitch never heard anything else about the subject until Erika brought BJ home one day to Altoona and introduced him as her husband.

It was just one of those nights that newly married Erika was at home in the apartment but feeling especially down. She wanted more from her husband already. By now, she knew BJ a little bit better. She was scared to push BJ in any direction. Scared, not of him abusing her—but of losing him. Their first year together had been "exciting," she later explained to a government agent. "We did cocaine and ecstasy five days a week," she admitted.

One party after the other.

Coke. Sex. Bars. Booze. Wild nights.

Being married to a SEAL was fun and exhilarating for the first twelve months, but was this it? Erika wondered. Routine, sporadic sex, drugs, and then waiting for your husband to return from wherever the navy had sent him this time around. She wanted more out of life.

As the marriage seemed to burn itself out, and running from the cops after initiating high-speed chases wasn't satisfying BJ's thrill-seeking nature, BJ and Erika began burglarizing Hooters restaurants and small businesses and retail stores in and around Altoona. They'd even started a side business on eBay selling the hot merchandise. Erika later said in letters that she was making up to $2,500 per week selling the stolen items—and loving every minute of it.

Erika not only participated in the burglaries, but she loved the high of being able to break into an establishment and steal things at will. It gave her a sense of power, authority.

Still, there had to be more to this guy.

More to life.

More to being married.

BJ shocked her one night, Erika later said. "I want kids," he said. It was out of the blue. She had no idea he was even thinking about it.

She was pleasantly surprised. "Kids?"

"Yeah. I want you to get pregnant."

What a turnaround. Overnight, the guy had gone from a criminal to someone who wanted to become a parent. This wasn't the BJ she knew. But then maybe he was ready to settle down and change. By now, BJ had already been discharged from the military. They had opened Memory Laine, their scrapbooking business. Save for the thieving and drugs, one could say, they were living a fairly contemporary married life.

But both were obviously bored.

It didn't take long. That first month passed and Erika missed her period. She was ecstatic. Maybe this was it? Maybe BJ was destined to become a father and everything would take on a new significance. She could live like her parents. Erika was not just an only child; she was the only child in the family. No cousins. Erika beamed with the glow of being a new mother. She was five feet six inches, plus, with BJ on her all the time about her weight, she had whittled herself down to almost nothing at ninety-five pounds. So, after three and a half months, she stood one night in front of a mirror and had herself a moment. BJ wasn't home. She relished having the child. It was going to be magnificent.

Wonderful.

She hadn't known it, but it was just what she had wanted.

In between her third and fourth month (Erika couldn't

recall the exact time when she was asked about it later), BJ came home with several of his SEAL buddies one night. They were drunk. BJ had "this look" on his face. He wanted something.

What have I done? Erika thought immediately.

"I don't want kids," BJ came out and said. "You thought I wanted to be a dad? You stupid whore. I don't want no kid."

Erika was confused. "You *what?*"

"You heard me. Get rid of the kid."

She started crying. She knew it wouldn't do anything. But she couldn't help it.

"Beej—"

"Either we get it out, here and now—I'm going to dig it out of you with a coat hanger—or you go to the clinic in the morning. Your choice."

BJ walked away.

Enough said.

No more discussion about it.

The following morning, BJ drove Erika down to the local clinic and she got the abortion. It was one of the hardest things she had ever done. She had taken a life. The baby had been alive that morning, kicking and moving in her womb, and now it was gone. Dead. Just a piece of garbage in some medical disposable waste site. They didn't even know what it was: boy or girl. And now they never would.

The abortion issue had never meant much to Erika. Heck, since she'd married BJ—who absolutely disbelieved in and despised God and religion altogether, shunning and exclaiming that Jesus Christ was a fake and a fraud— Erika hadn't even thought about it much. But here she was, heading home after aborting her child, knowing exactly what all those women before her had gone through.

Later, she would get a tattoo of a cross on her stomach to pay homage to the child.

On the way home from the clinic, Erika later explained to a friend in a letter, she sat with her head down on BJ's lap and he petted her hair as he drove.

I was 100% sedated . . . , she wrote.

"It's OK now, Lainey," BJ said. He was rubbing her ears and talking sweetly. "You passed the loyalty test. Everything is going to be OK." He said he was going to "take care" of her now that she had proven her devotion to him. He had to "make sure" that she would "pass the test" and because she had, she would "be his wife forever." It was why he had to do it, BJ explained.

"Everything's gonna be OK now, Lainey."

When he returned home one afternoon shortly after that, BJ saw that Erika had a sad look about her face. She was hurt. How could he be so coldhearted and cruel? What had motivated him to manipulate her to such an extent?

"Why?" she asked him.

According to what Erika later recalled, BJ said, "I never wanted a kid to begin with, Lainey. I just wanted to see how far you would go for me."

From BJ's perspective, Erika had perhaps passed the ultimate test. He knew now that he could trust her. He could ask of her the most intimate, the most personal, and the most horrible of things to do, and even though she might kick and scream, he understood that she was loyal and would likely do whatever he asked.

Now, that's one story of the abortion. A friend of Erika's tells a completely different version of this event in Erika's life.

BJ had lived in North Carolina with some friends, a

SEAL buddy and his wife. For a while, even after they were married, Erika lived with them. But they had, according to the friend, "moved out by this point. . . . We had heard they were having problems and she had been causing him a lot of problems by then with the military, calling his command and getting in his business."

BJ's SEAL buddy's wife was pregnant. Erika knocked on the door one day to have a chat with her. She had just been to her therapist, she said, whose office was close by.

Erika's pupils were so dilated, the friend recalled, you could barely see the color of her eyes.

"I just wanted you to know that I was pregnant and we (meaning she and BJ) decided that I should get an abortion. He's been doing so much coke (cocaine) and I've been popping so many pills, it was better this way. . . . It probably wouldn't be safe for me to have a baby." She even said she'd just discussed it with her therapist, and the doctor agreed.

"Well," the friend said, "you did the right thing. Don't feel bad about it."

Was this Erika covering for her husband's craziness? Her friend didn't think so. Erika seemed fairly sincere that day.

"The only people that truly know what happened are them."

17

"911 . . . ?"

If what Erika later said is true, sometime around 2:30 A.M., Joshua, Geney, Erika, and BJ walked along the beach up to the Rainbow Condominium and entered room 1101, BJ and Erika's spacious, elegant flat, after stopping at the Atlantis, where Geney and Joshua were staying.

When they first got inside, Erika later explained, Geney and Joshua were overwhelmed by how nice the place was.

"Wow. Look at this," Geney marveled, looking around, walking in and out of various rooms.

Erika walked toward the refrigerator to get beers for everyone. As she did that, BJ, Joshua, and Geney sat down at the glass table just off the kitchen, broke out the marijuana Joshua had brought with him, and began chitchatting.

Geney soon got up. "I don't want to change down here," she said.

The plan had been for everyone to smoke a joint, get into their bathing suits, and then take a swirl in the hot tub.

"Go upstairs, then," Erika said. She pointed. The master bathroom (with the hot tub) was right at the top of the stairs, to the left, off the bedroom.

Joshua and BJ sat and smoked. A few minutes later, Geney came back down the stairs and sat with them. As Erika later explained the scene to Detective Scott Bernal, "I'm not even paying much attention to them or sitting with them because I have no interest in smoking."

Erika was not a fan of marijuana; again, her thing was snorting Xanax.

The one thing about Erika was that no matter where she went or what she was doing, all of her personal belongings were organized. She had a place for everything. One drawer was just for blue jeans; another for underwear; another for bras; another for T-shirts of a certain color; and so on. Moreover, she had always put things in the same place so she knew exactly where they were—it gave her a sense of power over her obsessive-compulsive disorder (OCD). She could essentially relax.

While Geney and BJ were at the table smoking, Joshua got up for a moment and wandered around the living room. Erika began looking for her brown Hooters bag, which she always kept in a certain place inside the condo; then she noticed her purse was sitting on the "other side of the room," where she said she would have *never* put it herself. Putting the two together, in Erika's panic-stricken, drug-induced, alcohol-soaked mind, she said later that she believed at that moment that someone had taken the Hooters bag—and, worse, moved her pocketbook.

Where is my shit? What the hell is going on here? Erika thought.

Without telling anyone, she started looking around the first floor of the condo. As you walked in, the laundry room was right in front of you. To the left of that were two bedrooms, a bathroom attached to one. Walking down a short hallway toward the east end of the condo, off to the right was a set of stairs leading to the second floor, almost directly across from the kitchen. From there, there was that glass table with six chairs, in back of which were three bar stools against a counter/bar opening into the kitchen. Before the balcony, which spanned the entire width of the unit, were two roomy rec areas with couches, end tables, entertainments centers, and a television.

After a moment, Joshua sat back down at the kitchen table. The three of them were having a good old time: Joshua, Geney, and BJ. Laughing and drinking beers and just talking.

Erika was beginning to go into full-scale panic mode, without telling anyone, she later claimed.

She looked in a few obvious places to see if she could find her pocketbook, but it wasn't there. Under the white cushions of one couch; under the sky blue cushions of the other couch.

Nothing.

So she ran upstairs.

When she got into the bedroom, her purse was sitting on the counter by the bed. But when she looked inside, Erika noticed that her little red Coach handbag, in which she carried anything of value—including her $10,000 Canary diamond, cross, wallet with all her credit cards, cash, and her pill case—was missing.

It wasn't inside her purse, where she had always kept it.

At least this was the story she told Detective Bernal. "All this stuff is missing and I don't know where it is," she later explained. "I don't want to freak out, because they're all sitting downstairs smoking, and I'm like, 'I'm not gonna make a scene, I'm just gonna try and find my stuff.'"

By this point, Erika started flipping out, running around, overturning pillows and blankets and looking inside cabinets, the bathroom, the closets. That feeling was coming on: of not being able to control the situation. She sensed an anxiety attack in the works if she didn't find that Coach handbag with her valuables in it.

Her heart was racing.

Her pulse beating.

Faster.

Steadier.

"So, at that point," she continued to Bernal, "I decided to call 911 because I seriously thought that they (Joshua and Geney) were trying to pull some scam where they were stealing those things. I had showed those things to Geney earlier that evening. And the drugs were gone and these people have marijuana, so, of course, they do drugs themselves to some extent. So they would be *interested* in one or two hundred pills of the Xanax."

In total alarm mode now, Erika began frantically searching for her things once again. There were two strangers downstairs in her condo, and now her jewelry and her drugs and her money were all missing.

What am I supposed to do?

Not once, she later claimed, did she think of notifying BJ, a U.S. Navy SEAL, who could have likely taken on Geney and Joshua by himself and made them admit to where the items were. Nor did she think to confront Geney and Joshua herself.

Instead, she contemplated calling the police, knowing that they all had drugs.

* * *

With the feeling that Joshua and Geney had stolen her things and that she and BJ had somehow invited a pair of thieves into their lives, Erika said later that she then picked up the telephone (without telling anyone) and dialed 911 from the upstairs bedroom. Granted, this bedroom is almost directly above where Joshua, Geney, and BJ were sitting at the glass table. The place wasn't big enough to where you could go upstairs and not be heard. The walls and floor, moreover, were not sound-proof. Unless she whispered, the three of them down-stairs would definitely have heard Erika's end of any conversation. If not plain, easily decipherable words, at the least mumbled words that would, without a doubt, send BJ into a "Who are you talking to at this time of night?" mode. Erika had made private calls from the condo before, she later said. And those were all made from her cell phone, either from the upstairs outside balcony or the outside balcony downstairs.

According to telephone records, the first 911 call Erika made was at 3:01 A.M.

"Hello," the operator said. "Ocean City Police."

"Hello . . . ," Erika said. She was not whispering. In fact, she was talking fairly loudly.

"Yes?"

A clicking sound could be heard in the background.

"Hello . . . hello. . . Ocean City Police."

"Yes," Erika responded.

"Ma'am, did you want the police?" the operator said in a rather frustrated tone.

"Yes, I did, sorry . . ."

"Where?" the operator started to say, but Erika inter-rupted.

"Yes, I did, but I think there is another person on the line right now." Erika paused. All of a sudden, she sounded sleepy and out of it. Drunk. High. She did not sound as if she was in some sort of frenzy over her missing jewelry and money. She was actually calm. "Hello?" she said, trying to get whoever had possibly picked up the other line in the condo to respond. There was a telephone in the kitchen (attached to the wall) right by the glass table.

Then there were a few seconds of silence.

"Do you have a direct line I can call you back at?" Erika asked the operator.

The dispatcher gave Erika the telephone number.

Erika had trouble with it at first, repeating the numbers slowly, so the operator repeated it even slower, like she was talking to a child.

"OK," Erika said. "Thanks."

They hung up.

Next, Erika later insisted, she heard someone coming up the stairs, so she hid. With her fears alleviated a few moments later, she called 911 back—this after reassuring herself that no one was coming.

This seems to be an odd representation—or, perhaps, *mis*representation—of the facts and doesn't gel with what was later learned. Erika's husband was downstairs at this time getting high with their new friends. Her husband, a former SEAL who had graduated at the top of his class, was a trained killing machine. This was the same guy who had been trained to handle and subdue people with his bare hands. The same man, she claimed, she didn't want to ever be apart from. BJ Sifrit was downstairs. Both Erika and BJ had guns. Upstairs, in the bedroom, in one of the drawers, was a loaded .45-caliber weapon. Erika could have easily armed herself. Somewhere in the same room where Erika was standing was a .357 Magnum.

But Erika claimed she picked up the telephone and called 911 a *second* time (which she did), because she was frightened and scared that Geney and Joshua would get away.

"We believe," two OCPD detectives later told me, "that Joshua and Geney were already dead when Erika called 911."

And one more time, the operator picked up, asking, "911, what's your emergency?"

"Yes, I have an emergency at my apartment," Erika said during that second call. This time, she sounded quite calm, and, although a bit tipsy, she did not sound panicked in any way.

More important, she was not whispering.

"What kind of emergency do you have?"

"Umm . . . there are people in my house that I don't know . . . and," Erika said, sounding more out of it than she had previously, "my purse is suddenly missing . . . and I think I'm going to have a robbery here. . . ."

What one detective theorized later was that Geney and Joshua were already in the bathroom upstairs, shot dead and lying on the floor. And this phone call was a way to cover up the noise those shots had made, if someone in the condominium complex, awoken by the pops, had called 911.

Going back to Erika's story, what she told 911 made little sense. Her purse wasn't *missing*. Her jewelry bag inside her purse—so she later claimed—was the item that had turned up missing. And her last comment—"I think I'm going to have a robbery here"—reflected the incoherent state Erika was in at the time.

But even more revealing, why did Erika say she didn't know these people? She had spent the entire night with them, knew their names, where they worked, where they were staying. Furthermore, if it was a true emergency, as she had later purported it to be, why didn't Erika simply say, "There's an emergency here, send somebody fast"?

"OK, there's people in your apartment at this time?" the operator asked, hoping to clarify.

"Yes."

"I'll connect you to the police. Stay on the line."

"Hey," Erika said.

"What?" the operator responded before making the connection.

"I'm upstairs inside a bedroom, where they don't know where I am. . . ."

This was another strange comment. BJ was supposedly still downstairs smoking a joint with Geney and Joshua.

Why didn't Erika mention BJ?

BJ, Joshua, and Geney certainly knew where Erika was; they had seen her dart up the stairs after standing around downstairs while they rolled and then began smoking that joint—this was according to what Erika later told police herself. How could they *not* know where she had gone? In addition, if Erika was panicking, why hadn't someone—BJ, especially—followed her up the stairs? Why would BJ, Geney, and Joshua continue partying by themselves, with Erika freaking out upstairs? The way in which Erika later spun the story, she was in and out of it all night, snorting Xanax, blacking out, snorting more, blacking out, and coming to. How was she now, well after 3:00 A.M., sober enough to not only make all of these decisions, but then later recall them with such exactness?

"OK, I'll connect you to the police," the dispatcher said. "You can tell them, OK?"

The phone went dead for a moment as the dispatcher connected Erika to the OCPD. After some ringing, a new operator came on the line and asked what the situation was.

"Hi," Erika said in an unsteady tone, almost as if she was ready to fall out at any moment, "there are peop—" she began to say, but before she could finish the word, perhaps conveniently, the phone line went abruptly dead, as if someone had cut the line or had hung up the phone. Studying the telephone and where it was inside the upstairs bedroom, one would have a hard time ripping the line out of the wall. The phone was in the center of the bed headrest. There was a hole drilled in the headrest, in which the phone cord went down toward the floor and plugged into the wall jack in back of the bed. To rip it out of the wall, one would have to jump on the bed, grab the bulky table phone, and pull it out of the wall. It could be done, certainly, but it would take time and energy, neither of which Erika had at this very moment.

Just then, Erika later claimed, Joshua came up the stairs and started asking her what was going on. He was by himself.

"Hey, what's wrong?" Joshua supposedly asked.

"Nothing . . ."

"Who were you talking to?"

Erika later told Detective Bernal, "Joshua was being all sweet, almost like he knew that I knew what was going on, and he was trying to smooth me over by coming on to me."

At that moment, Erika claimed later, Joshua put his hands around her waist and started to kiss her neck, allegedly saying, "What's the matter? We're all having a good time here. What's the matter?"

"My shit is missing. Where is my stuff?"

"What are you talking about?"

"Look, my stuff is gone! My purse was not where I put

it. It was moved. And everything of value is out of it— and my Hooters bag is gone!"

Erika was getting heated. Angry and verbal. Causing a scene.

"Come on, what are you talking about?" Joshua said. He backed away from Erika at this point.

Erika got scared, she later said, and yelled, "Beej! Beej! Come up here."

BJ and Geney ran up the stairs immediately after Erika yelled, according to Erika's version of the night.

The implication she made when they arrived was that Joshua was causing her some sort of problem by putting the moves on her.

"What's wrong?" BJ asked. He was looking at Joshua, then at Erika. "What is this? What the fuck is going on?"

"Beej, my shit is missing," Erika said. She sounded mad. Upset. She was suggesting in her tone that they were being robbed. This was the first time, she insisted later, that she had let any of them know that she believed her things had been stolen.

BJ's SIG SAUER .45 was downstairs inside the Jeep, where he had always kept it. Erika thought it, too, was missing.

"Beej, all of our stuff is missing—where is your gun?"

"Lainey, you know," BJ said, indicating that he always kept the gun in the Jeep. "What do you mean?"

"Tell me where your gun is, Beej!"

"Well, it's not where I put it!" BJ said, picking up on what Erika was trying to say.

They were playing a game now with Geney and Joshua. BJ even stomped around in a circle for a moment and confronted Joshua, getting right up in his face, screaming like a drill sergeant, "Where's our shit? Did you fucking take our shit?"

"Everything is gone," Erika said. "Our pills. Our cash. Our jewelry."

It's odd that a SEAL would misplace or allow his gun to be stolen—a gun, mind you, that BJ had kept in a holster on his side or in the crook of his pants most of the time that he and Erika were in Ocean City—the same gun, in fact, he had on him at Seacrets earlier that night.

Erika said she was getting scared. The situation was quickly becoming uncomfortable. She knew when BJ was about to snap and go off on a tangent. He was almost there. That look in his eyes. The way he was staring at Joshua and Geney.

He was planning something.

"Give me your gun," BJ said to Erika. On the top of the bed headrest was Erika's .357 Magnum. She admitted later that she had put it there herself after walking into the condo from Seacrets earlier that night.

"Lainey, give me your gun!" BJ said again more forcefully.

"Beej, I don't think that's necessary."

"Fuck it. If you're not going to give it to me, I'll get it myself."

Geney was beginning to cry and shake. Joshua was standing tall and firm. According to Erika, she stood motionless, afraid of what would happen next if she handed BJ her gun.

So BJ grabbed the gun off the shelf near the headboard of the bed and began pointing it at Joshua. Waving it around. Walking around him.

"When he took that gun," Erika later explained, "I knew he was going to kill them."

18

"Guilty Pleasures"

Erika once confided to an Internet friend, a pharmacist she had met on eBay while selling some of the merchandise she and BJ had stolen, that she absolutely loved "tragedy theatre plays," Arthur Miller and the like. "Chilean wine, beer and vodka" were her drinks of choice. She didn't know the guy all that well and felt funny describing what she called "guilty pleasures," but what the hell! She considered his being a pharmacist very "sexy," and said she felt comfortable opening up to him.

Erika said she couldn't get to sleep at night without having at least one glass of Chilean wine "B4 bed." She also liked her "sex any way, every way."

I'll try anything once, she wrote.

Apparently, she was bored with her marriage. While BJ was off playing military guy, here was Erika telling a stranger what she liked to do in bed. It hardly played into her later story that she was heartbroken and totally out of her mind whenever BJ went away.

Men in uniform and men on Harley-Davidson motorcycles turned her on, as did cleaning the house naked.

Sleeping naked, always.

Watching porn and going to strip clubs.

Lots and lots of mirrors.

Eating hot wings and getting really messy.

She explained that she loved feet and tanning every day. She liked to straighten carpets when she saw that they were out of line. She had been diagnosed with OCD, Erika explained, and was taking a mixture of Paxil and Xanax to fight off the urges to preoccupy herself and her life with *everything*. For example, before she left the apartment she and BJ lived in outside Altoona, Erika had a system to check and make sure the doors were locked. She would twist the upper door lock nine times and the lower lock twelve times every day, rechecking each. It really wasn't about locking the door, but more about the number of times she checked the locks that made her feel confident the doors were secure. What was more, she would walk around the kitchen and check the oven and the doors of other appliances before leaving the house, constantly worrying that she had left the stove or another appliance open or on.

BJ picked up on this behavior soon after they started living together. According to some who knew Erika, it wasn't long before BJ began the process of using Erika's insecurities and disorders against her. He'd wait until she got to work, for instance, knowing it would drive her mad and ruin her day, Mitch Grace later said, and then ask Erika, "You sure you locked the doors?"

"What?"

"I think the doors might be open."

"Huh?"

"Maybe the oven is on, too."

It got to a point where Erika would call her father just about every morning and ask him to drive by the apartment to check the locks. Mitch had done it those first few times. But after a while, he said, it got to the point where it became a waste of time, so he lied about doing it to pacify Erika and her demons.

19

The Abuse Excuse

Whereas Erika certainly had her hang-ups, it seemed they fueled the passively sinister character stirring in BJ during the early stages of the marriage. For one, there's no doubt that BJ Sifrit had a death wish. He wasn't afraid of doing just about anything. He'd routinely antagonize people from different races and ridicule people with disabilities. He and Erika would be driving around town, Erika at the wheel, and BJ would stick his head out the window and pull out Erika's .357 Magnum and shoot up a street sign or, especially, a stop sign.

Then they'd both have a laugh about it.

Two rebels. Erika was at BJ's side by this point. The baby incident was in the past. She'd gotten that cross tattoo and was done with it. If she couldn't beat BJ and turn him into the ideal husband—the white-picket-fence life she'd always dreamed of. She might as well join him.

And that's exactly what she did.

But during their second year of marriage, BJ became

abusive, Erika later told a government agent. What first started out to be mild comments about her weight, or a jab about what she wore, evolved into BJ focusing his insults on specific areas. For one, BJ liked to tease Erika about her hair. Because it was kinky and tight and short, he'd often pull her aside and say, "Nigger hair."

Erika took it. Said nothing.

They'd be out and Erika would be hungry and BJ might refuse her food, calling her "fat ass" and "overweight."

According to Erika, he was molding the perfect woman that other men would not be attracted to. Short hair. Skinny as an anorexic. Feeble and quiet. What man would want her? She'd be all his.

But then, in another interview months later, Erika would tell a completely different story, saying that BJ wanted absolutely nothing to do with her: sexually, romantically, emotionally. He was a shell of a man. Quiet and passive.

When the insults started to bounce off her, and she became immune to them, Erika later insisted, BJ began "to smack me around a lot," she said.

"You're a cool wife," he said one night, "for going to strip clubs with me."

For BJ, strip clubs were, in fact, a place to kick back, relax with a few beers, and stare into the nothingness of a fantasy. When he met up with his SEAL friends, the strip club was the ideal spot to catch up, or just blow off some steam. There was one night when BJ hooked up with his SEAL friend Charles Atwood (a pseudonym). They were in Virginia Beach. It was 1999, shortly before BJ had even met Erika. BJ still had a good standing with the navy. Atwood and BJ were in SEAL Team 2; both had been stationed at Virginia Beach together. According to what Atwood later said in court, he and BJ were great friends.

"One of the closest friends I had on the SEAL team."

Atwood was feeling down on this night. He and his wife had just split up and he needed to talk to a friend. BJ had always been there for his fellow SEALs. All SEALs supported one another and backed one another up. BJ encouraged his friend to talk about what was bothering him. SEALs stuck together. If there was anything he could do to help, consider it done.

"Maybe I should send you to go whack my wife," Atwood told BJ jokingly.

BJ laughed. "Sure!"

"What's the going rate, anyway?"

"Oh, I don't know—twenty . . . thirty thousand dollars."

"I'll send you down there to get rid of her, and I'd be up here for a good alibi."

They chuckled. Had a good laugh. Clanked beer bottles.

"It was a 'joke,'" Atwood later remarked. Nothing more. He was upset. He was having a beer with a friend at a strip club. They were both SEALs at the time. (Atwood would later be discharged himself, like BJ, but under far different conditions: "other than honorable" (OTH), stemming from an incident where Atwood pulled a few bulletproof vests out of a trash bin on base and sold them.)

About a half hour into the conversation, the two men started talking SEAL stuff. SEALs are known as an elite group of military men trained to "kill and destroy." It's part of what they do and what they are trained (for as long as thirty months) to do under any conditions. Inherent in the secretive nature of conducting covert missions, which some might think only happen on Hollywood sound-stages, is learning how to sneak up on an enemy and annihilate him. Then remove his body and get rid of it.

Whenever SEALs get together, Atwood later explained

in court, they generally talked about things that might make the average person uncomfortable at the least, appalled and suspicious at the most. As BJ and his friend talked, they began discussing the best way to get rid of a body after making the kill. They'd moved on, apparently, from killing problem wives and were now focused on what to do with the body postmurder.

"We got into the topic of how to dispose of a body, involving laying down plastic on the floor, and that's where you would take the body and then quarter it," Atwood said in court, "and then remove the body in bags."

After taking a pull from his Bud Light, Atwood said, "I tell ya, BJ, I'd dump the corpse into the ocean."

Far out to sea. No one would ever find it. It seemed like a logical thing to do. Something that anyone might come up with after a round of beers.

BJ smiled. He had a more elaborate plan, he said. Something that took more guts, but was ironclad, he claimed, when it came to the authorities ever finding the body.

"What's that?" Atwood wondered.

"Well," BJ began, "I'd lay out plastic on the floor, then I would perform the dissection there with a knife, quarter the body or bodies, cutting off the legs, arms, and head. Then I'd wrap those pieces of body parts in bags and put them in different Dumpsters throughout the month, or to different Dumpsters throughout the city to avoid detection."

It was a bizarre comment, but then talking about the disposal of corpses was unusual talk to begin with, so Atwood really didn't think anything of it then. It was just the way SEALs talked outside the job. A way they dealt, essentially, with killing as a profession.

20

"I'm Sure in
My Brain . . ."

With Erika's .357 Magnum in hand, BJ pointed the barrel at Joshua and then Geney. After thinking about it for a moment, he said, "Take off your clothes."

"What . . . come on . . ." Joshua pleaded.

"Take off your fucking clothes, I said," BJ murmured through clenched teeth.

So Joshua and Geney obliged.

When they were naked a moment later, BJ asked both of them: "Do you want to die?"

And so as Erika explained it, when her husband pointed her gun at Joshua and Geney, and began barking out orders, she knew—right then and there—that he was going to kill them. It was something, she said, he had been talking about for some time: killing a fellow human being. It was as if their whole lives together had led up to this one moment. All those times they sat at home and watched *True Romance* and *Natural Born Killers*, bored with domestic life, had come down to this one moment.

"Oh, my God," Erika claimed to have said at this point. "I had no idea what was going on."

Yet, instead of running out of the condo and trying to find someone to stop her husband, Erika said she froze, and didn't know *what* to do.

Erika went through their clothes, she said later, thinking it would pacify BJ and lull him into a calmer mood, and that maybe she'd find the jewelry and the situation would resolve itself.

"I just kind of kicked their clothes around to make BJ think I was looking for the shit," Erika told a government agent. "But didn't really, because I knew it wasn't in their clothes."

Of course not. They had been wearing bathing suits. They had never left the apartment. Where in the world did BJ or Erika think they had stashed the merchandise? Besides, why would Erika even say this? How did she know the jewelry wasn't in their clothes?

"It's not here, Beej," Erika said.

"Son of a bitch," he seethed.

"Why are you doing this?" Joshua said. Same as BJ, Joshua was a military man. He had spent eight years in the army, traveling as far as Korea. At six foot one, he wasn't a small dude by any means. He had a black belt in karate, yet was never one to flaunt it or brag about what he could do. As two military men, Joshua and BJ were far different, however. Joshua had gotten out of the army with an honorable discharge; whereas BJ, it was well stated, had gotten into some serious trouble and, after a court-martial, pleaded guilty to a litany of charges. In fact, one report said that back in October 2000, BJ was convicted at "a special court-martial of two charges of going AWOL, three charges of insubordination, one charge of drunken or reckless driving, and one charge of wearing unauthorized insignia." Based on those charges, BJ was given a bad-conduct discharge, three months' prison time, forfeiture of his $600-a-month pay, and a reduction in rank. After an appellate review, the navy issued a notice that BJ's discharge had been finalized. Later, however, BJ would say he did it all—staged the crimes—for Erika's sake because she couldn't survive in the world without her hubby next to her all the time—and the navy was interfering with that. It was best for both of them if he left the navy.

As Joshua and BJ stood, toe to toe, BJ had that crazy, drunken, evil gaze in his eyes, Erika later speculated: *Make a move and I'll kill you!* He had crossed a threshold, for sure. And once BJ set his mind on something—especially where pride, ego, and crossing him were involved—there was no turning back until he felt confident the situation was under *his* control.

"I'm sure in my brain," Erika said later, speaking of that moment, "he's gonna go crazy. He's gonna do something fucking crazy, because he doesn't care about the shit that's missing. He was jumping at the opportunity to whack somebody. He's always wanting to kill somebody, 'Let's do this, let's do that.' So I'm freaking out because I know . . . I almost *know* what's coming."

Geney grabbed Erika by both her arms and started shaking her, according to what Erika later told the government agent, saying, "We didn't take your stuff. . . ." Geney sounded sincere. She was begging Erika to believe her. "We'd never *do* that."

BJ started to laugh.

"We've been good to you guys all night," Geney continued. "We paid your bus fare. . . . We're drinking. . . . We'd never do that stuff to you."

BJ was thinking again. Erika could tell. He had

something on his mind. He was quiet. The wheels were spinning.

After a few intense moments of uncomfortable silence, BJ finally said, "Get in the bathroom," using the gun as a wand to direct Geney and Joshua toward the door.

Joshua and Geney started toward the bathroom—and then ran as BJ hurried after them. But Joshua was quicker and managed to get himself and Geney into the bathroom first, slamming the door shut behind them, and then locking it before BJ had a chance to catch up.

21

Military Man

BJ was the oldest of Elizabeth Sifrit's two children (he has a younger sister). By the time he met Erika, BJ's parents had been married for close to twenty-eight years. BJ grew up in the Midwest—Iowa and Minnesota—but during his sophomore year of high school, the family uprooted because of his dad's job and moved just outside Houston, Texas. At Cypress-Fairbanks (Cy-Fair) High School, whose school motto seemed to fit with BJ's future, "Bobcat Fight Never Dies," BJ was a competitive swimmer. He was not a lazy kid and often had several jobs: YMCA swimming instructor, grocery store worker, lifeguard.

One job BJ took to, like a shark to blood, was when he worked for a locksmith. He just seemed to relish the work. A friend said that she was once locked out of her house, her new key wouldn't work. It took BJ just a few minutes and he had the key fixed. Friends described coming home and finding BJ sitting on their couch, watching television. "He could get through any lock."

BJ's mother and father—good, hardworking people, according to those who knew them—adored their son and thought he was the model child.

"His parents were great people, as was his sister," said a former friend. "They had a very good relationship with BJ, that was obvious."

During his senior year, eighteen-year-old BJ decided he wanted to pursue a life in the military. At first, he wanted to join the marines, an admirable profession only the "few and the proud" were able to make a career out of. BJ's personality seemed to juxtapose perfectly with the marine's *"Semper Fidelis"* motto, loyalty and commitment, or, "Always faithful." This phrase summed up the drive and dedication BJ had in his heart at the time. He wanted to serve. He wanted to make a difference. He wanted to earn his liberty for his country. The military was the best place to sustain that compulsion and, at the same time, fulfill what is a noble vocation. Yet, as he thought about it and discussed it with his mother, father, and recruiter, the navy seemed to be a far better fit for BJ's character. Sure, he'd make a hell of a marine, but after getting very high scores on his recruiting tests, it was made clear to BJ and his family that he had qualified for SEAL training if he opted for the navy—in particular, a nuclear-engineering program the navy was offering then.

BJ did his basic training outside Chicago in Great Lakes and then shipped out to field training in Coronado, California, just outside San Diego. It was here where BJ endured the rigorous twenty-five-week conditioning program any future SEAL is required to complete. Many drop out at this point; this is the period of the training that separates, as SEALs like to say, the men from the boys. In fact, out of the 160 candidates enrolled in BJ's class, he and only seventeen additional recruits would ultimately graduate. BJ was named honor man of the class, a position designated by the group commanders to the top performer of the class. So dedicated and tenacious, BJ had not only made it through hell week and the rest of SEAL training, but he had finished on top. Several of BJ's former SEAL peers later reported that he could spend all night drinking at a bar, get home at 3:00 A.M., sleep for two hours, show up for drills, and have no trouble running ten miles and completing the day's maneuvers. Meanwhile, some of his SEAL peers, heading off to bed at 8:00 P.M., eating rice cakes and drinking energy shakes, had trouble keeping up after five miles.

For BJ, indeed, it was mind over matter. He had read that the powerfully dedicated mind could accomplish anything—and he proved it.

After SEAL graduation on August 15, 1997, BJ was sent to his first SEAL platoon in Norfolk, Virginia, where he kept in close contact with his mother, father, and sister, flying home any chance he could and, if not, calling nearly every other day, just as he had in San Diego.

By the end of the year 1998, BJ had completed medic training in North Carolina, another twenty-five-week, intense training course (Corpsman Training Delta 18), where he learned everything from working on injured soldiers in the field, to conducting autopsies on cadavers. Next to God, most field soldiers will say, the corpsman is the soldier's best friend.

During this part of his training, BJ conducted between "six and twelve" dissections, he later explained, of cadavers. At first, that initial cut, BJ said, "was awkward." The first time he had worked on an expired human body was not the most pleasant thing he had ever done. "But you got used to it." It was the nature of every part of the SEAL training: All of it seemed impossible if you sat down and went through it on paper, or in your head, thinking about what you had to do; but you made it through because you didn't think about what you were doing. Instead, you just did it.

The field training—making wounds look real—was something the military went to great lengths to stage for its SEAL candidates. They had what were called "Hollywood kits." With fake blood and special effects, the military made the scenes look as gruesome as possible.

After a while, a SEAL became immune to the effects of the injuries and brutality of what he was involved in. Regarding battlefield triage injuries, "I was told to treat [injured soldiers] like machines . . . and I would be the mechanic and try to fix the problem," BJ explained in court. A soldier would never look at it as his best friend lying there injured, fighting for his life. A corpsman took emotion out of it. He did the job and moved on to the next situation.

And that was that.

After a while, a soldier with his guts hanging out of the side of his body was not what a medic saw; he took himself out of the situation and understood that it was something he needed to fix, like a broken robot.

Beyond the graphic Hollywood effects and cadavers BJ worked on during training, live beings were brought in, too. This was where things got really weird during training, BJ later said.

"I worked on mainly goats, but also pigs."

As the training drew to completion, corpsmen were asked to take part in, as a final exam, a final training exercise (FTX). In BJ's case, it was a "realistic [helicopter] crash scene with multiple casualties." In this exercise, the trainers brought in several live goats and, as BJ explained it, "some were injured intentionally more than others." Some were dead. Others were maimed and hurt beyond repair.

It was BJ's unit's job to help save as many animals as they could.

"But in the end," BJ said, "they all died."

Another part of BJ's training included serving on an EMT ambulance squad in New York City and a stint in an emergency room at a Manhattan hospital for one month, where he witnessed people die and people maimed and people in all sorts of real life-threatening situations.

During BJ's first three years in the military, he put up stellar performance numbers and records. Bar none. He had a reputation that few ever achieve, earning a good-conduct medal and expert marksmanship status with a rifle and .45-caliber pistol. According to his military record, his career was running swimmingly, but then things started to change for him when, he later said, "I met Erika."

Indeed, if you believe BJ's version, once he hooked up with Erika, his military life quickly spiraled out of control, like a plane that had lost its wings. It had become unmanageable very rapidly, without him even realizing it.

"BJ was not a violent person," said one former friend who knew BJ before he met Erika. "I felt completely safe around him all the time—except for maybe when we got into a car and he was driving." This woman, whose husband was a SEAL buddy of BJ's, had spent four months alone with BJ in her home. He lived there. "BJ was just quiet and very shy with girls," she said. "He would not even approach a girl in a bar. He'd ask me to approach the woman for him."

But then, Erika came around—and everything changed. Erika was so obsessed with BJ, said this same former friend, "that she asked me not to look at him, and definitely not talk to him." BJ was ten minutes late coming home one day after taking off with a SEAL buddy to go look at guns. He was right down the street from the home. Erika came in and "freaked out. She let out this bloodcurdling scream and threw her frozen pizzas all over the kitchen floor.

"'Where is he? Where is he?'"

Calm down. He was right around the corner.

Erika called his cell phone. "What are you doing?"

"I'm just down the street. You know where I am and what I'm doing. Relax."

She wouldn't calm down.

Come home, come home, come home. Right now.

She called BJ at least fifteen times, her friend said, until he finally shut off his cell phone.

BJ was soon faced with a choice: Erika or the SEALs?

BJ's parents had never met Erika, nor had they even heard of her when BJ called shortly after the wedding to announce that he was now married.

"August 21, [1999]," BJ told his mother over the phone. He sounded happy. "We met three weeks ago." Recalling the incident later, Elizabeth Sifrit had tears in her eyes, her voice scratchy and weak from the pain of having to recall how her son's life took such a nosedive into chaos.

BJ's problems in the SEALs started as early as 2000, merely months after he ran off with Erika to Las Vegas to get hitched. Mrs. Sifrit got a call one day. She was informed that her son had gotten into some sort of trouble, and by July 2000, she later said, "I knew he was going to select out of the SEALs."

* * *

One of the incidents involving Erika that added to BJ's list of growing problems with the navy took place in Alaska. BJ was in the Northwest as part of his Mountain and Arctic Warfare training, a rigorous test of endurance, patience, strength, and emotional stability. Only the tough survived the SEAL Alaska maneuvers—and BJ was certainly expected to complete his training without any problem, given his extraordinary performance rating up to this point, and likely to exceed expectation.

BJ was not allowed to tell Erika where he was going, whenever he went on training maneuvers. None of the SEALs were. It was policy. Part of the navy's disciplinary tactic of getting these soldiers ready for what could be the most covert operations in the world.

In some strange sort of code, which BJ and Erika had worked out before he left, BJ was able to get Erika the exact location of where he was stationed.

So Erika, lovestruck and going crazy back home without her husband around, flew out to Alaska the next day.

BJ snuck her into his room.

Part of BJ's training involved his corpsman work. He was trained in field medicines. He often had various amounts of narcotics, and even morphine, hanging around his room, for which he was responsible. Well, lo and behold, BJ got caught with Erika in his room—where his medicine bag was just sitting there, easily accessible.

A big no-no.

Later, a rumor would circulate that Erika and BJ had actually broke out the morphine and used it while she was out there; but if this happened, it was not included in the extensive report the military made of this breach of conduct. In that report, BJ was reprimanded and given a second chance. He was told to "thoroughly familiarize yourself with the Navy's rules and regulations concerning the storage and distribution of medicines both in the team area and while on training evolutions. . . ." Beyond that, BJ was told to report to his superiors for a good old-fashioned tongue-lashing. BJ was ordered to "keep the SEAL Team TWO Command Master Chief advised of [his] progress until directed otherwise."

BJ spent some time building up his reputation and standing again. But then soon after, things really went downhill when he was stationed at Camp Lejeune, in North Carolina, with Erika. By this point, Erika was putting a tremendous amount of pressure on BJ to spend more time at home. She had no concept of what a military wife was supposed to do, or how to act—better yet, a navy SEAL wife. Meeting BJ, Erika knew what she was getting into, yet she couldn't handle the time apart. It was turning her inside out to see BJ go away.

So, with Erika going crazy and causing BJ all sorts of trouble, according to BJ, he and Erika devised a plan to get him tossed out of the military so he could open a business with Erika and work side by side with her all day long—essentially giving her what she wanted.

On August 30, 2000, BJ walked off the base, leaving his "prescribed . . . appointed place of duty," a report of the incident noted. When he was confronted with the offense during formation by his staff sergeant and the hospitalman first class on duty, BJ shouted, "Fuck you!" to both of them.

The entire unit looked on in disbelief.

That sort of disrespectful, foul language didn't go over well with his superiors. Later that same day, when confronted with the offense by his gunnery sergeant, BJ took things a bit further by calling the sergeant out. When the officer failed to respond to BJ's insults, BJ said, "I see that you're all talk and no show." Then he walked forward into the guy, "pushing his body against [the] Gunnery Sergeant. . . ."

From there, BJ walked to the barracks, packed his things, and waited for Erika to pick him up outside.

Leaving the base without express permission from a superior was a direct violation of the law. BJ had not been authorized to leave.

He was in big trouble.

Exactly what he and Erika wanted.

When he returned the following morning near eight o'clock, BJ was walking through camp talking on his cell phone, which was, again, a direct violation of camp policy and code.

"Put that away, Petty Officer Sifrit," his superior said.

BJ stopped. "No." Then kept walking.

"Put that away, Petty Officer Sifrit."

"Fuck you!" BJ scolded, and walked off.

"What did you just say?" one of the officers nearby asked.

BJ quieted down some and smiled. "I said, 'Fuck you.' Did you *hear* me this time?"

During his court-martial, BJ was asked why he had used such language, upon which he answered, "I didn't have a reason—I just disrespected them, sir. I have no reason, sir."

"You have no justification for it?" asked the military judge.

"No, sir."

BJ and Erika had talked about how he could get kicked out of the navy on a "bad-conduct charge" because, according to BJ, she didn't want him to wait for an honorable discharge, which could take months, maybe even up to a year. This way, if he got himself kicked out quickly, he could do a little time in the brig and be done with it all.

The problems had initially started a few days earlier, on August 18, 2000, when BJ had taken off from the camp at a high rate of speed in his Chevelle on his way to get a haircut. Taking off, BJ floored the gas pedal and barreled out of the gate, which was manned by marines. Without stopping, at a speed of, he later said, "fifty miles per hour," BJ laughed as he drove through the gate. The marines stood guard at the gate, stopping each vehicle exiting or entering the camp, but when they spotted BJ hauling ass, they, of course, had to jump out of the way to avoid being hit and possibly even killed.

After his haircut, BJ went back to the base and did the same thing on the way back in.

At one point, BJ had been thrown in the brig, and his mother, Elizabeth, flew into town to hire a lawyer to get him out. Erika was "hysterical," going ballistic at the notion that her husband was in jail. At the apartment one night after a military hearing on BJ's account, Erika and Elizabeth got into an argument over what was going on and how BJ was going to get out of the brig.

Elizabeth was BJ's mother. She didn't need *some woman* he had just met and married telling her what to do, and how to handle the situation. More than that, BJ had made it clear later that it was Erika who had gotten him into so much trouble in the navy, with her constant need to meddle in whatever operation or maneuver he was involved in. Erika pulled her gun on Elizabeth, who had locked herself in the bedroom and called 911.

In the end, BJ got what he wanted. As a hospital corpsman second class, BJ was demoted several pay grades, forced to forfeit his $600-per-month salary, confined for a period of ninety days in the brig, and, exactly what he and Erika had wanted to begin with, booted "from the United States Navy with a bad-conduct discharge."

22

The Civilians

There is no doubt that Erika was the dominant partner in the Sifrit marriage. She had caused BJ great problems within the navy, and because of her unstable behavior, BJ had opted out of the navy. According to BJ, he could have obtained what is called a "separation in lieu of trial" (an administrative discharge), but Erika *insisted* that they take the case to trial and plead guilty with "assigned military counsel," instead of a much-respected, thirty-year, seasoned trial attorney Erika had hired early on in his case, whom Elizabeth was now paying for—that is, until the hired lawyer was fired.

On top of that, in order for Erika to "get her husband back," as one source later put it, "as quick as possible," BJ pleaded out to that "bad conduct" charge and was discharged dishonorably. But he could have—if he had fought it—stayed in the navy and continued on with his career. As he saw it, however, why bother? Why go back into the navy and be right back in the same position a month, or a year, down the road, with a wife who went crazy every time he walked out the door?

According to Erika, the second year of the marriage was when everything went wrong and her fairy tale turned into a nightmare. After the baby episode and BJ's court-martial and time in the brig, having him around her all the time turned out not to be what Erika might have expected. The scrapbooking business, which Erika's father had financed, was eating up most of Erika's time. She was now working seven days a week—all day long and well into the evening. Business wasn't great, but she was keeping the lights on. One of the only setbacks was BJ, who would actually scare customers away, Erika and Mitch later insisted. He'd be sleeping in the store on the floor, or on a chair, and customers would walk in and then turn around and walk right back out.

It was right around this time, Erika said later, that she found out BJ had cheated on her a second time. Because of his repeated infidelity, Erika went into a severe depression and realized that she had built her life on the foundation of a guy she didn't even seem to know. It was a devastating wake-up call for her. Between working all the hours and dealing with BJ, Erika found herself at the psychiatrist's office in town, wondering how to fix everything.

It was the winter of 2001. Dark, cold, lonely.

"I received mental counseling for mental conditions to include OCD and anxiety order," Erika later told law enforcement.

As the sessions carried on, Erika's doctor prescribed what she later referred to as "a lot of medications . . . that just did not work."

Nothing seemed to deaden the pain or the anxiousness of worrying what BJ might say and do next, and how the business would survive the economic post–September 11 downturns hitting America. Add to these pressing issues, she and BJ were burglarizing various retail stores and selling the merchandise, and Erika was walking around with a huge monkey on her back. She knew that the cops could show up and arrest them both at any moment. But you ask Erika or those close to her during this time and you get the idea it was all BJ's doing—that his behavior alone was what sent Erika running off to a therapist, and eventually being placed on antidepressant meds. Not that she was burning the candle and committing felonies and abusing drugs and alcohol.

23

"What . . . Did You Do?"

Joshua Ford and Geney Crutchley were in the bathroom, likely pacing around, scared for their lives, wondering what to do. The bathroom was rather large. To the left was a stand-up shower; to the right a closet. Most of the floor space had been taken up by the hot tub, which was situated in the northeastern corner with a blue tile step in front, a blue tile deck along the wall by the large window looking out onto a balcony. On the opposite side of the hot tub was a countertop running the span of the wall, which had a three-drawer vanity underneath the right side, and an area in the middle and on the left side of open space.

This bathroom had hosted some great times in the past—not only for Erika and BJ, but for other couples who had rented the condominium before them. But now, BJ and Erika had a couple they had just met and partied with, both now being accused of being thieves, inside the bathroom as their prisoners.

They had kidnapped them. And Erika Sifrit was certain that her former navy SEAL husband, drunk and angry, with an immense chip on his broad shoulder, was going to kill them.

According to Erika's version of what happened next, after Joshua and Geney locked themselves in the bathroom, and BJ stood by the door pointing the gun toward them, she "ran downstairs and started looking for the stuff in hopes that I would find the stuff somewhere, that it was just misplaced, praying that I'm gonna find it and come back upstairs and say, 'Here's the stuff. See, it's okay. Don't do anything, period.'"

But that's not what happened next, Erika said.

Instead, while she was downstairs looking for her Coach purse, panicking, fearing BJ was going to snap and kill them, she frantically turned over couch cushions and looked in drawers and on tables and underneath the couches. She was startled by . . .

. . . shots.

Several loud cracks she knew had come from her .357 Magnum.

And then, as she stopped what she was doing, she heard BJ thumping at the door, trying to kick it open. How she knew this—she never said. But as she was downstairs, Erika later insisted, hearing those noises, knowing BJ had begun his killing rampage, she ran back upstairs quickly.

"What the fuck did you do?" she claimed she asked BJ as she watched him trying to kick the door open.

"It's hard for us to believe this scenario," Detective Scott Bernal explained to me later. "We found Erika's prints on the outside window of the bathroom." Thus, if BJ had kicked the door open as she ran upstairs, there would have been no reason for her to even be on the opposite side of the bathroom window, which you had to lean over the handrail of the balcony to get at. "No, instead, we believe," Bernal added, "that at this time, when Geney and Joshua were locked in the bathroom, Erika was looking in the window and directing BJ, telling him when to shoot Joshua and where."

Continuing along with Erika's first version of this tragic event, she said that BJ then stormed into the bathroom and went straight for Joshua, who had already been shot in the arm and was holding a towel on the wound.

Erika said she was pacing in the bedroom: "I did not even want to look in the bathroom."

Then, she said, BJ pointed the gun at Joshua's head and said, "Now you gonna tell me where our shit is?"

Joshua wouldn't answer at first. He was obviously in a lot of pain. Geney was terrified, screaming and crying, shaking. Then Joshua said, "I was in the army, you're in the navy, man. Why are you doing this? Why are you doing this to us?"

BJ got right up in Joshua's face at this point, Erika later explained, and said to him, "See you later, motherfucker!" Then he shot Joshua in the head, which dropped him to the floor.

Erika said she was still in the bedroom when she heard the shot and the *thump*.

Joshua did not die immediately, however, according to Erika.

"Come in here," BJ said excitedly.

Joshua was "bubbling, and there was blood coming out of his mouth," Erika explained.

"No," she yelled from the bedroom to BJ. She didn't want to see it. She didn't want to be a part of it. She didn't want to know what he had done.

So BJ came out of the bathroom. He looked at Erika. She had a wet patch easily visible on the front of her pants.

She had pissed herself.

"He started making fun of me," Erika recalled.

"You fucking pussy," BJ said, laughing. "You pissed your pants? Oh, my God." He couldn't believe it.

As BJ continued to laugh, Erika started shaking, she later insisted, and crying.

With Joshua on the ground, his legs straight out in front of himself, Geney had used his body for a shield and curled up into a fetal position, crouched underneath the open area underneath the countertop across from the hot tub. She was naked and whimpering and crying, scared for her life.

The determined gunman, Erika insisted—and keep in mind that BJ was qualified as an expert marksman with higher ranking in the military for shooting than most anyone else in his unit—missed his first shot at Geney. This, mind you, was while he was standing at point-blank range. The bullet hit the ground and lodged itself in the tile.

"This is impossible," Bernal later said. "Think about this. BJ is standing right in front of Geney, Erika tells us, and he misses. No way. You see, it's those little mistakes that a liar makes that can expose her."

Pissed off that he missed, BJ then held the gun up to Geney's left shoulder and shot down at her, "through her lung," Erika said, "and it went straight down through her, like he shot her down and hit her" on the top of the left shoulder.

There was blood everywhere by this point, Erika said. On Geney's arms. On the floor around them. All over her body.

The blinds were spattered with blood—apparently from the shots.

The walls. Behind the hot tub.

"All over the place."

This, with just a few shots from a .357 Magnum.

Again, Bernal said, it doesn't make sense.

Where Geney was curled up underneath the countertop, there was a pool of blood underneath her body, Erika explained, but she couldn't tell at that point if BJ had slit Geney's throat or not. At this point, all she said she knew was that BJ had shot the two of them, and that she had played no part in any of it.

With both Joshua and Geney now dead, BJ walked out of the bathroom and told Erika, who was again pacing in the bedroom, "You go out on the beach right now and you see if they threw our stuff over the balcony, or if there are any cops out there because of the shots."

(Erika had explained that there was blood all over the place, especially the floor in the bathroom. And she was certain that she and BJ had gone in and out of the bathroom. Yet, crime scene examiners found zero trace of blood or even bleach on the carpets outside the bathroom.)

BJ then explained to Erika—again, if you believe what she later said—that it was possible Geney and Joshua had tossed the stuff over the balcony in hopes of grabbing it on their way home.

"Go now, check that out."

Erika reluctantly left.

Interesting enough, as Erika told this part of her story to Bernal and the state's attorney (with her lawyer sitting by), she floated something out there that she needed them all to hear.

"He wanted me to go look for the police because, number one, he was afraid people heard the shots, and, number two, he was afraid from my 911 call that someone might be stopping by . . . and I swear I called 911 *before* any of that happened. I thought that they were stealing our stuff. I did not do that to cover up. I never even heard of anybody doing that to cover up. I wouldn't even think that."

"I cannot be away from you," Erika said she pleaded with BJ when he demanded she go outside and take a look around.

"You go and get the walkie-talkies (which they had used to communicate when doing burgling jobs) out of the Jeep and you bring one up here to me. I'm gonna sit here and watch these bodies."

So she went and retrieved the walkie-talkies, and took a quick look around the beach.

But didn't find anything.

"So we looked all over the place," Erika later said, ". . . and it (her missing purse) was underneath the bed in the master bedroom on the balcony side."

So all their stuff—the large Hooters bag with the gun, jewelry, pills, her wallet, their cash, and everything else—was underneath the bed upstairs in the master bedroom, Erika explained.

Sitting, listening to her, Bernal had the feeling that she was lying about everything. Later, after the interview, Bernal went back and measured the clearance between the bed and the floor.

Half an inch.

She was lying.

As they both stood there staring at their stuff, Erika recalled, with two dead bodies in the bathroom, BJ started to make fun of her again, calling her a sissy for pissing in her pants. Then: "These bodies are going to start stinking," she claimed BJ told her. "We need to get rid of them."

And that's when things, Erika said, took an unusually graphic, terrifying turn for the worst.

24

All Jacked Up

BJ was fired up, Erika said, when she arrived back upstairs and they had found the belongings they thought Geney and Joshua had stolen. But now, she explained, BJ was faced with the growing dilemma that they had two bodies to get rid of, and nowhere to dispose them. Also, they had a bathroom in a rented condo that was full of blood.

"Go downstairs and get me some garbage bags," BJ said to Erika. She could tell his wheels were spinning; he had an idea.

"He was, like," she said later, "acting really, really rash. He was, like, all pumped up and just telling me what to do and calling me a pussy and, like, 'Go do this' and 'Go do that.' All jacked up."

Erika ran down the stairs and brought back the bags. Tossed them on the countertop inside the bathroom.

"They're white, you stupid bitch," he said. "What am I

gonna do with white bags? They're fucking white! Go get me *black* ones."

Again, all this traveling in and out of the bathroom by the pair of them, and not one trace of blood was ever located anywhere else in the condo besides this bathroom.

"I don't wanna leave, Beej. I cannot leave. I'm too scared. I cannot drive. I don't want to leave." (Erika added later, "It was four in the morning.")

"Go get some black garbage bags *right* now." BJ wasn't asking.

Erika left. She said she went to a dollar store right around the corner from the condo. (This seemed unlikely. A dollar store open all night? Didn't make sense.) Nonetheless, Erika said she got the bags—maybe at an all-night convenience store, later she couldn't recall which—and returned.

By then, BJ had managed to get both bodies, she claimed, into the hot tub by himself. Erika had spread the bags out on the countertop in the bathroom, where she had put the white ones earlier.

"Come . . . come over here," BJ said next. "I want you to look at this."

Erika looked at Geney and Joshua. Their eyes were glassy and glazed. Blood was all over them, all over the inside of the hot tub, all over the floor.

"Are these the first dead bodies you ever seen?" BJ asked.

Erika whimpered.

"Why don't you take a minute and look at it. It's a pretty sight, ain't it? Just take a minute and look."

"No. No. I'm going downstairs."

"Yeah, well, that's probably better, anyway. Because if the police come, then *you* need to be down there and *you* need to distract them so they don't come upstairs."

"Please don't yell for me," Erika said, "until you have

this stuff gone, because I don't want to see anything. It's making me sick. I don't want to see."

"Go downstairs on the couch and wait until I call you up here," BJ said.

What was odd to Erika, she recalled later, was that as BJ stood in front of her talking, a knife in his hand, waving it at her as he spoke, he was butt-ass naked. While she had gone to the store, he had undressed. It was as if BJ had shot a few deer and was preparing to dress them down.

He was in combat mode. Ready to take care of business.

25

The Inconceivable

Erika was curled up on the couch downstairs. She was holding herself, she later claimed, like a baby, rocking back and forth, scared to death.

Petrified.

Anxious.

"Lainey," BJ yelled from upstairs.

Erika looked toward the stairs.

"What?"

"Come up here."

Erika walked slowly up the stairs, she said. She had no idea what to expect. She knew that if she didn't go, BJ would come down. When detectives later looked at this and went through Erika's story, it became hard for them to consider the notion that Erika was that intimidated by her husband. She could have just as well run out of the condo and gotten help, or gone pleading to the police, telling them exactly what had happened. She had even left the condo at one point.

But she did none of that, of course. Instead, she gripped the railing of the stairs and slowly took those steps up toward BJ and his "little shop of horrors."

She explained later that she stood in front of her naked husband, who was now holding Joshua's head out to one side in one hand, and Geney's head out to his other side in the other hand. He was painted with their blood like a warrior. Smiling.

"Take my picture, Lainey," BJ demanded, according to Erika. He had an erection, too, she later claimed. He was standing there in front of her with both of their heads out to his sides. Their headless corpses were inside the hot tub. "Get your camera and take my picture. Do we have a digital camera?" BJ asked. "I'd like to send this photo around to my buddies." He laughed.

Erika was sick. She had her hands over her mouth. "You asshole," she said, "don't call me back up here again."

"You sissy," BJ said, mocking her. "You're a baby."

She ran back downstairs, and "I vomited in the bathroom down there." She didn't have anything in her stomach, so she began dry-heaving, a fluorescent yellow mucus coming out of her. "It was the grossest thing I had ever seen in my whole life," she said later, recalling seeing BJ holding the two heads, standing in front of her with that erection.

The heads were BJ's trophy, Detective Bernal remarked. "His crowning moment of the kill."

The knives BJ had used to decapitate Geney and Joshua, and eventually to dismember them, Erika explained, had been gifts.

"The two knives he used were identical Spyderco knives. We had got them for Valentine's Day, matching ones—they were silver . . . Spyderco blades, just, only about three and a half inches long—that's what's so sick!"

Erika was downstairs on the couch again, crying,

holding her hands over her ears. BJ was taunting her from upstairs. Yelling at her. "Baby. Sissy. I cannot believe you are *not* watching me do this."

Erika went back upstairs at some point. BJ pointed to the walls. "Isn't that so cool?" he said. "Just like in the movies."

He was referring to all the blood spilled on the walls. It was like someone had tossed gallons of red paint everywhere in a fit of artistic rage.

"I felt like I was actually watching myself in a movie," Erika later explained. "I was literally in shock. I know that's a cliché, but it's the truth."

If what she had seen already wasn't shocking enough, what happened next might seem as though that Hollywood movie had taken an even darker, more evil turn.

There was blood now covering the entire floor of the bathroom. The headless corpses were still inside the hot tub. According to what detectives later said, Erika told them that BJ then took Geney's head, propped it up on the water spout, grabbed her headless corpse, and then had sex with it while Erika was "forced" to watch.

But even that wasn't the worst.

Erika had run back downstairs and started pacing. BJ called her back upstairs.

She went, thinking that he was finally finished with whatever he was doing.

By now, BJ had cut off the arms and legs from the bodies. He had placed them in the garbage bags Erika had purchased earlier. Joshua's torso, however, was up on the edge of the hot tub and BJ needed help lifting it into a bag.

"No way," she said. "I cannot help you do that. I can't do it, Beej."

"Help me move this." BJ had his hands on one end of Joshua's torso. "Come on now. Help me out here."

When she refused again, BJ picked it up like a sack of potatoes, heaved it over his shoulder, and moved it himself.

"Sissy."

When he was done putting Joshua's torso into one of the big black bags, he walked over to one of the other bags with the legs inside, opened it, and cracked the leg in half with his foot, as if it were a piece of wood. Staring at Erika, he said, "Can we have this for dinner?"

"What?"

"I want you to cook this."

Bernal later asked Erika, "Did you?"

"No."

"Did *he* cook it?"

Erika wouldn't answer.

"Did he *eat* any part of these two people?" Bernal wanted to know.

"Not to my knowledge."

"Do you know if he drank the blood?"

"Not to my knowledge."

Back inside the bathroom, Erika said, BJ was fixated on cooking the leg. He had always talked about eating human flesh, she said. It was a turn-on for him to even talk about it.

"If I cut the meat off," BJ said, "will you cook it?"

"No. No way, Beej."

"Go downstairs and get the kit bags," BJ said after Erika apparently talked him out of cooking and eating one of Joshua's legs.

Kit bags were BJ's old SEAL canvas bags, larger in size and obviously a lot stronger than plastic. Joshua's torso wouldn't fit into one of the garbage bags the way BJ had wanted. The kit bags, about five or six feet long, would do the trick.

The way in which Erika described the bathroom at this

point of the night was indeed worse than any scene out of any horror film. You couldn't walk in that bathroom without splashing blood all over, she claimed. There were organs, she added, just floating in a pool of blood inside the hot tub. Body parts all over the place. Bits of flesh and bone on the floor. Blood on the walls. The blinds. The countertops.

Everywhere she looked. Red.

After BJ packaged the body parts in bags, he said they were going to have to dispose of the bags in Dumpsters somewhere.

By now, it was six o'clock in the morning. The sun was up. They had all these bags with body parts and they needed to get them into the Jeep so they could drive somewhere and dispose of them.

Erika took one last look at everything, she claimed, as BJ smiled and teased her. For a moment she just stood with her hands over her face, wondering how the night had turned into such madness.

BJ had these plastic storage tubs he had put all of the bags into. This way, they could get them downstairs without leaking blood on the concrete or inside the Jeep.

"I'm taking a shower," he told Erika. "Then we're packing up the Jeep and taking off."

26

Dump Site

Erika claimed to have passed out in the Jeep on the way to the first dump site. She said she had snorted so much Xanax throughout the night and into the morning that it knocked her out. She and BJ had been up by this point for twenty-four hours. They were driving north on Route 1, heading toward the next major beach town, Rehoboth. It was a little more laid-back in Rehoboth. More private. Lots of supermarkets and large department stores. Residential neighborhoods.

BJ was thinking . . . *Dumpsters*.

When Erika woke up the first time, they were parked in the back of the Hotel Blue. "Where are we?" she asked, coming out of it, opening her eyes, looking around.

BJ got out. There were people around.

Then he got back into the Jeep. "We're gonna keep driving."

Erika went back to sleep.

It was a "considerable amount of time" before she

woke up again, because Erika looked at the clock in the Jeep the second time she got up and about forty minutes had passed.

When she opened her eyes, the Jeep was parked. BJ was not in the vehicle by her side. Her heart raced for a moment. She looked around. *Where is he?*

BJ was outside the Jeep putting everything into two different Dumpsters.

"Get your ass out here and help me!" BJ had yelled at one point, but Erika refused.

She said she never got out of the Jeep, and never helped him, but instead she lay back down and tried falling asleep.

After BJ was finished, he jumped back into the Jeep and started to drive. Looking both ways, pulling out of the back of the supermarket, he said, "You know where we are?"

"No," Erika said.

"Delaware."

"Oh."

"We're going to come shopping here tomorrow. I'm gonna bring you out here to the outlets."

The trip would serve two purposes: he wanted to make sure the Dumpsters were emptied, he explained, and a good shopping excursion at the outlets was something Erika could probably use at this point.

As they drove, Erika began falling in and out of it again, still tired from her night of horror, and coming off so much Xanax and booze. She and BJ had been going in high gear for about eight hours, up all night.

At one point as they drove back to the condo, BJ looked at Erika, she later said, and, as calm as could be, he said, "I've never been that excited in my life."

"What do you mean? What are you talking about?"

"Sexually, you know." BJ was referring to killing

and then dismembering Joshua and Geney. It had stimulated him.

BJ had split up the bags and placed them into two different Dumpsters, each about forty yards apart from each other. He had even jumped inside the Dumpsters and sprinkled sloppy joe mix and various rotting foods over the bags so that no one got curious and opened up the bags.

Because he had worked at a grocery store when he was in high school, BJ knew that the large chain grocery stores emptied their Dumpsters two or three times per week. He knew that the particular Food Lion in Delaware he had chosen would be on the same schedule. He also knew that because rotten meat and other foods had been tossed out with regular garbage fairly regularly, the smell of the decomposing body parts wouldn't cause anyone much concern. The smells were expected, in other words.

When they got back to their condo at the Rainbow, BJ said, "Let's take a nap."

He plopped himself down on the couch and slept for "three to four hours," Erika later told detectives.

Erika had told BJ before his nap that there was no way she could clean up all the blood. He could sleep as long as he liked, but she wasn't about to go upstairs again. It was too damn eerie and disgusting.

As BJ slept, Erika went into cleaning mode, which is something she did whenever anxiety hit, like hunger pains. She started rearranging and fixing things downstairs in the condo. She didn't need sleep because she had slept pretty much the entire ride to and from the dump site.

When she was finished, she woke BJ up and told him, "You need to get this blood out of here. It's starting to smell. It's making me sick. You need to go up there and clean."

BJ smoked some of the marijuana he claimed Joshua had brought to the Rainbow and then went upstairs and started the gruesome task of trying to get the bathroom to look normal again. To BJ's delight, he and Erika still had almost the entire week left to their stay. The next couple expected at the condo wouldn't arrive until the coming Saturday morning, about six days away.

Most of Joshua and Geney's personal belongings had gone out with their bodies in the Dumpsters. But BJ, Erika later described, wanted to keep certain things for "trophies." Their IDs and Social Security cards, especially. Seeing that BJ could use them in the future if he needed identification for "something illegal," he had tossed them aside and kept them.

"He talked about [how] he wanted to wear the ring," Erika explained. "He saved the bullet, which he wanted to make a necklace out of. . . ."

The bullet was from Joshua's torso. According to Erika, BJ had carved the bullet out of Joshua so he could save it.

Later that day, they went to the local hardware store in Ocean City to buy cleaning supplies. The bags of supplies were heavy, and Erika said BJ made her carry them upstairs.

"You must understand," she explained to Detective Bernal, "when we go for groceries at home, he goes grocery shopping with me and leaves eight bags of groceries in the car and goes upstairs and sits on the couch. Like, I carried all the cleaning supplies up to the bathroom, or they never would have gotten up there."

Upstairs, BJ took a gallon of bleach and poured it all over the blood on the floor.

"That's not going to do anything," Erika told him.

"I know. They have that stuff that they spray to see if there's blood." It was almost a joke to BJ, she said. Like he was having fun with the entire idea of cleaning up the murder scene.

Later, as she was explaining this to detectives, Erika was laughing about the memory. "I'm sorry," she said, "there's nothing funny, but he dumped Clorox . . ." And she started laughing again.

"Clorox," BJ had said, "will cover up DNA, but they'll still be able to spray luminol and tell where the blood was."

BJ then got down on his knees and started scrubbing the floor. He was kneeling in about an inch of blood—high as a junkie, Erika said.

Looking back up at Erika as she stood just outside the bathroom, he said, "Help me."

"No way. I cannot clean up that amount of blood. You need to clean up the basics of it . . . the guts and the [left-over body] parts off the floor."

Erika walked over to the toilet and vomited.

Every time BJ would "come down from his high," he'd go back downstairs and smoke another joint.

Instead of helping BJ, Erika lay out in the sun on the balcony, making sure not to lose her tan. Back home, she went to the tanning salon every day. Why waste a moment in the sun—seeing they were in Ocean City already—and she was determined not to help BJ?

After a few hours, BJ was able to get the bathroom to a point where, Erika later described, "it looked like somebody had had a bloody nose or something. It didn't even compare to what it had been."

The next day, Tuesday, BJ and Erika went to the Home Depot and purchased paint and a new bathroom door and other supplies they needed to get the bathroom back to as normal as it was going to get—without gutting it and starting over. Any garbage they accumulated, bloody rags and paper towels and "body organs" and tissue and "guts," as Erika called them, along with wood molding too darkened by blood to be painted over, were tossed into trash bags or put directly down the garbage chute in the condo's main hall.

Throughout all this, Erika later insisted, BJ made her take photos, documenting the entire bathroom remodeling job. She said she was scared to say no to him, because he was acting so crazy. Looking back on the entire week, Erika, the scrapbook queen, had documented everything on film, even after the murders: the trip to Home Depot, everywhere they had stopped to eat or drink. And just about everything else they did together. In no way was she forced to take these photographs.

"And so you have to understand that this entire time everything he's asking me to do, I'm—I'm incredibly frightened to even tell him no, because I've never . . . I've heard him say things and I've seen him do crazy things . . . I was snorting Xanax . . . I cannot even tell you how many."

Still, looking at the facts, it's hard to agree with Erika. In almost all the photos taken of them together (by a passerby or stranger they met up with and befriended) during this period (before and after the murders), they are smiling, hugging, and kissing. There are even photos of Erika eating chicken wings and drinking beers and playing miniature golf and getting a tattoo of a cobra on her hip, where BJ later said she had made the "first cut" on Geney (which she later backed up during an interview with a government agent). There's one photograph of Erika and BJ each with a pile of crab legs in front of them—and this photo was taken about twenty hours after the murders.

While they were running around Ocean City like two newlyweds on their honeymoon, drinking and drugging and gorging themselves on all-you-can-eat crabs and pitchers of beer, Erika was wearing Joshua's ring, a tiny little blood spot on the inside arc of it, on a chain around her neck. And Geney and Joshua's IDs were in her purse. In no way was BJ forcing Erika to do any of this. Her own photographic documentation of the events before and after the murders, along with her behavior in the coming days, spoke to an entirely different scenario—one that put Erika Grace Sifrit at the helm of this ship, sailing her and BJ into a week of thrill-seeking madness, which they had both been leading up to for quite some time.

27

The Real Me

Questioning Erika, OCPD detective Scott Bernal had a tough time wrapping his mind around the idea that she was just some sort of innocent bystander who stood behind her violent husband because she was scared to death of what he would do to her. But as Erika talked about her marriage, which was based on lies and violence and threats, she explained that for her it was more than any of that—much more.

"Because I didn't think that anyone else would want me," Erika said when Bernal asked her why she had stayed in the abusive relationship, and why she never went to the police. "He loved me. He laid down with me at night. He worked with me. He, you know . . . Why would anyone else want me? I didn't want to be alone."

Erika further explained that "during that whole week, I was petrified of him. I didn't know, day to day, what was going to happen after that week. . . ."

Erika and BJ's crocodile was named Alabama. She

loved having these types of reptiles in the house. BJ thought that snakes were "associated with the Devil," Erika said, which was one reason why he enjoyed having them around.

Further along, Erika told a story about BJ, something he had once said regarding hurting people. There was a "true way" to hurt a person.

"If you want to hurt someone or there's someone you hate," Erika said, "you just go and kill their whole family so that they have to live without them, and you film it and you film you. . . . You film you torturing their family and then you mail them the tape, and they have to live without their family forever, and they have to watch the way that their family died—being tortured."

28

Killer Wife

In the middle of their ten-day vacation in Ocean City, two days after they had spent the night partying with Geney and Joshua, murdering and dismembering them, BJ and Erika met up with a new friend, Todd Wright.

BJ and Erika had gone back to Seacrets, drinking and drugging and having a good time, on Wednesday afternoon, and found themselves there well into the night. Todd seemed pretty drunk, but he was fun. What had started as a day of just sitting outside in the sun, banging back beers and shots, had turned into a night of heavy and hard drinking with Todd.

Erika was acting crazy, BJ said later. Totally out of it. Their new friend, Todd, was even drunker.

At some point that night, well before midnight, one of the bouncers from Seacrets approached BJ and Erika and asked them to leave. Erika was out of control. Stumbling all over the place. Slurring her words. Laughing at people.

There was one point where BJ had done a shot of tequila and vomited right there in the bar.

Erika broke out her camera and photographed it for a scrapbook she was going to make of the trip.

BJ had no problem leaving. They had been there for about ten hours already.

Erika snapped. She started yelling and screaming. Swearing. Spitting.

BJ walked over and restrained her. "I'll kill you . . . ," Erika screamed at one point as the bouncer began to now insist that they collect their belongings and get the hell out of the bar. As he did that, Erika took her gun out of her purse and began waving it around, saying, "I'll kill you. . . . I'll kill you!"

"Come on, Erika," BJ said, "let's go."

"I stopped her," BJ later recalled in court, "I mean, why not . . . of course I stopped her."

The bouncer was prepared to call the police after catching BJ trying to pick the lock of a bank machine inside the bar. BJ, however, grabbed Erika as she was laughing and waving the weapon, pulled her away, and, with their new friend, Todd Wright, left the club.

29

Fish Tales

Near midnight, as Erika, BJ, and Todd were out on the road after leaving Seacrets, Karen Wilson (a pseudonym) was at home when she began receiving telephone calls—sixteen in all. It was Todd, her friend. He was "falling-down drunk," Karen said later, and wanted her to meet him and his two new friends at another Ocean City bar. He just wasn't sure which one.

"Stop calling me," Karen said during one of the calls.

"Come on . . . ," Todd said.

"Stop it."

After being talked into it, perhaps just to get Todd off her back, Karen agreed to make the drive down to Ocean City from her home in Delaware, which took about a half hour. Todd had said something about being stuck on the side of the road with his new friends and not being able to change a flat tire. All of them were so drunk, he stammered, that they had no idea what to do. In fact, BJ was out there at one point trying to get the

Jeep lifted up on a jack, and Erika was, of course, taking photographs, documenting the little mishap.

Erika later said BJ knew how to do it, but he was just "too damn lazy." This does not mesh with the photograph of BJ sitting on his ass on the concrete, trying to get the Jeep off the ground after taking the tire off it. Apparently, it had fallen off the jack.

When Karen made it to the outskirts of Ocean City, she pulled over and answered her ringing cell phone. She had first called Todd to ask him where they were. He wasn't sure, when she had spoken to him last, but he said he'd find out and call her back.

"I don't know," he said. "We left one bar . . . You're not going to believe what happened. I've been hanging out with this couple all night. We got a flat tire."

As Karen now understood it, they were too drunk to change the tire. They had been sitting off to the side of the road, waiting, trying to decide what to do next. The guy Todd was with—meaning BJ—had gotten the tire off the Jeep, but couldn't get the spare on.

"Name off a few streets around where you're at," Karen told him, "and I'll come and find you." She couldn't believe what was happening. Why in the world was she getting involved with this mess?

Karen and Todd finally agreed on meeting at Phillips Crab House, a decades-old establishment on Philadelphia Avenue in Ocean City.

Karen was right down the street. "I'll be there soon."

Describing her friend Todd Wright, Karen later said, when he got into the car, he was "incapacitated," drunk beyond anything she had ever seen. "Cross-eyed and stumbling."

When she and Todd arrived at the Jeep, where Erika and BJ were waiting, two blocks south, Karen got down on the ground herself and changed the tire. BJ had removed the flat tire, but he couldn't manage to get the spare onto the rim and attach the screws. He and Erika were laughing and stumbling all over the place like two junior-high kids drunk for the first time.

When Karen was done, BJ and Erika walked over and thanked her.

"Can we buy you . . . a drink for helping us out?" BJ asked.

It was strange how he and Erika seemed so out of it one moment and OK the next. Not quite sober, but coherent enough to communicate. How could they not figure out how to change a flat tire?

Karen felt "uneasy about the whole situation," she later said in court. Something about the couple wasn't right. It was her intuition, telling her to stay the heck away. Not only were they drunk, but Karen saw a bit of craziness in their eyes.

"I'd rather not," she told BJ.

Todd stumbled over. "Let's go get another . . . drink . . . ," he tried to say. "Come on, Karen."

"You really don't need another drink," she told her friend. "Let's just go home."

Erika said, "Oh, come on, just one, *please?*" She held up a finger. "Just *one* drink."

"Let's just go with them," Todd pleaded. BJ and Erika were pressuring him to get Karen to take them up on the offer. "Come on, just one drink."

"All right," Karen said reluctantly. "Just one."

It was late. Well after midnight now. So they drove to Fish Tales, only a few blocks away from Phillips. Karen was going on a trip in a few days. It had been planned for some time. The last thing she wanted to do was stay out all night.

One drink and I'm out of there.

After entering Fish Tales, as was her normal course,

Erika took out her camera and started snapping photos of everyone.

"Come on, Karen, get in there with Todd and BJ, so I can take your photo."

Karen balked.

"Just do it."

She did. At no time did Karen ever notice BJ insisting that Erika take photographs. It seemed to Karen that Erika was doing it all on her own, directing everyone and truly eager to document the night.

At one point, Karen noticed that BJ had a bloody lip, bloodstains on his lower teeth, and some swelling near his chin.

"What happened to you?"

"Ah," he said, "I hit my mouth on the steering wheel when we hit a curb and got that flat tire." He was so drunk, he explained to Karen, he couldn't see where he was driving.

Karen had Hawaii on her mind. She was flying out of town in two days. She needed to phone a friend who was already there, she told Todd, and give the girl her flight information. So she excused herself from the bar, where they were all sitting, and went outside to make the call.

When she returned a few minutes later, Todd had spilled his drink, drank the drink Karen had ordered (but hadn't touched), ordered her another, and drank half of that.

Whatever was left over, Karen dumped out.

I'm out of here.

Indeed, it was time to leave. Karen needed to get home. She told Erika, "You guys should probably call a taxi. You're in no shape to drive."

"Come with us," Erika said. "You drive us."

"No, no, no. You guys should really go. Call a taxi."

The Rainbow wasn't far: a straight shot, south on the

Coastal Highway for about five miles. Erika and BJ could take a taxi home, then get a ride back in the morning to pick up the Jeep.

"Please, can you just follow us back to our condo?" Erika pleaded. She sounded desperate.

"I don't know. . . . Let me go talk to BJ," Karen said. She wanted to see if BJ was in any shape whatsoever to drive. Maybe he could drive and she'd stay close behind. Once they got to the Rainbow safely, Karen could take off with Todd and call it a night. Get away from this crazy drunken couple.

But after taking one look at BJ, Karen could tell he was in no shape to get behind the wheel of his Jeep.

"Trashed," Karen later said. "Intoxicated beyond belief."

Erika, whom Karen was already calling "Lainey," after Erika insisted that she be called by her nickname, was in far better shape. She seemed up and more alert.

"I cannot control Erika," BJ said to Karen as they talked.

"What?" Karen said. It made no sense. "What are you talking about, BJ?" Erika was in far better shape than he was, Karen thought, to drive a vehicle.

But that's not what BJ meant.

"Erika, my wife," BJ continued. "I can't control that girl. If she wants to drive and . . . and . . . she gets pulled over, my girl packs heat." BJ slapped himself on the side where he kept his gun in his shoulder holster. "Heat, I said. She'll kill a cop."

Karen realized at that moment that she was entirely out of her element. She couldn't believe what she was involved in. Or what she was hearing. It was clear that one of them—either BJ or Erika—was going to drive back to the condo. And there was nothing she could do to stop them. So the best thing she could do for the situation was to follow them and make sure they made it back without killing themselves or someone else. How, in fact, she was going to do that was another question entirely.

"Follow us, Karen, please?" Erika pleaded. She was begging again.

"Well, listen," Karen said, "if you guys are going to drive, I might as well follow you."

And so they left. BJ and Erika in their Jeep, and Todd and Karen in her vehicle.

Karen kept her distance. BJ was driving, or, rather, trying: swerving in and out of lanes, slowing down, speeding up, riding the brake, and just bouncing the Jeep all over the road.

Todd was sitting next to Karen. He was totally out of it. "His eyes were rolling back in his head," Karen said of Todd.

When they pulled into the parking lot of the Rainbow about eight minutes after leaving Fish Tales, BJ ran up to Karen's driver's-side window. He looked like he wanted her for something, and didn't want her to leave.

"Hey," he said, "I need your help. Lainey is *totally* out of it. Can you help me carry her upstairs?" Erika and BJ were staying in the penthouse, the top floor of the Rainbow, he explained to Karen. If she could just help get Erika into the stairwell and into the elevator, he would greatly appreciate it.

"Let me go talk to her and at least say good-bye and see how she is," Karen said, putting her car in park and shutting it off. The last thing she wanted to do was extend the night.

When Karen got out of the car, Todd came to and fell out of the passenger-side door and onto the pavement. The three of them then walked over to BJ's Jeep, and BJ opened the door and grabbed Erika, who appeared to be unconscious. When BJ tried picking her up, she slipped from his grip and hit her head on the Jeep door.

"Hey, you guys need to be careful," Karen said. "This is your wife, man. You're tossing her around like a rag doll." It seemed that BJ didn't really care about Erika's well-being, or he was too drunk himself to notice what he was doing. Either way, it seemed he was struggling to hold Erika up, making it appear as if there was no way he could manage getting her into the elevator and up to the condo by himself.

Perhaps it was part of BJ and Erika's plan all along: to get Karen and Todd upstairs. All things considered, BJ was a powerfully built man compared to Erika's deteriorating frame of approximately one hundred pounds. If he had wanted, BJ could have picked her up with one arm, Karen with the other, and carried both of them to the elevator himself, drunk out of his mind or not.

Inside the lobby, BJ talked Karen into helping him get Erika upstairs. Todd was right behind them, stumbling along, mumbling to himself.

When they got to the door on the top floor, Erika suddenly came out of her drunken stupor and started rummaging through her purse, looking for her keys, as if she had been alert the entire night. She grabbed her keys out of her purse and opened the door on the first try. No problem.

It was strange how she had just snapped to attention. Quite a bit different from just moments ago when she was deadweight and seemingly unconscious.

As they walked into the penthouse, Erika placed her purse on the table and went straight for the laundry room, where she noticed that the washing machine wasn't working. She'd apparently put some wash in before she and BJ had left earlier that night, and the clothes were still soaking wet.

"You need to *fix* this, Beej," she yelled into the other room, where BJ and Todd were waiting, "so we can *finish* the laundry." Little did Erika know then that Geney and Joshua's hair had clogged up the machine; they had washed some of the clothes that had been lying on the bathroom floor at the time BJ cut up the bodies.

Once inside the condo, Erika took Karen by the arm and led her into the living room.

"How 'bout a tour?" Karen asked. She was amazed by the size and splendor of the penthouse. She had never seen anything like it before.

Erika smiled. "Sure, come on."

As they walked around, Erika began to talk about the building itself. "My dad built this building and made this penthouse *just* for me," Erika bragged. She seemed completely sober now. It was strange. Just a moment ago, Erika was passed out in the Jeep. Now she was playing Martha Stewart with Karen, showing her around the penthouse as if she owned it.

"Really? No kidding." Karen was impressed. What a place.

"Yes."

"I run a [clothing business]," Karen said.

"Well, let me show you some of my bathing suits and blouses."

By this time, BJ and Todd had grabbed a few beers and were sitting at the kitchen table drinking. Erika came out of another room with all sorts of different shirts and blouses and bathing suits. She and Karen then walked into another room, where they started going through the clothes and talking about their favorite pieces of jewelry.

Girl stuff. It was the first time that night that Karen had felt a connection with Erika. They had something in common.

"I have this ring my grandmother gave me," Erika explained. "It's in my purse."

Erika then started searching around the room for her purse, but she couldn't seem to find it.

Karen was curious. She thought Erika had put it on the table when they walked in. But, then, maybe Erika had put it in her bedroom upstairs?

"Look, we really need to find this purse," Erika said. She was becoming quickly unraveled. Anxiety settled on her like bad news. "It's *very* important that we find this purse," she said again. And then a third time. "My grandmother's ring is inside it."

There were other items inside that purse Erika was worried about: Joshua and Geney's IDs, for starters.

By now, BJ and Todd were part of the conversation. "What's going on?" BJ wondered, taking a pull of his beer. Todd was still drunk, falling in and out of it.

Erika was now completely animated and disheveled. "Beej, we *need* to find my purse. . . . *Those* people, their IDs are in my purse."

Those people? Karen wondered. What did Erika mean by "those people"? Yet, she could tell the phrase had some sort of dark, important meaning to Erika and BJ that they both understood by the mere mention of it.

"We need to find that purse," BJ said.

"Let's spread out," Karen suggested.

They began looking around the main floor of the condo, overturning pillows from the couch and cushions, underneath the kitchen table, in the kitchen, wherever they had been after they walked into the condo. Karen thought maybe someone was being funny and decided to toss the purse over the balcony, so she walked outside and looked down.

She couldn't see anything but a long, shadowy drop to the beach; she heard the subtle sound of the ocean waves crashing into the sand and the constant swoosh of the wind.

After hunting through the main floor, to no avail, Karen and Erika went upstairs and started looking around. When Karen came to the bathroom, where the hot tub was located, she noticed that the bathroom door had been taken off its hinges and placed there next to the door frame.

"It had what appeared, to me, to be a bullet hole in the door," Karen said later, recalling that moment when she saw the door for the first time. "But I didn't realize it was a bullet hole until later, when things began to make more sense."

30

Purse Strings

BJ came upstairs as Erika and Karen were searching for Erika's purse and suggested that someone go down and look in the Jeep. Standing there and thinking about it for a moment, Karen knew Erika's purse was not in the Jeep.

"We couldn't have gotten into the condo without her keys, which were in her purse," she said.

Indeed, Erika had opened the door to the condo. To do that, Karen remembered specifically, Erika had to go into her purse to find the keys.

Nonetheless, Karen and Erika went downstairs under BJ's persuasive urging and began digging through the Jeep. By now, Erika was frantic.

Hysterical.

Manic.

She needed to have that purse. It was as if losing it had sobered her up completely. She was in a seemingly possessed state now, wildly running around, mumbling things to herself, stressing to Karen that there was nothing more important than finding the purse.

After not finding it in the Jeep, Karen and Erika rushed back upstairs. Karen walked in first. Looking toward the stairs leading up to the bedroom and bathroom, where the hot tub was located, she saw BJ and Todd standing there on the small landing. BJ was standing in back of Todd. He had a weird look about him. Cocky and peculiar, like he knew something that no one else did.

Karen looked at BJ closer. Inside the front of his trousers, he had a large handgun tucked into his pants.

It startled her. *What is this?* Karen hated guns of any sort. How did a gun become part of this night all of a sudden?

Karen was not one to react with great drama to situations that terrified her, she later explained in court. So she said nothing and instead continued hunting for the purse. And as they turned over couch cushions and looked behind appliances once again, BJ walked up to Karen and grabbed her by the face with his large hands and pulled her, nose to nose with his face, as if he was about to kiss her. But the force he used and the agility of the gesture made her aware that it wasn't meant to be comforting or even erotically romantic.

"It's very, *very* important that we find *this* purse," BJ said stoically, with as much fear as he could manage to put into the words. He seemed stone-cold sober. Intimidating and frightening. There was no doubt, Karen now knew, that BJ needed to recover his wife's purse, or there was going to be a major problem.

More than that, Karen had a sinking feeling as BJ held her face in his hands that he was now implying that she or Todd had stolen the purse.

"BJ, look, there's no reason for me to take her purse," Karen said as BJ released the firm grip on her face. "I helped you put your vehicle back on the road. . . . I'm not a liar or thief."

BJ reminded her that it was *very* important to him and Erika that they locate the purse. Nothing else mattered at this point.

Furthermore, there was nothing she could say to change that.

"Why would I steal it? I have my own money," Karen said.

After a while, they were all upstairs near the bathroom. BJ was getting angrier by the moment. Stomping around. Mumbling things to himself. Making sure Karen and Todd were well aware of the fact that he had a gun. He'd take the gun out and hold it for a time, then put it back into his trousers. Todd was standing by Karen's side.

Erika was rubbing her head. Thinking. Not saying anything. She and BJ and Geney and Joshua were in this same predicament, not even five nights ago, and she knew how that night had ended. Yet she stood and she didn't say a word as BJ worked himself into a state she knew would ultimately lead down one road.

"If you're ripping us off," BJ said in a terse, harsh, threatening tone, "we've had *other* people try ripping us off. If you've ripped us off as the *other* people who were here, I'll do the same damn thing to you that I did to them." BJ was now staring at the bullet hole in the bathroom door, which they were all standing near. The danger was clear. "These people," he continued, "were bad people. . . . I'm ridding the earth of bad people. They came into *my* place and ripped *me* off! No more will they do that."

Karen and Todd would die the same way as the other couple had, BJ implied, if it turned out that they were thieves. According to what Karen later said, BJ wanted to make it clear that there was a price to pay in *his* world for thieves and liars.

A deadly debt.

At this point, BJ had his gun in his hand, but, Karen said, he never pointed it directly at her or Todd. He waved it around and used it as an instrument of intimidation. Just the sight of it was enough to quiet Karen and Todd down.

BJ became calm for the moment and ordered everyone to get back downstairs and continue searching.

"Now!"

After they spread out, Karen noticed that Erika was in the bathroom by herself, so she worked her way into the same room and cornered Erika. She wanted to talk to her privately about her concerns. This wasn't right. BJ walking around the house with a gun, threatening everyone. Maybe, Karen thought, if she just spoke to Erika, woman to woman, Erika could "get a handle on BJ." Maybe she could even talk some sense into Erika about what was happening. It seemed to Karen that Erika could perhaps tell BJ what to do and he'd oblige. Like she held some sort of power over him.

"Hey," Karen whispered, "I don't like to be around guns. They scare me. They make me really uncomfortable. I'll do whatever I can to help you find your purse, but you're going to have to ask BJ to put that gun away."

Erika walked out of the bathroom without saying anything. It was as if she didn't care, or didn't even hear her. And when she ran into BJ in the living room a moment later, Erika patronizingly said loud enough so everyone could hear, in a whiney type of voice, mocking Karen, "BJ, can you *please* put your gun away?"

Then Erika laughed.

"She spoke very nonchalantly," Karen recalled later,

"like it was nothing for him to be holding this gun like this."

BJ put the gun back into the front of his pants. "Keep looking," he said.

A while later, as they searched every nook and cranny of the suite, Karen was in the front bedroom frantically searching, when she heard a loud voice coming from another room.

"Oh, look . . . what . . . I . . . found. . . ."

Karen walked out of the bedroom and saw that BJ had pushed a cushion from the couch forward and pulled the purse out.

Thank goodness it was over. The purse had been in the couch the entire time.

Or had it?

Although Karen was thrilled, the find made little sense to her. Karen had looked in that same area of the couch several times. Inside and out. She'd turned up nothing.

31

Guns Don't
Kill People . . .

Erika and Todd went out onto the balcony on the first level of the condo and sat down on the lawn furniture to chill out for a while after the stress of finding the purse was over.

Karen and BJ sat down at the glass table, off the kitchen. The table was large, with four chairs. In the middle was a wicker basketlike pot with sand and seashells. You could look down through the center of the table into it. The atmosphere in the condo was a bit more calm, now that BJ had located the purse. As they got settled at the table, BJ asked Karen, "So why are you so afraid of guns?"

Karen didn't hesitate. "Nobody likes a gun pointed at them, you know."

Who could argue with such a statement?

BJ kind of laughed a little bit. He was thinking how to answer. Then, "Well," he said, "guns are portrayed as bad on television. Most people don't understand how they work." BJ pulled himself closer to the table, took the gun from his waistband, placed it on the table in the middle of the two of them, and started to take it apart. "Let me show you how this works," he said. "This is a SIG SAUER nine millimeter. It's my gun." BJ then got up and went into one of the other rooms and pulled out Erika's .357 Magnum and placed it on the table beside his, adding, "This is a revolver. . . ."

Karen could have cared less. She didn't like guns. Did the guy not get it?

As they sat and talked, BJ took the Altoids tin on the table in front of him and a bag of cigarette tobacco next to it and opened both. He explained there was marijuana in the tin. Then he started to mix the two—the marijuana with the tobacco—into a rolling paper he had cradled into a V in one hand. As he was rolling the joint, he said, "This is a little gift left over by the people who were here the other night." He gave Karen an eyebrow raise.

Karen knew who BJ was talking about when he said "the people," because, she recalled in court later, "he had made several references throughout the night regarding two people being over to [the condo] a night or two [before]." These were the people he needed to "rid the earth of," he had made a point of saying throughout the night.

On the glass table to the left of where BJ was sitting was a rolled-up twenty-dollar bill and what appeared to be some white lines of powder, which Karen took to be cocaine. BJ cleared up the confusion.

"Xanax," he said. "Lainey has an anxiety disorder, but she prefers to snort it."

Erika and Todd had come back into the condo by this point, and Erika asked BJ to get some pills out of her purse and crush them up. After doing that, he called Erika over, but he never touched the Xanax himself.

Erika bent down, snorted a few lines, came up, and smiled. Then she sat on BJ's lap.

Todd was standing in back of where Karen was still sitting.

"We need to go have some sex," BJ said, kissing Erika, grabbing at her.

OK, Karen thought, *that's my cue to leave! It's been an exciting evening, but . . . time to go.*

Karen stood up, turned to leave, and said, "Do you want me to take Todd with me or leave him here?"

It appeared the party was just getting started again.

"You can leave him here," Erika said.

"Fine," Karen answered.

With that, she said good-bye, walked out the door, got into her car, and left.

As Karen made her way back toward Delaware, just a few blocks from the Rainbow, her cell phone rang.

Now, who could that be at this hour? It was pushing 3:00 A.M. Karen needed to get home.

"Why'd you leave me here?" Todd said.

Karen wanted to wring his neck. "You were taking too long—"

"Pick me up."

"You'll have to meet me on the street. I'm not going back up there."

Karen turned around. When she got to the Rainbow, Todd was outside, stumbling around. She got him into the car—and he quickly passed out.

The following morning, Karen got on a plane for Hawaii and tried to forget about the ordeal, having no idea of the horror she and Todd Wright had narrowly escaped. In fact, it wouldn't be until she returned to the mainland ten days later that she learned what Erika and BJ might have done to her and Todd, had BJ not found that purse.

Part III

Oh, the Mistakes We Made

32

Missing

Martha "Geney" Crutchley was "very punctual," her friend Gloria Bancroft (a pseudonym) later explained to police. "I was the one that was late, and if I was five minutes late, she'd call me."

It wasn't that Geney was anal about people always being on time; it was more that she was concerned something had happened if someone showed up late to a meeting or a dinner date.

An underwriter, like Geney, Gloria had worked with Geney at an insurance company outside Fairfax City, Virginia, for the past five years. Not only was Geney a good friend of Gloria's, but she was also her manager. The weekly departmental meeting on Wednesday morning, May 29, 2002, had come and gone, and Gloria was getting concerned. Geney was never one to miss that meeting—not ever. In fact, so punctual was Geney that in all the years Gloria had worked with her, Geney had not only never missed a meeting, but she had never been late.

Gloria had spoken to Geney on the previous Friday as Geney and Joshua made their way to Ocean City. It was a quick call, Gloria later said.

"How's everything going?" Geney wanted to know, meaning at work. Then, "Are you coming to Ocean City to meet us?"

Gloria had mentioned something about maybe meeting up with Joshua and Geney at some point that weekend.

"No, I can't," Gloria said. "Sorry, I have something I need to do."

It was the last time Gloria spoke to Geney.

When Geney didn't show up for work, and there was no answer at her house, Gloria and a friend took a ride over to Geney's mother's house to see if she knew anything, or if she had possibly heard from Geney and Joshua.

She hadn't.

So Gloria and Geney's mother started calling friends.

No one had heard from Geney.

Or Joshua.

"We got really nervous," Gloria later explained.

Feeling that she had to do something, Gloria mapped out the way to Ocean City and began calling hospitals along the route Geney and Joshua would have driven. She thought maybe Geney and Joshua had gotten into a car accident.

But she ran into one "no" after another.

So Gloria contacted the Virginia State Police (VSP). A trooper told her to call her local police department, and she ended up filing a missing persons report with the City of Fairfax Police Department.

Late into the evening on Wednesday, Gloria ended up talking with someone at the OCPD and then giving a detective there a photograph of Geney and Joshua. "So they would find them and bring them home," Gloria later said. That was Detective Scott Bernal, who was on the case.

33

Greene Turtle

On Thursday, May 30, 2002, BJ and Erika woke up and decided that they had better get that door fixed and painted. BJ had purchased a new door at Home Depot already, but it needed to be painted and hung. Time was getting short. A new couple would be checking into the room on Saturday.

"I'm going to lay out," Erika said. It was a bright and sunny morning. She wanted to work on her tan.

When BJ finished, he asked Erika what she wanted to do.

"Take me tanning," she said. She had purchased a week's worth of tanning at a local salon and didn't, she later told police, "want to waste any of it."

BJ sat at the table and smoked a joint.

And now he had the munchies.

"Let's go to Hooters," he suggested, "and get some wings."

Erika went tanning while BJ went into the restaurant

and ate himself a pile of hot wings and fries and drank a pitcher of beer. When she met up with him at the table after her tanning, BJ was white as a ghost. He looked pale and sick.

A moment later, he was vomiting.

Erika paid the bill and they left.

Back at the Rainbow, BJ slept off his high on the couch downstairs as Erika e-mailed a few people and took care of some business on eBay.

BJ was still out cold when she was finished. So Erika went over and shook him awake. "Can you get up, please? I would like to do something today."

"Yeah, yeah, yeah . . . ," BJ said.

After BJ collected his bearings, he told Erika he wanted to go over to the Greene Turtle, a local watering hole that served crabs and all sorts of different brands of beer.

"I saw a sign out front," BJ said. "They have Guinness."

As they walked into the Turtle, both stopped at the front door and marveled. There in front of them was a missing persons flyer asking for help in locating Geney and Joshua. In the surveillance videotape that police later viewed, they couldn't believe it as Erika stopped, smiled, and proceeded on into the restaurant after looking at the photograph, like it was just another night out.

BJ took a look and followed behind.

They stayed at the Turtle for most of the night, Erika said, listening to the DJ, drinking, and snorting Xanax in the bathroom.

BJ was pretty wasted again, as was Erika.

When it came time to leave, Erika said, she "assumed" that they were going home to the Rainbow. She allowed BJ to drive. He could barely see two feet in front of himself, but she was no better.

As soon as she got into the Jeep, Erika claimed, she passed out.

While she was out cold in the Jeep, Erika heard banging on the window. She had no idea where they were.

"Get up," BJ was saying. He was standing outside the Jeep. "We're at Hooters."

Erika was in and out of it. Her head was leaning against the window. BJ started pounding on the side of the door. "Get up. Get up. Come on."

Erika said, "What?"

"Get your ski mask." The Jeep was backed up to the Hooters gift shop, which is directly next door to the restaurant.

"BJ, are you crazy? Isn't there an alarm?"

BJ had a green bag in his hand. "Take this," he said as Erika got out of the Jeep. "No alarm. I already picked the lock. The door's open."

Erika looked over. Indeed, the door was wide open. What they didn't know, however, was that the OCPD did routine patrols throughout the city all night long. Also, there was a silent alarm BJ had tripped.

Erika followed BJ into the gift shop and they began robbing the place: cigarettes, T-shirts, mugs, anything and everything they could get their hands on. Erika made trips back to the Jeep as BJ walked around the inside of the shop, pulling things out he wanted her to take.

Both were armed. BJ had his SIG SAUER in his shoulder holster, and Erika had her .357 in the crook of her back, tucked inside her pants.

34

Busted

Police officer Jason Hardt was employed by the Winchester Police Department (WPD) in Winchester, Virginia, about a four-hour, 225-mile ride directly west of Ocean City. During the early-morning hours of May 31, 2002, however, somewhere after midnight, Hardt was working his summer job as a seasonal police officer with the OCPD.

Like most seasonal cops, Hardt enjoyed the gig.

The beach.

The babes.

The surroundings.

The action.

Hardt was riding with OCPD officer Freddie Howard that night when they got a call to check out a tripped alarm at 123rd Street, which is downtown in a little strip mall.

"Hooters restaurant," dispatch said.

As Hardt and Howard came around the corner and

pulled into the parking lot, they noticed there was a Jeep Cherokee backed into a parking space in front of the Hooters store. Two people were in the process, it seemed, of burglarizing the place.

"Are they placing merchandise from the store into their vehicle?"

As the two cops pulled closer to the Jeep, the woman sat inside the Jeep in the passenger seat and didn't move, while the male, attempting to get into the Jeep at that moment, stepped away from the door.

Erika and BJ. Caught in the act. Their reign of burgling Hooters restaurants all over Pennsylvania, Maryland, and Delaware now apparently coming to an abrupt end.

Howard and Hardt got out of their vehicle quickly and told BJ not to move.

BJ stopped and put his hands up. "Can't we just put the stuff back?" he said. "We stole it. We stole it. But we can put it back."

For some strange reason, BJ thought he could talk his way out of it.

Howard immediately grabbed BJ by the arms and handcuffed him. After that, he patted BJ down and found his SIG SAUER semiautomatic handgun tucked into the front of his trousers, inside a holster. BJ was also wearing one of those vestment-type shoulder holsters. There was no second gun inside that holster, but BJ had placed two magazine clips, fully loaded, inside the holster.

The gun tucked into BJ's waist was loaded. "It had a clip in it," Howard later said, "and there was one [bullet] in the chamber."

BJ Sifrit was armed and ready for a firefight.

The officers looked inside the Jeep and it was crammed with all sorts of Hooters merchandise and dozens of packs of cigarettes in display racks that BJ and Erika had obviously stolen. Another few minutes and they would have probably been long gone.

Howard asked BJ to have a seat on the ground in front of the store as Officer Hardt, meanwhile, went around to the other side of the Jeep. As he approached Erika, he noticed that she was leaning over to grab something inside the Jeep.

"Let's see those hands . . . ," Hardt said sternly.

Erika stopped.

"Exit the vehicle, ma'am. Show me your hands and get out of the vehicle—right now."

Erika got out of the Jeep with her hands up. Hardt quickly handcuffed Erika and brought her around to the back of the Jeep.

As Hardt began to pat Erika down, he noticed that she had what appeared to be a Buck knife, the type that folds in half, clipped to the front left pocket of her blue jeans. As he worked his way around toward her back, he felt what he knew to be a handgun tucked nose-first in the crack of her ass.

Hardt slowly took the weapon out and placed it on the asphalt away from where they were now standing.

"Can't we just . . . put this stuff back?" Erika asked pleadingly. "And you guys just let us go?" She was getting nervous. But no more so than any other suspect caught in the act of what was a class-A felony.

"What?"

"Can't we just—"

Hardt paid her no attention, but instead instructed Erika to sit down by a brick wall near the store.

Officer Howard, certain that BJ wasn't going to cause any trouble, began searching the inside of the Jeep more thoroughly. In the center console, he found a .45-caliber Heckler & Koch handgun, which was also fully loaded.

"Damn . . ."

Were Erika and BJ expecting some sort of shoot-out? They were certainly armed for it.

Underneath the gun was a lock pick, one of the tools BJ never left home without. Beside the lock pick were two ski masks and a pair of gloves.

At some point, while Hardt and Howard were analyzing the scene and making sure there weren't any other people involved (accessories), Erika called Hardt over.

"Officer, Officer," she said hurriedly.

Erika needed something. She was moving around and crying, and looked totally out of it.

"What is it?" he asked.

"I have . . . I . . . I have anxiety problems," Erika said despairingly. "I haven't taken my medication and I need it, and I need you to get it for me in my purse."

Erika had been snorting Xanax all night long.

"Where is your purse?"

"In the front seat of the Jeep."

By this point, there were other officers arriving on scene. One of the sergeants, Hugh Bean, had been called in. Hardt called him over to speak to Erika.

She told Bean the same thing, adding, "I need my Paxil and Xanax. It's in my purse."

"Where is it?" Bean asked.

"The front seat of the Jeep. I need those pills."

From where he was standing, Bean looked over at the Jeep. With the light from the gift shop shining into the console area of the vehicle, along with his flashlight, Bean could see Erika's purse sitting there inside the vehicle.

"I take it twice a day," Erika said. "I had one this morning but missed my dose at ten tonight. Please."

"OK, ma'am," Bean said. "Just try to relax."

"I'm having a panic attack . . . I need it!"

"Where, exactly, is the medication?" Bean wanted to know.

"Inside my purse, in a brown leather pouch inside the purse. The pills are in bottles, but they're not labeled. I need a pink and [a] white pill."

Bean walked over to the Jeep and began digging through Erika's purse, searching for her prescription. Bean found the pink pill right away, but he couldn't locate the white pill. In any event, regardless, Erika wasn't getting any of these pills.

As Bean dug through Erika's purse, he uncovered four spent .357 shells and one live round. It seemed strange that they'd have four spent shells hanging around in the Jeep.

"Huh?" Bean said to himself. "This is odd."

Bean continued searching. He saw what he believed to be a change purse, a small zipper bag. After opening it, he located "several IDs."

What is she doing with all of this stuff?

Bean was struck immediately by the photographs of the two people on the driver's licenses he found inside Erika's purse. He had been working on the night the missing persons case had been filed for Joshua and Geney, and as he sat there inside Erika and BJ's Jeep, he remembered that he had filed some paperwork that night and happened to run into the flyer with Joshua and Geney's photograph. All good cops—and Bean certainly could be included, with over twenty years on the job— keep their radar up all the time. They pay attention to what's going on around them in the squad room. It takes a team to solve cases.

"If it wasn't for Sergeant Bean's awareness on that night," Detective Scott Bernal said later, "this case may not have been solved."

Bean continued looking. He found Joshua and Geney's Social Security cards inside Erika's purse, and a

Bally Total Fitness Club ID with Joshua's photograph on it.

That looks like . . . , Bean thought.

Sergeant Bean walked over to his car and got on the radio. "Get me the captain."

When the captain came on, Bean said he thought he had found some information on a couple arrested for burglary that might have something to do with that missing persons case the OCPD had been investigating the past few days.

The captain told Bean what to do.

Bean called in the CID of the OCPD, got out of his car, and told his officers, "Shut this scene down."

Detectives were on the way.

35

Hostages

Captain Jeffrey Kelcher took control of the investigation, calling in Detectives Richard Moreck and Scott Bernal, who already had been looking into the missing persons case of Geney and Joshua.

After going through the Jeep and putting together the connection between Erika and BJ and the missing couple, Kelcher told Moreck and Bernal that they needed to get over to the Rainbow Condominium and check things out there.

"Immediately," he said. "They might be being held and might need medical attention."

Before that, Bernal walked over to Erika and sat with her for a moment, first advising her of her Miranda rights.

Erika signed the form, saying she understood.

"Are you willing to speak to me without a lawyer?" Bernal asked.

"Yes," Erika said.

He showed her where to sign.

"Where'd you and BJ meet Crutchley and Ford?" Bernal asked.

"I have no idea who or what you're talking about."

"OK . . . one more time . . . where'd you and your husband meet Crutchley and Ford? The two people whose identifications we found in your purse."

Erika looked puzzled. "Not sure what you mean."

Bernal went to his car and got a copy of the missing persons flyer.

"I never saw them before," Erika said defiantly.

"Come on . . ."

"My husband might have put those IDs in my purse. And if he did, it was because he found them."

"Why would you have spent bullet casings in your purse?"

For Bernal, who had worked several homicide cases before this one, it was rather obvious that two and two made four: spent bullet casings and IDs from a missing couple probably meant someone had been shot.

"My husband shot my gun and gave me the casings to show me how my gun worked."

It seemed that Erika had an answer for every question.

With all the evidence the OCPD found inside the Jeep, it appeared to them that maybe Erika and BJ had taken Geney and Joshua hostage and were holding them at the Rainbow against their will.

Bernal was concerned. He and Moreck decided to head over to the Rainbow right away with a team to see what they could find.

36

There Are
No Coincidences

State's Attorney Joel Todd's home phone was ringing. Although he didn't know it yet, the OCPD was on the other end, calling with some news about the missing persons case that detectives had been investigating since the night Geney's friend Gloria had called and reported Geney and Joshua missing. Leading up to Memorial Day weekend, 2002, Worcester County state's attorney Joel Todd had been briefed about what had turned into a nagging, strange missing persons case the OCPD just couldn't understand, or let go of. For locals, especially in law enforcement, Ocean City is a small region. For that reason, Todd told me later, "I am probably made aware of things more often than my counterparts are in larger metropolitan areas."

In any event, Todd had been briefed about the calls the OCPD had been receiving regarding Geney and Joshua. But Todd, of course, busy with more cases than he could handle, stuffed the information in the back of his mind and went about his immediate business. What could a state's attorney do, essentially, for a missing persons case?

Now, though, here it was, the middle of the night, and Todd's ringing phone was telling a different story. It was Detective Sergeant Richard Moreck.

"Hey, Joel, it's Sergeant Moreck, with Ocean City. Sorry to wake you up, but we've made an arrest of two people in a burglary. And get this, they had identification of those two missing people on their person."

It was well after midnight. Todd was still half asleep. "OK," he grumbled, "let me get up and I'll be right over."

It was important for Todd to get over to the OCPD so he could begin consulting detectives on how to handle the case from this point on. It's not every day a burglary arrest turns into a connection to two missing people. Every step detectives made from this point on—if things turned out the way everyone had hoped they *wouldn't*— would be scrutinized at some point by a judge, jury, and, more important, defense attorneys.

Still, it didn't take a supersleuth to consider that something had happened to Geney and Joshua, and that Erika and BJ, having been caught with Geney and Joshua's driver's licenses and other personal items, had had something to do with it.

Now dressed and wide awake, Joel Todd got into his car and headed over to the OCPD. Although he didn't realize it just then, it was the first hour of what was slated to be a twenty-three-hour workday for him.

37

Probable Cause

Finding those items of Geney's and Joshua's on Erika and BJ after their arrest gave the OCPD the opportunity to use an "exigent circumstance" clause in the law to go right into BJ and Erika's condo without a search warrant.

"They went in under this exigent circumstance to see if there are any people there alive," Joel Todd said later. "The OCPD had found flex cuffs, ski masks, and that kind of stuff on the two suspects."

Which was enough to cover them under the law.

Detectives were "hoping," Joel Todd said, it was a hostage situation. "Because, let's face it, you normally wouldn't need flex cuffs and ski masks if you're going to have dead people. You would generally only need those items for live people."

Early the following morning, OCPD detectives, with uniformed officers and emergency medical technician (EMT) backup in tow, busted into room 1101 at the Rainbow, and conducted a quick search for any live people.

Upstairs, Moreck went into the bedroom. After searching that room, the corresponding balcony, and the bathroom with the hot tub, he found no one. But as Moreck passed that glass table in the kitchenette area downstairs a few moments later, he saw two spent rounds of ammunition just sitting there.

Both had what appeared to be flesh and blood on them.

Son of a bitch.

"One of the projectiles," Moreck said later, "was significantly more damaged than the other. . . ."

More than that, one of the spent bullets had what appeared to be blood on it.

And it smelled.

Moreck called Bernal over. "Look at this."

There was human tissue on the bullet, too. It was as if someone had extracted it—or even dug it out—after firing it into a person's flesh.

With that, probable cause had been established. It was time to get a judge to sign a search warrant so they could get the forensic team into the room, as well as some more uniformed officers, and go through the condo more thoroughly.

38

The Robot

While in lockup, BJ Sifrit was tight-lipped, living up to the SEAL code of ethics when taken into custody: "Name, rank, and serial number," said one investigator, referring to how quiet BJ had become that night. He knew his rights and he knew that not saying anything would serve him down the road.

On the way back from the room, Bernal called the station and requested that BJ be brought to the CID interview room from his cell. Bernal wanted to give BJ a crack at explaining his situation (or possible involvement) in this entire scenario, based on what Bernal and Moreck had learned while sniffing around the Rainbow rooms.

Bernal's colleague, Detective Brett Case, who had also been part of the Crutchley/Ford missing persons search earlier that week, was on the opposite side of the two-way glass as Bernal sat with BJ. Case was a tough cop. He not only looked the part—with his steely gaze and the tall frame of an NBA basketball player—but Case had an amiable way about him. A guy like Case was an asset to any investigation. Sitting with him, just chatting, he had a way of making you feel like you had known him all your life.

Bernal had seen BJ's type before. "Shy on appearance," Bernal said, "but totally driven inside. Whatever BJ set his mind on doing, he proved to himself he could do it." It was a challenge, in other words, for BJ to set his mind on something and then go for it.

Bernal read BJ his rights. BJ signed off. Then Bernal said, "I'm an honor man, like you," referring to their military connection, but BJ wouldn't bite on the common-ground rapport Bernal was trying to build.

"Talk to my wife," BJ said a number of times.

"You want to tell me what's happening here?"

"Like I said, talk to my wife. *She* knows."

"What about you, BJ, what's *your* part in this?"

BJ said, "Hey, can we talk off the record?"

"We're legally bound by this form. . . . We cannot really speak 'off the record.' You can waive your rights, however, and talk to us without an attorney."

BJ thought about it. Sat back in his chair. "I want to talk to a lawyer."

Bernal got up and walked out of the room. Case and a few other OCPD officers were waiting.

"Take him back to his cell. We're done here."

39

The Trade-off

Erika Sifrit was another story.

After an immediate breakdown, in which she kicked and screamed and said something about not being able to live without her husband, she sat down with Bernal and said she wanted to cut a deal.

"A deal?"

"I will trade information about [the missing couple] to drop all of the burglary charges against me," Erika told him.

Bernal was floored by this.

Burglary? Why burglary?

40

Girls on Film

As crime scene technicians, detectives, and uniform officers began to go through room 1101 at the Rainbow Condominium complex, they began to see the disturbing picture of what had possibly taken place inside the bathroom, six days prior. Of course, no one at that moment knew or foresaw how cruel and violent and brutal these murders would actually turn out to be, but a clear portrait of a terrible crime became apparent almost immediately.

For starters, Geney and Joshua's Atlantis room key was found on a small table in the living room. Beyond that, police began to rip apart the bathroom upstairs, and what shocked them most wasn't all the blood they had uncovered, but that some of it was still tacky and wet. Moreover, roll upon roll of film—along with photographs of BJ, Erika, and, yes, Geney and Joshua—were quickly located. The one thing about Erika was that she documented just about every major event in her life. Apparently, murder—and the attempted cover-up—was one of those events.

The most telling area of the condo was the bathroom upstairs. On the wall, for example, leading to the toilet, was one drop of blood dripping down alongside the vanity. In fact, when technicians ripped out the vanity itself, all along the floorboard (or toe-kick) was a channel of dark and thick dried blood. It appeared as if the blood had found its way into the channel between where the tile floor met the vanity toe-kick.

Moreover, the door leading into the bathroom had just been painted, that much was obvious.

Even more disturbing, when detectives took out one of the drain spouts in the bathroom sink, the water stopper itself, from the bottom up to the top, was drenched red with blood. There was also a piece of someone's scalp with black hairs still attached, stuck inside the drain, along with more fresh blood.

After a careful examination of the grout, it was hard to find a place where blood hadn't stained it. On the side of the vanity were spatter and smudges of blood, as though there had been some sort of struggle there.

The mattress upstairs in one of the bedrooms had a large stain, about the size of a garbage can lid, on one end of it.

Over in the corner of one room was a blue Playmate cooler. Inside were two of Erika's massive, three-inch-thick, five- to six-foot snakes.

In the laundry room were new bottles of Drano. Fresh cans of paint. KILZ stain sealer. Rollers. Sandpaper. Paintbrushes. Tarps.

Someone had done a little remodeling recently, cops figured as they looked at the stuff.

The clothes dryer's lint catcher was filled with hair and tissue and what appeared to be coagulated blood that had gelled up like veal stock put in the refrigerator.

Inside a duffel bag downstairs was Erika's stash of

Yellow Jacket speed pills she had purchased from the Internet and stolen, as well as more Xanax.

But it was all the blood that concerned detectives most—and the fact that there was no sign of Geney or Joshua. There had been a struggle for life in this condo, detectives were certain. And it appeared that the only two to walk out of it alive were sitting in prison not saying anything all that much.

41

Fifty-Fifty

Detective Scott Bernal went in to see Erika again, after BJ had asked for a lawyer and she had made it known that she wanted to cut a deal for the burglary. For Bernal, a seasoned investigator who had made it his business to study the body language of the suspects he interrogated, the way a person shifted and moved was key to how an interview went forth and how he would proceed with questions. Bernal closely watched a suspect's body and how she reacted to certain questions. He'd ask a question that he knew the answer would be "no" to and carefully watched how the person reacted. Then he'd ask a question he didn't know the answer to and see if he got the same result.

"You can never control your body language," Bernal said later. "It's instinct." Once Bernal was questioning a man for a series of burglaries. He asked the guy, "Did you do this one?"

The suspect shook his head "yes" while answering "no."

"You cannot control how your body moves when you

speak. In that sense, Erika was easy to read," Bernal said. "She lied so much that we knew exactly when she was lying, because she couldn't stop herself from the way her body moved."

The other aspect of a good interrogation is quite simple, that is, where it pertains to questioning someone who you know had had at least some involvement in a crime. The guilty will always minimize their involvement. No matter what. Even if a suspect is giving a confession, he or she will always diminish his or her culpability. It's human nature.

"All Erika cared about, truthfully," Bernal added, "was that you liked her."

Once Bernal picked up on that, he used it to his advantage.

As Bernal sat down and began talking to Erika that second time, she told the same story she would begin to add to over the course of the next several weeks: Geney and Joshua had stolen her purse. They all searched the condo together. Couldn't find it. Erika was standing downstairs in the living room, BJ was upstairs with Geney and Joshua, when she heard BJ shoot both of them.

"I was asleep when he put them in plastic bags and took them from the condo unit," she said.

"Look," Bernal said to Erika, "I know BJ told you not to talk, but I spoke to him and he realizes what he did. . . . Being in the navy, he feels guilty. He confessed."

Erika had a quizzical look about her face. She didn't say anything.

"I already know the truth, Erika, I just need to see if you're going to lie to us."

Her jaw dropped to the floor.

"Why do you need me, then?" Erika asked smartly after a moment of reflection. She wasn't taking the bait.

"I just need to see how honest you're going to be. That's going to matter a great deal in this case, Erika. We want to see how truthful you can be with us."

A test.

Erika started crying. "Do you like me? . . . Do you like me?" she asked, tears streaming down her cheeks. "Do you think I'm pretty? Do you like me?"

"Of course, Erika. We just want the truth here."

"Do you like me?" she kept asking. "Am I really pretty?"

"Erika, why wouldn't I like you? You've done nothing wrong to me."

That seemed to pacify Erika's minor sense-of-worth meltdown.

"What we need to talk about, Erika, is what you and BJ did to the other couple."

She shook her head as if to say she was ready.

"Are the bodies in the bay or the ocean?" Bernal asked.

He had assumed from listening to Erika—whom he knew to be lying—that she and BJ had dumped the bags into the water. Moreover, looking at the crime scene itself, Bernal and his colleagues were certain that whatever had happened to Geney and Joshua wasn't some sort of spontaneous crime that just came to Erika and BJ on the spur of the moment. The forensic unit had found a tremendous amount of blood present in the bathroom upstairs. However, in no other area of the condo—save for the laundry room, which could be expected—did any sign of blood turn up. "That told us," Bernal said, "that some sort of planning had gone into this crime. Otherwise, you would have seen bloody footprints tracked all over the condo."

"Neither," Erika said, wiping away tears, meaning that Geney and Joshua's bodies were not in the water.

Ah, finally some truth, Bernal thought. He had been paying strict attention to her body language.

"Where are they, Erika?"

"I cannot tell you."

"No?"

"But I can show you."

"Let me ask you," Bernal said, "what are the chances that Geney and Joshua are still alive? Give me a percentage if they're dead or alive. Sixty-forty? Seventy-thirty?" Bernal was a smart cop. He had been down this road before. You always want to put a limit on responsibility. He knew percentages meant absolutely nothing. A person is either alive or dead. But somehow, by putting it in this manner of speaking, it made the suspect always feel better.

Erika thought about it. "Fifty-fifty," she answered.

By telling Bernal "fifty-fifty," Erika was actually saying that Geney and Joshua were dead. "Because look," Bernal remarked later, "if you know they are alive, they're alive. There's no two ways about it."

"I want to talk to BJ," Erika said. "I want to talk with BJ." She started crying again.

"BJ said you're on your own, Erika. He doesn't want to talk to *you*. He's already covered *his* ass."

"What can you do for me?" Erika asked.

"I need to find these people, Erika. If they are still alive, and we can help them, that's a hell of a lot less serious charge against you. What if they die while you're in here?"

Erika didn't say anything.

"What do you want to go to jail for?" Bernal continued. "Because you *are* going to jail. You have to decide, Erika. Murder charges or something else?"

It was close to sunup. Erika was tired.

"What can you do for me with the burglary charge?" she asked once more.

Bernal was again confused: *Burglary charge? Why is she worried about the damn burglary charge when two people are missing and presumed dead?*

42

Pulling Teeth

The OCPD needed to move quickly. Public defenders for BJ and Erika had been contacted to help consult both of them in regard to what to do next. It was well into the early-morning hours of Friday, May 31, 2002, by this point. The public defender's office had decided to take on BJ's case because it believed BJ was facing the more serious charges, but they also sent in an attorney to speak with and advise Erika.

No one really knew what was going to happen over the next few days. Two things, however, remained absolute. For one, BJ and Erika would face a judge on Monday morning for a bail hearing. Right now, they were being charged with burglary. And, yet, Erika had indicated a desire to trade off some information she had about Joshua Ford and Geney Crutchley for the state to drop any possible burglary charges against her. The fact that the couple could be dead, and BJ and Erika charged with those murders, never entered the picture at this point. Strangely enough, Erika indicated a concern more for getting out of the burglary, not for anything associated with the missing persons case that was at the focal point of all the discussions.

"Anybody, whether it's my daughter or anyone, if you know you're facing murder charges," Mitch Grace told me later, "you are not going to go in and give the police the information to use against you and say, 'Drop the burglary charges.' Wouldn't you want to cover yourself on the charges you *knew* to be going against you? At that moment, I think she didn't even begin to think she was going to be charged with murder . . . because BJ killed them."

In that regard, State's Attorney Joel Todd, who had been advising the OCPD throughout the night, was more than willing to drop all the burglary charges against Erika for information about two missing people.

"I'll trade burglary for murder any day of the week," Todd told me later.

The other problem Erika and BJ faced as the light of Friday morning broke over Worcester County was that throughout the night, the OCPD had uncovered a boat-load of rather hard evidence at the Rainbow condo against the now-infamous duo from Altoona, beyond what they had found inside Erika's purse and the Jeep at the burglary scene.

Bernal had gone in and had spoken to Erika several more times before her appointed legal defense attorney showed up. During one conversation, Bernal asked Erika why BJ had a swastika tattooed on his chest. They were worried that maybe the missing couple had been part of some white supremacist plot by BJ and Erika to kill anyone they didn't see fit to live.

"He loves Hitler," Erika said. "I read him Hitler's biography. . . . We both agree with Hitler's beliefs."

"Erika, if these people are still alive, we need to find them as soon as possible."

"I know more than I'm telling. I had stuff missing. My pills were thrown over the balcony. They tried to steal my purse and throw it over the balcony."

"Every time we found out another piece of the truth," Bernal remarked later, "Erika gave up just a *little* bit more of what she knew."

43

Black and White

Mitch Grace and his wife, Cookie, were just beginning their day by opening up Memory Laine for Erika and BJ, whom they knew to be on vacation in Ocean City, when their lives changed forever. As far as Mitch and Cookie knew, Erika and BJ would be back from their vacation late Saturday night after attending a reptile show somewhere in Pennsylvania.

As Cookie went about her normal morning duties inside the store, the phone rang. Mitch was out in front smoking a cigarette.

After a moment on the phone, Cookie looked as if the life had been sucked from her. She turned white as wool. It was Erika on the other end, letting her know that she was being held in Ocean City on burglary charges.

Cookie screamed. Then cried.

Mitch turned around quickly, stubbed out his cigarette on the ground below his feet, and rushed back into the store.

"What is it? What's happened?"

Cookie dropped the phone receiver.

Mitch went for it . . . "Hello, what is this?"

Erika explained. Mitch bowed his head. He couldn't believe what he was hearing. Erika was crying. She said she needed them right away.

"Get here as soon as you can."

All throughout the morning as Mitch made plans to hire a private jet to fly him and Cookie down to Ocean City, he shook his head and began to think, *Damn it all! That BJ finally got Erika into trouble.*

44

Lawyer Up

By noon, Mitch was climbing the walls, worried and unhappy with the fact that a court-appointed attorney was advising his daughter. He wanted Erika to have her own attorney. Maybe she could get out of jail on bond? What Mitch didn't know immediately was that the OCPD had not only uncovered driver's licenses of the two missing vacationers inside Erika's purse, but also several pieces of jewelry that belonged to Geney and Joshua. This would make bond pretty unlikely.

Things happened quickly after Mitch realized his daughter needed an attorney—hopefully, someone who knew his or her way around Maryland law. Mitch called a law firm in Altoona that had represented several contracting companies under various circumstances. Someone in the firm knew a guy in Baltimore. In fact, the guy Mitch spoke to in Altoona about finding a lawyer in Baltimore owned the Rainbow Condominiums in Ocean City, where Erika and BJ had been staying that week.

Mitch's friend back home called down to Baltimore.

"Look, Mitch Grace is a friend of mine," he said. "His daughter got into some trouble in Ocean City. They need a good attorney."

Right away, the attorney in Baltimore recommended a guy by the name of Arcangelo Tuminelli, a well-known lawyer in Baltimore legal circles since 1979. The idea that a double murder could have taken place inside the condo would likely make BJ and Erika good candidates for the death penalty—if they were involved and ultimately convicted. When Baltimore attorneys heard the words "capital offense," the name Tuminelli generally came up.

Mitch got Tuminelli's number. Tuminelli's friends and his colleagues called him by his nickname, "Arcky." He wore flashy sharkskin suits and played the role of high-profile defense attorney like he wrote it. The cases other attorneys would rather not touch were his specialty. Generally taking on only federal cases, Arcky once represented a man involved in a five-defendant trial where large quantities of heroin had been found—four of the five received life sentences while Arcky's client walked out of court a free man. Yet, to Arcky, winning didn't necessarily mean that a client walked out of his or her jail cell into freedom. For Arcky, winning could just as well mean saving a condemned human being from death row.

Arcky showed up at his Baltimore office late on Friday afternoon. As he walked in and began checking his messages, going through his mail, Arcky's secretary flagged him down and said, "Have you heard the news?"

"No, what? What are you taking about?"

"There was this Pennsylvania couple arrested for a burglary and they think maybe they might have had something to do with a missing couple from Virginia."

The news of Erika and BJ's arrest had hit the wires and

was being reported in the Baltimore area and locally in Ocean City. So far, there wasn't much of a story, but reporters had put together the two cases, nonetheless.

Arcky was intrigued. "No kidding . . ." He put his mail down.

"Yeah, and someone is calling *you* about the case," his secretary said.

"Huh?" Surprised and intrigued at the same time, Arcky was curious.

"His name is Mitch Grace," she said. "He wants you to call him right away."

Arcky looked at the number. He was up to his neck in caseloads. He didn't need to take on a new job. Although, something about it spoke to Arcky's intent and instinct—he had a feeling the case was going to be big. And interesting.

Mitch answered. He sounded confused and desperate. More of a father worried sick about his daughter than anything else, Mitch wanted to make sure his daughter was being taken care of. And he considered the idea that a public defender couldn't do that for her.

"Mitch and Cookie," Arcky said later, "were terrified at the prospects Erika faced."

Their little girl was in a jail with hardened criminals. Women who had committed sick acts and egregious crimes. Her parents were scared for her well-being. Mitch and Cookie made it clear to Arcky right away that it had been BJ who had caused this entire mess. They were certain of it. The marriage was doomed from the moment she brought the guy home and introduced him as her husband.

Arcky explained to Mitch that he was working on a brief for another case and it had to be filed as soon as possible. He didn't have time to focus on Erika right at the moment. He couldn't just drop everything and take on her case. But it did interest him, he explained, and he said he wanted to help Erika.

Mitch talked a bit about where Erika's case was, as far as her arrest and incarceration. Something told Arcky that Mitch was under the impression that a good lawyer was going to be able to bond Erika out of jail and get her back home.

"When is the first hearing scheduled?" Arcky asked.

"Monday morning . . . a bail review hearing, as I understand," Mitch answered. "Can you get down there immediately?" Erika needed someone to be with her. An attorney to tell her what to do, to protect her.

"I have to get this brief done, Mr. Grace."

Mitch said he understood. "OK, call me when you can get down to see her."

45

A Picture's Worth . . .

Back at the Rainbow Condominiums, the OCPD was still digging through room 1101 in an intense search—one of which was producing results that led to more questions than answers. In plain sight, there on the coffee table, was drug residue and a rolled-up twenty-dollar bill. It wasn't much, but it explained a lot about what was going on inside the condo. In the ashtray was a roach and marijuana. In the bedroom was a scrapbook that Erika had obviously been working on. Inside the book were photos of Erika and BJ at various locales around Ocean City. When taken into context, the photos were strange and telling. In one, BJ is standing in the parking lot of Home Depot, smiling. He's wearing a brand-new black shirt, white pants, flip-flops. In another, Erika and BJ are both smiling, hugging each other, as the Atlantic Ocean acts as a backdrop. There were photos of BJ and Erika taken inside nightclubs and at restaurants. In several of the photos, Erika is wearing a

Hooters T-shirt. In another, she's showing off what is a tattoo of a cobra on her hip, which she had obviously just gotten done.

But then, as one of the detectives was looking at the photographs, there it was: a photo of Joshua Ford and Geney Crutchley. Joshua is holding a Seacrets cup, both he and Geney are smiling. There was even a photograph of Erika laughing, eating shrimp. Around her neck is a cross and a man's ring. More interesting, in another photo, Erika is playing miniature golf: she's kissing what is a large model of a green cobra. Then there was a snapshot of Erika standing side by side with a Hooters waitress, smiling and pulling the girl closer to her.

All of the photos, it was soon determined, had been taken after Geney and Joshua had been reported missing. It was as if after meeting Joshua and Geney, Erika and BJ had officially started their vacation. Here they were, in one photo after another, living it up, smiling, laughing, drinking, eating, playing golf, lying on the beach.

Having the time of their lives.

Back at Worcester County Jail, detectives kept up the pressure on BJ, but he just wouldn't talk. True to his SEAL training, BJ said he wasn't going to say anything, except to his lawyer.

When pressed, however, BJ smiled and echoed one sentence, over and over: "If you want to know what happened [to Geney and Joshua], you need to ask my wife."

Meanwhile, Erika had confided in Detective Bernal that Geney and Joshua were murdered. She said the murders had taken place on the beach after an argument. BJ accused them of stealing their belongings.

Bernal was intrigued. "Really? Where did this happen?"

"BJ did it on the beach," she said.

With all of the evidence pointing to the bathroom, and the fact that Erika's body language spoke clearly to what the truth was, Bernal shook his head and allowed her to talk, but he knew damn well that she was lying through her bleached-white teeth.

46

Let's Make a Deal

The OCPD had Erika and BJ nailed on the burglary. *Literally* caught in the act. Erika was now saying, however, that it was BJ who had masterminded the entire Hooters burglary.

"OK," Bernal said, "what about Crutchley and Ford?"

Erika quieted down. She was obviously distressed and emotionally unstable. She hadn't slept much over the past twenty-four hours. Her dad had told her that an attorney was going to be in to see her as soon as he could get away from another case.

Hold tight. Don't say anything else.

OCPD detective Brett Case was beginning to show up with Bernal during the times when Bernal started to put a bit of pressure on Erika. They knew Erika would crack. It was just a matter of time.

"BJ killed them," she said at some point that afternoon. "I helped him dispose of their bodies." She was crying hysterically. Erika was down below one hundred pounds, arguably borderline anorexic. Although, in a letter to a friend in the coming weeks, Erika would talk about how everyone thought she was anorexic, but she said her weight had nothing to do with her eating habits—that it was based more on her drug and drinking addictions. In any event, there was nothing left to Erika, essentially. Her face was skeletal and gaunt. Her cheekbones cut sharply. Her ribs were visible. Her once beautiful, kinky hair was matted and falling out. "I was downstairs," she explained, when "it" happened, implying that she in no way witnessed the murders.

But didn't "it" happen outside on the beach?

Erika was changing her story again.

Either way, she was not around when BJ killed them, she insisted.

"Do you mind showing us, then, where you helped him dispose of the bodies?"

Erika nodded yes, adding, "I will." She seemed unsure, however, and made it clear that in exchange for this information, she wanted to be certain she wasn't going to be prosecuted for the Hooters burglary.

Joel Todd allowed Case and Bernal to go back in and tell her, sure, they'd drop those burglary charges if she brought them to the bodies.

Case and Bernal got a car ready. Bernal wanted a female officer to ride with him and Erika. He didn't want any trouble with Erika. Case would follow.

Within the hour, they were on their way.

Erika sat in front and directed Bernal where to drive. She again kept asking, "Do you like me? Am I pretty?"

"Erika, we need to focus on this."

"Am I a bad person?"

"Where are we going, Erika?"

When they arrived at the second location, a Dumpster in back of strip mall near the condo, Erika appeared to be uncomfortable. This happened after going back and forth with Erika for some time, even once bringing her back to the station because she was talking in so many different circles. Erika finally told Bernal she would take him to the right Dumpsters. And here they were. Bernal was even inside the Dumpster himself, pushing garbage around.

But still, nothing.

Pissed off, he went back to his car, where Erika was waiting with another officer.

"What's going on? You gonna tell us the truth here, or what?"

She didn't say anything.

"What is it?" Bernal asked.

"This is it! He cut them into six pieces and put them into bags," she yelled.

Bernal was astonished. Speechless at first.

"Can you please repeat what you just said?"

She repeated herself. Then, "Do you think I'm a bad person? I don't know why BJ did this. I'm pretty sure this is the Dumpster. . . . I was pretty drunk. I don't know."

Bernal and Case went over to the Dumpster and opened it up. The Dumpster had garbage inside it.

They next drove into Delaware.

At one point, they stood in back of a small strip mall near several Dumpsters. Erika was looking across the street at a Food Lion parking lot.

"Why are you looking over there?" Bernal asked.

"No reason."

"Was it here?" Bernal asked, frustrated. He was referring to where they were standing.

"No . . . I don't think so . . . I don't know . . . ," Erika said.

Bernal drove Erika back to the OCPD. As they worked their way down Route 1, Bernal knew that Erika wasn't being totally truthful with them.

"Listen, Erika, we aren't playing the same game here. We know the bodies weren't dumped there. Now, come on, where are they? When are you gonna start telling us the truth?"

"I'll show you. They're farther down into Delaware. I don't know, I was sleeping."

They drove.

"I played college basketball," Erika said as they turned around and went on their way back to Delaware again. "Everybody loved me. I love BJ so much. Do you like me, Detective?"

"I have no reason not to, Erika, but we need to find these bodies."

Here she is looking at double murder, Bernal thought, *and she cares about what I think.*

Just then, Bernal's cell phone rang. It was Detective Richard Moreck. He had something. "It definitely happened in the bathroom of the condo," he said. "We've confirmed that."

Bernal hung up and continued driving. After a minute, he said to Erika, "You know, all you've done is ask me if I like you and how pretty you are and talk about your college basketball days. I want to know, what do you think of yourself?"

"Oh, me? I'm a great person. Everybody likes me."

"Do you always try to do the right thing?"

"Yes. Always."

"Then let me ask you, when in the hell are you going to stop lying to me? Do you think that I actually believe that this happened out on the beach? Do you think I know or don't know that this happened in the condo? I'm curious what you think."

"OK, OK, OK . . . it happened inside the condo, in the bathroom," Erika finally admitted.

"Are you sure you threw the bodies in Dumpsters? I

don't want to be led on some wild-goose chase here. Are
you sure your husband didn't just toss them into a ditch
somewhere?"

Erika turned red. Seething through her teeth, she
lashed out at Bernal. "How fucking dare you! My husband would *never*. He would never throw a body in a
fucking ditch. That's how they found my friend Krista."

"Krista who?" Bernal asked.

"Krista Ruggles."

Bernal's heart skipped a beat. He had not worked the
case, but had heard enough about it to know the details.
Krista was a friend of Erika's who had been murdered in
Ocean City. It was still an open case. But Erika's reaction
told Bernal that Erika was definitely involved in Geney
and Joshua's murders. He had hit a nerve.

Erika pointed out a Dumpster in the back of a grocery
store, which was actually across the street from where she
and BJ had put the body parts. The problem with this
new location was that detectives found out that the
garbage from this particular Dumpster, the one Erika
was now lying (or was confused) about, had been
dumped in two different landfills, which meant they'd
have to search two separate locations.

47

The Great Pretender

According to several sources, throughout the weekend of June 1 and 2, Mitch Grace had a tough time stepping back and letting the attorney he hired to work on Erika's case "do his job." "Micromanage" is probably too strong a word to describe Mitch's input; but for one, records indicate that he was calling Arcky Tuminelli all weekend, constantly asking what was going on and, at times, trying to direct Arcky regarding what to do next.

As he had promised, Arcky spent Saturday and Sunday finishing the brief he had due in another case. Late Sunday afternoon, however, he finally finished, e-mailed it, and then began to focus exclusively on Erika's case. It was close to eight o'clock on Sunday night, June 2, when Arcky left his house outside Baltimore and headed south to Snow Hill, where Erika was being held in Worcester County Jail. Dealing with Mitch all day, and now into the night, had been difficult. But Arcky understood the guy was simply worried about his daughter. What father wouldn't be? Arcky had been schooled in legal defense long enough to know how to deal with people like Mitch. The guy's daughter was in jail facing serious charges—maybe even murder. He had every right to question and call on the man he had retained to represent her.

In learning more about Erika's case, based on what Mitch had told him, Arcky was sure that Erika had said too much to the police already, sending them on a mission to find what she had admitted by the end of the weekend were "bodies and body parts," as opposed to "missing people."

Big difference.

By Monday morning, Arcky knew, dozens of cops would be searching dump sites in Maryland and nearby Delaware looking for the bodies, based on what Erika had been supposedly telling them. If the OCPD located Geney and Joshua's bodies, any type of bargaining Arcky could possibly do for Erika was history. She would have no carrot left to dangle in front of the state's attorney.

Still, everything depended on the assumption that Erika was telling the truth—which Arcky, as any good defense attorney would agree, wasn't so sure about.

Arcky's secretary had gotten the prosecutor's name, cell phone, and home numbers. Worcester County state's attorney Joel Todd was going to be prosecuting Erika and BJ, Arcky was told. Todd had been with the OCPD all weekend, advising and talking detectives legally through questioning Erika and BJ. Worcester County is located on the Eastern Shore of Maryland, tucked there in the armpit of southern Delaware.

Beyond being the president of the Chamber of Commerce in Berlin, and the onetime president of the local bar association, Joel Todd was a seasoned prosecutor with a terrific, almost ironclad, track record, Arcky knew. The guy was hard to beat in a courtroom, no doubt about it. In addition, Todd's assistant, E. Scott Collins, was a hotshot veteran trial lawyer himself.

Completely bald (by choice, perhaps), wearing his glasses and speaking with just a touch of a Southern drawl, Joel Todd embodied the academic prowess and intellectual suave his job sometimes required. Todd had been the state's attorney since 1995 and the assistant state's attorney since 1985. His experience preceded him. He knew the ins and outs of Maryland courts, especially in his own county. If Erika Sifrit knew where to find the bodies of Geney and Joshua, Todd felt it was his duty, as well as his responsibility, to get that information out of her and bring those bodies back home to family members.

Arcky learned with a quick phone call to Todd that he was extremely interested in learning exactly where the bodies had been dumped. There was some indication by this point that Erika might have been lying about the locations she had taken detectives to earlier—and that she was playing games. This infuriated the police, of course, but they knew Erika was going to break down sooner or later. Otherwise, she would have done what BJ was doing: keeping his mouth shut. Little by little, as Bernal kept asking Erika questions, she started telling the truth.

Just that Sunday morning, for instance, Bernal had asked Erika, "If BJ told you to tell me where the two victims were tossed, would you do it?"

"Yes," she said, "but I have to know what will happen to me. I have to be with my husband."

"Not possible," Bernal said.

"What can you do for me?"

After speaking briefly with Todd, agreeing to meet at the Worcester County Jail, Arcky called Mitch and told him he was on his way down to see Erika. Snow Hill, Maryland, Arcky explained, was a good three-hour trip from Baltimore.

He had better hurry. Because the more time the OCPD had with Erika, the tighter the noose around her neck was getting.

"We'll meet you there," Mitch said.

The Graces believed Erika had played no part whatsoever in the crimes. Whatever had taken place beyond the burglary was BJ's doing. By this point, the newspapers were running with the story. It was being widely reported over the weekend that the OCPD had been searching for the bodies of a missing couple from Virginia. On June 1, that Saturday, the *Washington Post* published a story by reporter Jamie Stockwell under the headline 2 CHARGED IN KILLINGS OF MISSING VA. PAIR; PA. COUPLE ARRESTED. The article explained the initial charges BJ and Erika faced: . . . *first-degree murder in the deaths of two Fairfax City residents who had been reported missing.* Jay Hancock, a spokesman for the OCPD, had released a statement on behalf of the OCPD, in which he said, *"Extensive blood spatter, spent shell casings, and what appears to be human tissue were found in the 11th-floor penthouse that Benjamin and Erica Sifrit of Altoona had rented at the Rainbow Condominiums."*

Those words, "human tissue," sent shock waves throughout the community.

Mitch and Cookie were overwhelmed with disbelief, shock, and grief—suffice it to say—when reports that BJ and Erika could have been involved in dismembering two human beings started circulating. One former friend later said that Mitch was quickly soured by the media coverage. And later, he put others into that same box, making anyone, and everyone, who did not believe in his daughter into an enemy, saying, "Look, you take the media, lawyers, and investigators, put them in a brown paper bag, shake it up, dump it out, and you get the same thing! They all take your words and turn them into what they want them to sound like."

Looking at Erika's upbringing and background, the Graces had to think: How could something like this happen? How could Erika allow herself to get involved with this guy and end up in jail, facing such serious charges? The Graces had sensed a dark side to BJ the moment they had met him. There was always that strange gleam in his eye, that look about him that spoke of trouble. In no way did they want to believe that Erika could have had anything to do with what looked to be the most horrible crime imaginable. And yet, the truth was, no one really knew the horror that was about to be unearthed.

48

Hometown Girl

Erika's old high-school friend and AAU basketball teammate Kristin Heinbaugh had worked for a local Altoona newspaper for quite a few years leading up to Erika's arrest. Part of Kristin's job was to monitor the wire stories and look for anything that would be of interest to local readers. By coincidence, Kristin had been working on an unrelated Ocean City, Maryland, murder story for quite some time. On that Friday afternoon, after BJ and Erika had been arrested and processed, as Kristin was putting together stories for the following day's front page, her managing editor, who was standing in the middle of the newsroom, yelled over to her.

"Kristin, hold off on A-1, we have an Altoona couple arrested for murder in Ocean City, Maryland."

"OK," she said, and went back to searching the wire for any information about the crime. She had been working on that other story for so long, Kristin just assumed that her editor was referring to the same thing.

Kristin had no idea what Erika's married name was, but she did know that not a lot of women with the same first name spelled it with a *K*. It was rare to see that name. As she sat and watched the wire, the Associated Press ran a few sentences by: *Altoona couple, Erika and Benjamin Sifrit, arrested for double murder. . . .*

Huh? Kristin thought. *That's odd. I cannot believe this . . . but I don't know any other Erika with that spelling.* She doublechecked. *Yup, it is Altoona/Duncansville.* Erika and BJ's apartment was actually in Duncansville. Not many people knew that.

But Kristin did.

There's no way—this cannot *be her!* she thought.

Kristin picked up the telephone and started calling old friends to see if anyone knew Erika's married name.

Nobody did.

As the day went on, Kristin kept checking the Associated Press photo wire, hoping the OCPD would release a mug shot of the couple.

And then, sure enough, there it was: a mug shot of Erika and the man Kristin had seen her with at the mall a few years back.

"I was . . . I don't know," Kristin said later, "shocked. Speechless, actually."

She printed the photograph out and walked over to her managing editor and stood in front of him.

"What?" he said after Kristin didn't say anything.

By now, she was shaking, "trembling so bad," she recalled, "that I was unable to pick up my hand" and show him the photograph.

"It's Erika Grace," Kristin told her editor. "Mitch Grace's daughter."

Everyone in town knew Mitch Grace.

"Oh, my goodness," her editor said, looking at the photograph, "you're right!"

Kristin turned and walked back to her desk. She was so nervous, she said, and shocked that it was actually Erika in that photograph, her nose started to bleed.

"I was a mess," she said later. "I just could not fathom it. And as more of the case came out, I thought, 'OK, I still believe that it was his [BJ's] influence.' But apparently, as I would learn, she thrived on all of this. They had, we found out, committed a lot of burglaries around the Duncansville area, and throughout the entire county, actually."

This reaction echoed throughout the small community of which Erika had been a part for her entire life. Last everyone knew, Erika was a history major who graduated from a fairly decent college in Virginia. She was a local business owner. The daughter of one of the region's best known contractors. She had grown up with a silver spoon. Now everyone was supposed to believe she had taken part in a double murder and actually had a hand in dismembering two people. None of it added up.

49

Hubris

Part of what the OCPD had uncovered at the Rainbow, inside Erika's cache of photographs, proved that she had planned on perhaps putting together some sort of scrapbook representing all of her and BJ's criminal activities throughout the years. Among the photos, detectives were puzzled by several pictures of the inside of a house outside Altoona. The photos were from a night when BJ and Erika met some dude at a local bar and ended up going back to his house to play some pool and have a few drinks. While BJ kept the guy busy, Erika searched throughout the guy's house, checking things out, no doubt to see if he had anything worth thieving. Well, lo and behold, Erika took a series of photos in just about every room she entered. In one, she was smiling, sitting on the guy's toilet.

After they left the house, later that night, BJ and Erika went back. BJ was on his knees, picking the front door lock of the same guy's house. Either Erika and BJ were too drunk to realize it or they hadn't even thought about it, but the guy was home while they were trying to break in. Then again, maybe that was part of the game? Perhaps BJ and Erika, not getting anything out of breaking into retail stores and Hooters, wanted to up the ante and try it while someone was home?

As BJ was picking the lock, the dude opened the door and pointed a shotgun at his head. "What the fuck do you think you're doing?"

"Oh," BJ said, startled, "we forgot some things from earlier and wanted to retrieve them."

"Get the fuck out of here."

50

Circumspect

Arcky Tuminelli's niche was federal court. That was where his experience and skill in the courtroom was able to shine. Still, the Sifrit case was something Arcky saw as a challenge. As he viewed it, Erika was a "highly motivated, driven, accomplished athlete, intelligent," and not necessarily the type of person, with her background, that you would see involved in such a disturbing case. Arcky knew bad people. He sat across from them at conference tables in prisons and in courtrooms. He knew the smell of evil. In Erika Sifrit, at least during the early portion of the case, Arcky didn't see any of it.

Arcky was a philosophy major in college. Law wasn't even part of his outlook at the time. In fact, a decade after high school, college wasn't even in Arcky's plans. He had grown up in Baltimore, in the northwest section of the city, not too far from where the famous Preakness horse race is run every year—and he didn't go back to school until he was twenty-eight.

From Arcky's standpoint, Erika's case posed some significant legal challenges right out of the box, which he needed to get a handle on immediately if he was going to be of any help.

"You had what appeared to be a double murder," Arcky later explained, "by two people who—not knowing much about either one of them as I drove south—I believed, at least in Erika's case, appeared to be from this really stable, *good* family. This wasn't your typical murder case. There was something odd about it. Benjamin was the first in his class with the SEALs. Both of them were very interesting people. And then you have a suggestion that something happened with the bodies. So, in that sense, as a lawyer, as a trial attorney, it was unique. I've had murder cases—a number of death penalty cases, in fact—but never with facts lining up like this."

And so as he drove from Baltimore on that Sunday night, June 2, Arcky thought about the case. The plan was to meet up with Erika, Mitch, Cookie, and, eventually, Joel Todd and OCPD detectives that night. As he looked at Erika's background, nothing made sense to Arcky.

The hum of nighttime driving on a Sunday, when the roads are mostly clear, can do a lot for preparing the mind. Arcky began to analyze what he had been told. From what he understood, he could see BJ involved in the murders. A crazy SEAL, discharged from the service after a court-martial, had maybe gone nuts and snapped. It happened. The SEAL training alone, most people knew, was enough to make any good man crazy.

Yet, the delicate image Mitch and Cookie had painted of Erika didn't fit into that insanity mold that seemed to fit the particulars of what was beginning to look like a truly horrible crime.

Something was missing.

"And the more I learned," Arcky said later, "the more

interesting and complicated it all became, which was the challenging aspect of it all."

Nevertheless, regardless of what Erika had told her parents or even the police, Arcky believed he was in a good position. Erika apparently had some information that the state's attorney wanted. Arcky could use it as a bargaining chip, if nothing else, and possibly save Erika a lot of trouble down the road.

Inside the jail, near 11:00 P.M., Arcky got settled in one of the visiting rooms. He knew that Joel Todd and a few OCPD detectives were at the jail already, and had been questioning Erika most of the day. But before he sat down with Todd, Arcky needed to speak with Erika alone. He wanted her take on what had happened.

Tossing his notebook on the table, Arcky looked up and saw that the guards were bringing Erika in. She looked disheveled: crying, shaking, entirely unraveled.

Looking at her, Arcky was surprised by how thin Erika appeared.

They sat and talked. Within an hour, Arcky was aware of the details regarding what had happened the previous Friday night, and some of what took place over the weekend, when Erika and BJ were taken into custody. According to court documents (Arcky would not talk about anything he and Erika discussed), he was made aware of how Erika had spoken to detectives regarding where the bodies were dumped, and that BJ had murdered Joshua and Geney without her knowledge.

Of course, all of this information was contingent upon the idea that Erika was telling the truth. And Arcky certainly had no reason *not* to believe her. She seemed sincere. Mitch and Cookie, pretty shaken up by the entire incident, were upstanding people. They had reputations.

The irony in the case was tremendous. Had Erika and BJ simply left town—which they were scheduled to do earlier on the day they were caught burgling Hooters—they might have never been arrested, or even questioned about the disappearance of Joshua and Geney. But here they were: in jail, facing murder charges.

"Yes, I was there . . . but Benjamin did this," Erika told Arcky at one point, according to court documents. "I didn't know anything about it or that it was going to happen."

Arcky was being told that Erika had had nothing whatsoever to do with the murders, but had, in fact, helped her husband clean up the mess and dispose of the bodies.

As her lawyer, Arcky was equally concerned about *any* role Erika might have played in the crimes. OK, she wasn't there. She claimed not to see BJ kill the couple, but she *knew* they had been murdered, and, moreover, she had helped BJ, according to what she had told police already, get rid of the bodies. By themselves, those were pretty serious charges.

"I went with him when he disposed of the bodies," Erika confirmed.

Arcky wrote it down on his notepad, saying, "Listen, what these people are really, *really* interested in is where the bodies are."

Arcky had stepped out and spoken briefly to Joel Todd and several of the investigating detectives. He could tell from the conversation that they didn't necessarily believe Erika, especially Brett Case and Scott Bernal. She had taken detectives to two Dumpsters, where she said she had helped BJ dump the bodies. But detectives were under the impression that she wasn't being totally truthful.

Because of this, Arcky made it clear to Erika that if she came clean and was willing to cooperate, he could possibly cut her a deal.

Erika (right) and a team-mate give a thumb's up during what can be described as Erika's glory days of AAU basketball. (Courtesy of Kristen Heinbaugh)

Erika, as a teenager, was happy and vivacious. (Courtesy of Kristen Heinbaugh)

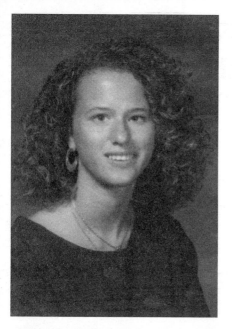

Heading into college, Erika Grace showed promise and excellence on the basketball court. (*Courtesy Hollidaysburg High School yearbook*)

As a youngster, Erika (center) was a prominent player on her local AAU traveling basketball team. She was away from her home a lot, yet never got into any trouble. (*Courtesy of Kristen Heinbaugh*)

OCEAN CITY POLICE
MISSING
PERSONS

Chief David C. Massey

DATE: 5-30-02   CC# 2002-006440

MARTHA MARGENE "GENEY" CRUTCHLEY AND
JOSHUA EDWARD FORD

CRUTCHLEY'S DOB: 9-1-50	FORD'S D/O/B: 9-8-69
HAIR: BLONDE	HAIR: DARK BROWN
EYES: BLUE	EYES: BROWN
HEIGHT: 5'7" – 5'9"	HEIGHT: 6'0" – 6'2"
WEIGHT: ABOUT 125	WEIGHT: ABOUT 220
TATOOS; ANKLE?	TATOOS: NONE

BOTH LAST TALKED TO FRIENDS ON SAT. MAY 25, 2002, BOTH WERE STAYING
TOGETHER AT THE ATLANTIS CONDOS. █████████████████BOTH WERE SUPPOSED
TO BE BACK TO WORK IN VIRGINIA ON 5-28-02. SHE DIDN'T SHOW OR CALL. HER VEH.
WAS STILL AT THE ATLANTIS ON 5-29-02. IT WAS TOWED TO OUR IMPOUND LOT.
CRUTCHLEY AND FORD'S BELONGINGS WERE STILL IN THE ROOM ON 5-29-02 AND
SEIZED BY OCPD/CID ON 5-30-02. AS OF 5-30-02, 1900 HOURS, CRUTCHLEY AND FORD
HAVE NOT BEEN FOUND. . IF YOU HAVE ANY CONCERNING THIS CASE PLEASE
CONTACT DET. BERNAL., 8171, 410-723-6610.

If you have information concerning the above individual, please contact the Ocean City
Police Department at 410-723-6610.

When Martha "Geney" Crutchley and Joshua Ford failed to show up for
work after the long 2002 Memorial Day holiday weekend, friends and
coworkers became concerned and reported the couple missing. *(Courtesy
of the Ocean City Police Department)*

After leaving college with a history degree and running away to Las Vegas to marry a man she had known for three weeks, the newly wed Erika Sifrit, now calling herself "Bonnie," was arrested with her husband—"Clyde"—on May 31, 2002, while breaking into an Ocean City, Maryland Hooters restaurant. *(Courtesy of the Ocean City Police Department)*

Wearing his trademark shoulder holster, staying true to his Navy SEAL training, Benjamin "BJ" Sifrit refused to speak to police after his arrest on the night of May 31, 2002. *(Courtesy of the Ocean City Police Department)*

Nearly 160 candidates entered Benjamin Sifrit's Navy SEAL training class, but only 17 graduated, with BJ as honor man. *(Courtesy of the United States Navy public record)*

After their arrest on May 31, 2002, Erika and Benjamin Sifrit took different sides regarding the incriminating evidence found in their Jeep Cherokee, which tied both of them to the missing persons case of Geney Crutchley and Joshua Ford. *(Courtesy of the Ocean City Police Department)*

These photo ID driver's licenses of Geney Crutchley and Joshua Ford were found inside Erika Sifrit's purse on the night of May 31, 2002, after she and BJ were caught in the act of burgling an Ocean City Hooters restaurant gift shop. *(Courtesy of the Ocean City Police Department)*

On the bottom curve of this ring—which belonged to Joshua Ford and was found in Erika Sifrit's possession on the night of her arrest—there is a small blood spatter mark that was later proven by DNA testing to match Joshua Ford. *(Courtesy of the Ocean City Police Department)*

Here is a photo the Ocean City Police Department took of Joshua Ford's ring, attached to a necklace owned by Erika Sifrit. *(Courtesy of the Ocean City Police Department)*

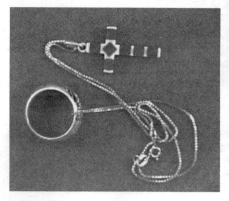

These plastic flex cuffs, along with ski masks, adhesive tape and several weapons, were found inside Erika and BJ Sifrit's Jeep Cherokee, leading Ocean City PD detectives to believe that Crutchley and Ford were being held hostage somewhere. *(Courtesy of the Ocean City Police Department)*

Here is the inside of Erika and Benjamin's Jeep Cherokee, showing how detectives found Erika's Coach handbag, where the gun used to kill Crutchley and Ford was located with other incriminating evidence. *(Courtesy of the Ocean City Police Department)*

Ocean City PD detectives found a serrated knife on Erika, clipped to the side pocket of her jeans. The knife was later found to contain bits of human flesh and blood. *(Courtesy of the Ocean City Police Department)*

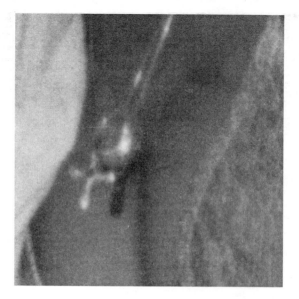

These two close-up photos proved that Erika Sifrit was wearing Joshua Ford's bloodied ring around her neck after Ford and Crutchley were reported missing. *(Courtesy of the Ocean City Police Department)*

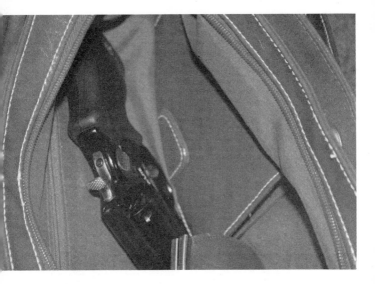

In the crook of Erika's back, tucked into her pants, police uncovered a fully loaded .357 Magnum revolver that was later proved to be the weapon used to kill Joshua Ford; and inside Erika's Coach purse, police located this .45 caliber handgun, along with four spent shell casings and one live round of ammunition. *(Courtesy of the Ocean City Police Department)*

Here are Geney Crutchley and Joshua Ford in photos taken hours before they were murdered and dismembered by Erika and Benjamin Sifrit. *(Courtesy of the Ocean City Police Department)*

After Erika turned on BJ and started talking to Ocean City PD detectives, cutting a deal with prosecutors, she explained where she and BJ dumped the body parts of Ford and Crutchley. In this Delaware landfill, police found one of Crutchley's legs and Ford's torso, both his arms and one leg.
(Courtesy of the Ocean City Police Department)

Here Erika holds one of her prize possessions—a python snake. *(Courtesy of the Worcester County State's Attorney's Office, Maryland)*

After Erika and BJ murdered Ford and Crutchley, dismembered their bodies, placed the body parts in plastic bags and a Navy SEAL duffle bag, and tossed them into several different Dumpsters in Delaware, they began what these photos prove to be a fun-filled vacation in Ocean City, asking passersby to snap their photo as they smiled and hammed it up for the camera. *(Courtesy of the Ocean City Police Department)*

After finding Ford and Crutchley's IDs in Erika's purse, police searched their condominium, where they immediately uncovered blood, hairs, and pieces of a human scalp inside this sink and a washing machine. *(Courtesy of the Ocean City Police Department)*

This photo shows Erika's python, but she and BJ also owned a cobra. *(Courtesy of the Ocean City Police Department)*

This blood stain on Erika and BJ's mattress is likely where BJ, naked and fully painted with Ford and Crutchley's blood, sat and explained to Erika that he had masturbated over their bodies before dismembering them. *(Courtesy of the Ocean City Police Department)*

This bullet, found inside Erika and BJ's room, contained flesh, hair fibers and blood belonging to both Ford and Crutchley. Erika was said to be saving it for a necklace she wanted to make. *(Courtesy of the Ocean City Police Department)*

Joshua Ford, 32, and Geney Crutchley, 51, were said to be building a life together in Fairfax City, Virginia, when they met up with Erika and BJ Sifrit on an Ocean City, Maryland bus. *(Courtesy of the Ocean City Police Department)*

A sweet deal, at that.

In turn, Joel Todd would probably want to use Erika as a witness in BJ's potential trial, and if all went as expected, Erika wouldn't face prosecution herself for the murders.

Erika indicated that she understood clearly what Arcky was telling her.

"As far as I'm concerned," Arcky said later, "she understood." Both Scott Bernal and Brett Case backed this up.

What was strange was that Erika had negotiated a deal already with the state's attorney through the detectives, before Arcky had even arrived. It was back on Friday night and early Saturday morning. She had made a promise to receive immunity from the burglary if she showed detectives where she and BJ had dumped the bodies. Why she tossed only the burglary on the table was the question no one could really answer.

"Apparently," Joel Todd said later, "she wanted to shoulder all the blame on Benjamin and get herself out of trouble completely. I recall when Detective Bernal came to me with her proposal, my response was 'I'd gladly trade a burglary for a homicide.' I'm like, 'Give me some information about these murders and I'd be glad to drop the burglary charges.'"

Why was Erika so concerned about receiving immunity from the burglary? A Hooters burglary was nothing compared to double-murder charges—the least of her problems, in other words. Apparently, Erika wasn't worried about any potential murder charges. It was as if she didn't think she needed to protect herself from those charges in any way whatsoever. And yet, after Arcky arrived and explained things differently, it was clear that she needed to rethink that earlier position.

And then the idea came up that Erika had not given detectives the right information, anyway. So perhaps she *did* know what she was doing when she cut that earlier deal and then lied to police about where she and BJ had dumped the bodies.

As would be the case in the coming days, it would be clear that it wasn't what Erika had said to detectives that mattered most. It was, instead, what she *hadn't* told them that was going to be of immediate concern.

51

Unfathomable

Detective Scott Bernal had gone in to see Erika periodically throughout that weekend. His goal was to see if she wanted to talk. He had to keep making himself available. There was one time when he was interviewing Erika with Joel Todd and Arcky present and Erika said something that in Bernal's almost twenty years of law enforcement he had never heard, and would most likely never hear again.

"After he cut Geney's head off," Erika said of BJ, "he—he . . . he put her head up on the corner of the tub, like propped it up, and then he had intercourse with her corpse."

Bernal studied Erika while she told this horrific story, as she went into great detail. She also said that BJ needed a certain type of stimulation to get him excited, and this was it, she said, killing people and chopping them up.

Bernal watched her body language as she told the story.

"It was the same as when she had told me other things of which I *knew* to be truthful."

52

Just Another
Roll of the Dice

Sitting with Erika, Arcky explained the situation in the simplest terms he could manage. From a legal perspective, two facts remained certain where it pertained to what he could do next: One, there was a double murder that somehow involved BJ and Erika. Two, Arcky had no idea, at this point, what the actual facts were surrounding those crimes. The truth of the matter was, Erika had told several different versions of one absolute: Geney and Joshua were dead, their body parts placed in two separate Dumpsters. Beyond those two knowns, there was a litany of unknowns.

It wasn't that Arcky didn't trust his client; like the detectives and state's attorney, he just didn't know what was true and what was false. That said, BJ not saying anything was actually working to Erika's advantage. Even after being briefed by his court-appointed attorney, BJ continued to be tight-lipped. Not a word. He wasn't interested in making deals or sharing information with police. He opted to wait for his chance to speak in court.

The other constant in this for Arcky, viewing the situation as a capital-crimes attorney, was the notion of how a double murder was going to play out in a court of law. In the state of Maryland, not all murders fall under the legalities for a potential death sentence. Mitigating factors involved in the crime rule. Murders that are subject to a prosecution involving the death penalty include deaths involving certain "aggravating conditions." One of those includes the act of two people being murdered around the same criminal event. In other words, if somebody kidnaps a couple, holds them hostage, and, for whatever reason, murders the couple during that additional (kidnapping) crime, the murder charges would be subject to the death penalty if a jury voted for such punishment. Same as if a bank robber kills someone in the event of a heist.

"Granted," Arcky commented later, "all I know for sure at this point is that we have two people dead. I don't know who did it. I know that Erika is certainly not admitting to it. But I know by then that she's told the police that Benjamin kind of 'freaked out' and he was the one responsible for the murders."

But Arcky was skeptical. He didn't feel that all the facts were being put on the table. All he could be certain of was that his client was somehow involved. Beyond that, he had to take Erika at her word and make decisions based on what she was telling him.

Before talking to Joel Todd about a possible deal, Arcky considered that Erika needed to be protected from the possibility of a death sentence, should it later turn out that she was somehow held partly responsible for killing the couple. In order to be subject to the death penalty, beyond killing a police officer or committing a contract murder, the individual being prosecuted has to be the *actual* killer. If things turned out different from what Arcky had been told, he knew enough about the law to make a decision to protect his client from herself and/or her own stupidity. One other problem was that Erika had been arrested at Hooters with a gun in her possession, while spent bullet casings and one live round (from that same weapon) were located inside her purse, among other items belonging to the missing couple. More than that, a serrated knife with "fresh blood" and "human flesh" on its teeth was stuffed inside Erika's front pocket. Her husband was telling the police, "Talk to my wife . . ." At best, it seemed as if the gun had been fired and the knife used. "By whom" could be the subject of argument later. But why was it in Erika's possession if she hadn't used it, or hadn't planned on using it? Also, the gun matched the spent bullets with blood and tissue found on them inside the Sifrit condo during the OCPD's search. In addition, why would Erika have a knife with human flesh and blood on its teeth tucked inside her left front pocket? There was no doubt in anybody's mind that when the lab came back with its results, the human flesh and blood on that knife was going to match Joshua, Geney, or both.

And then there was the necklace Erika was wearing: the OCPD had confirmed there was blood on a ring.

Walking in to speak with Joel Todd, Arcky's main objective was to negotiate a way to get the death penalty taken off the table, regardless of the outcome of the case later on. He needed to save Erika's life first. The second condition he demanded was that life without parole be taken away, which would give Erika the opportunity to get out of jail one day, if everything in the case went against her.

Nobody, save for Erika and BJ, knew what had happened inside that condo bathroom. In effect, Todd and Tuminelli were rolling the dice, Joel Todd maybe gambling a little more than his defense counterpart.

53

Midnight Special

It was close to midnight when Joel Todd and Arcky Tuminelli sat down to discuss and hack out a deal for Erika. This closed-door, midnight meeting would be subject to raised eyebrows and questions in the days to come, especially from BJ's camp. But it was, when all the facts later emerged, quite legally appropriate—not to mention something competing attorneys did all the time.

"If she gives you the information that would help you to find the bodies," Tuminelli explained to Todd after exchanging pleasantries, "death and life without parole *have* to be taken off the table. Period! No matter what you find out later."

By now, the OCPD officers were confident that Erika had led Bernal and Case on a wild-goose chase when she took them around to various Dumpsters. Erika knew damn well where BJ had dumped those body parts.

Joel Todd agreed, though apprehensively. According to both attorneys, Todd said, "That's fine."

"Now, that will be in exchange for the information you want," Tuminelli explained. "We also want Erika to be able to cooperate in any future litigation or trial against Benjamin. For that, we want a deal that she not be prosecuted for *any* count, any type of murder charge against either victim."

Todd looked unsettled by this. Was the guy crazy? It was a lot to demand—even more to agree to without stipulation.

Arcky Tuminelli was more or less doing his job, trying to cut the best deal he could for his client.

"Listen, Arcky," Todd said after some reflection on the matter, "the first part is fine with me . . . but how can I do the rest of that? She won't be subject to death or life, no matter what the facts are. OK. But how can I promise she won't be prosecuted for murder until we know that she did not participate in the murders?"

There was still that apprehensive notion lingering that Erika was not the innocent little Altoona businesswoman she might have liked to project.

"Let me go talk to her," Tuminelli said.

In good faith, how could Joel Todd and the OCPD be certain that Erika wasn't involved in the murders? This became the question of the night. Or, actually, early Monday morning. Todd couldn't allow Erika to slide on everything.

What if she signed the deal and then admitted to the murders?

Arcky spoke to Mitch first, who assured him that Erika was telling the truth. These were serious crimes, Arcky said. "We have to be sure she's telling the truth and not hiding *anything*."

"I know that my daughter is telling the truth," Mitch said sincerely. "I trust her. She'd never lie to me."

"OK."

Arcky walked in and sat with Erika. They needed to complete this deal as quickly as possible, but Arcky needed more facts. According to court documents, Arcky told Erika, "Listen to me. I can protect you from a life sentence and a potential death sentence, but I cannot protect you from murder charges, unless the state's attorney is confident you're telling them the truth."

Erika nodded. She understood.

Arcky demanded that Erika tell him the truth. He needed to know. No matter what the truth was, whether she was involved or not, it didn't matter. He needed to know the facts of the case so he could protect her.

Erika made it clear she understood and that she was telling him and her parents everything. Later, Mitch Grace backed up this claim, saying that his daughter was telling the truth. She'd had nothing whatsoever to do with the murders.

Arcky felt a slight twinge of confidence building.

"She knows better," Mitch said as Arcky headed back to meet with Joel Todd. "She's smart enough to know better. She's not going to lie to you."

After going back and forth with Joel Todd, discussing various ways in which they could all agree, Arcky Tuminelli was able to get a commitment from Todd that the state would not prosecute Erika for murder if she didn't have anything to do with the murders. In order for the state to be convinced Erika was telling the truth, Todd explained, she needed to take a polygraph.

"I cannot just go on her word, Arcky," Todd said at one point.

"I understand, Joel, I completely understand."

"I have to be satisfied. I need at least some assurances that she is being truthful."

A lie detector test would soothe some of those feelings for Todd. It wasn't infallible, of course, nor could it be used in court. But it would at least serve as a starting point. If Erika passed the polygraph, Todd would agree not to prosecute her for murder. Thus, all Erika had to do was pass a lie detector test, and she would be, literally, free and clear. She would walk away from jail, at least for the time being, out on bond and, in the end, perhaps for good. She'd face a few charges of illegally disposing of the bodies, but the major charges would be washed away like that salty foam along the Ocean City shoreline.

54

The Search Begins

Inside Joel Todd's office, Arcky Tuminelli and the state's attorney worked out the specifics of the deal, writing and rewriting an agreement until each party was happy with the content. They worked tirelessly into the early-morning hours of Monday, June 3, 2002.

Afterward, Arcky traveled back to Worcester County Jail and had Erika sign it. Mitch and Cookie were overjoyed that Arcky was able to negotiate such a promising deal. If all went well, Erika would face a handgun possession charge, beside an illegal disposal of bodies charge, at worst, and she'd probably be able to knock that down to time served with a plea. As Cookie and Mitch had wanted all along, their daughter might even be out of jail and back home within a month.

That morning, Erika gave the information everyone had been waiting for to Arcky. As it turned out, she was more help than anyone could have imagined. Not only did she give detectives the actual location of the dump site, but she explained that BJ had packaged the body parts in various SEAL bags, which were distinctively different from normal trash and duffel bags. This way, the OCPD knew exactly what type of bags to be on the lookout for when the sun rose on Monday and the real search began.

After Erika gave up the locations of the Dumpsters, town officials pinpointed a landfill in Sussex County, Delaware, about forty-five minutes from Ocean City. What turned out to be a significant breakthrough in the case was the way in which this particular dump site layered its trash. Each layer, or section of the site, was laid out by days of the week. In other words, in one quadrant of the site, a town in Delaware had its trash. Each layer was a week, each cube a day. They could backtrack right to the day of the week Erika said she and BJ had dumped the body parts and begin searching what was a specific section of the landfill.

By late Monday afternoon, while what was left of Martha "Geney" Crutchley and Joshua Ford was being searched for in a Delaware landfill, Erika and BJ Sifrit were brought into court to face a judge regarding bond. No one—save for maybe Mitch and Cookie—expected Erika (or BJ) to be bonded out of jail after what was being reported in the newspapers as one of the most disturbing, heinous, and shocking crimes to hit the region in over a century. With that said, Worcester County district judge Richard Bloxom agreed, refusing both accused killers bail of any kind.

When that issue was settled, Bloxom scheduled a preliminary hearing for Erika on June 17 and a June 11 hearing for BJ, both of which would take place in Ocean City District Court. Each faced two counts of first-degree murder, Bloxom explained, and were to remain held at Worcester County Jail pending those court appearances.

Walking out of court, Arcky knew that the hearing was a formality. He still had that deal on the table with Joel Todd. Erika would undoubtedly take and pass her polygraph, walk out of prison, and soon retire to Hollidaysburg, Pennsylvania, in seclusion at her parents' house until BJ's trial—where she would emerge to withdraw her marital privilege and testify against him.

55

What Remains

In total, fifty-five law enforcement officers from Delaware and Maryland planned to bring in lights and continue to search for Geney and Joshua's remains overnight. At first, it looked as if, Joel Todd later said, "the search was going to be like a needle in a haystack."

The problem was that too much time had gone by. Those Dumpsters had been emptied and they had a range—or a part of the week in one quadrant—where their contents could be, but it was such a large landfill that as the day went on, and with the hot and humid weather and the smell and rotting garbage and squeaking seagulls, it all became too much.

When Detective Scott Bernal got out to the landfill, it was around 4:30 P.M. The air quality, he recalled, was worse than he could have ever imagined. Wasps, bees, flies. "It was like shit floating through the air and it just stuck to you."

But then, one hour and twelve minutes into the search, someone found something.

"We did find human remains, but at this point they're unidentifiable," Delaware State Police spokesman Bruce Harris told reporters.

In truth, they had uncovered a leg, a torso, and two arms—all of which were badly decomposed, and yet eerily intact. One of the arms had a tattoo on it that family members of Joshua Ford had described. What were the chances that the body parts were someone else's?

"I would have liked them to continue looking," Todd added later, "but I absolutely understand why they stopped. So I cannot quarrel with them for not going another day. But I guess I'll always wonder if we continued looking would we have found other body parts or not."

Joel Todd could have made a decision at that point to prosecute both BJ and Erika together, but he would have had to use Erika's statements *against* BJ.

"Her statements include inculpatory information as to him—information that would be hearsay if I tried him by himself. And there's no way I could introduce her statement without including the information about him, which means that I had to do separate trials."

Regardless of the horrific nature of the crime and the way the press treated BJ and Erika as monsters (perhaps understandably so), on the surface things appeared to be going reasonably well for Arcky and Erika. It seemed that the deal Arcky had cut for Erika with Joel Todd and E. Scott Collins, his assistant state's attorney, would be consummated, and, within some time, life would carry on for Erika Sifrit.

56

Divine Intervention

Detectives Scott Bernal and Brett Case had their doubts about Erika. But they were cool with allowing Joel Todd to do his job. What they had to do now was build a case against BJ and Erika for the state's attorney. Collect evidence. Calculate it. Study it. Interview witnesses. And figure out exactly what had happened inside that bathroom on their own, without Erika interfering with her lies and constantly changing stories.

Bernal and his boss, Detective Sergeant Richard Moreck, attended the autopsies of Geney and Joshua on June 4.

Dr. Adrienne Perlman conducted the autopsy on what amounted to a human torso, two human arms, and one human leg. A lot could be learned from body parts. From just looking at them, it was easy for Bernal to tell that as BJ (or Erika, they weren't sure just yet) cut up the bodies, it was apparent where the knife had begun to dull. The first arm was cut clean off. The second arm looked as though it had been cut and torn off.

As Perlman put the torso on the table and readied it for X-ray, Richard Moreck stood and watched, with Bernal by his side. Bernal could barely take the smell. For some reason, it was getting to him today. For Moreck, however, it didn't seem to bother him.

"What is it?" Bernal asked Moreck. Bernal had his hand over his nose and mouth. He could tell Moreck had locked onto something important.

Moreck stared. The entire torso wouldn't quite fit on the autopsy area in which the X-ray was going to pick up; just a bit of the top section of the torso was not going to make it in the image.

Moreck leaned in. The smell was worse, the closer you got to the torso.

"The worst I had ever smelled in my career," Bernal said later. "With the decomposition and the dump, it was ripe in that room. Unbearable."

"Look at that," Moreck said. He was pointing.

"What?"

Moreck was focused on an area near the shoulder. "Get that in the image," he told the technician.

Sure enough, in that little area that would have been otherwise missed, there was another spent round, on top of the one Perlman had already recovered.

"There were several of these incidents," Bernal suggested later, looking up toward the sky as he spoke, "that led some of us to believe that something larger than ourselves was working alongside this investigation."

57

The Fighter

Brett Case drove out to Lewes, Delaware, one afternoon in mid-June to speak with the tattoo artist who had drawn the snake tattoo on Erika's side. The OCPD had several photographs of Erika getting a tattoo of a snake only a few days after Geney and Joshua were known to be murdered. Case wanted to understand Erika's and BJ's demeanor and attitude while they were there. The way in which they acted was going to be important to the case.

As Erika stood in front of the mirror, the tattoo artist explained to Case, she looked at herself and said, "I'm too fat. I look so damn fat."

She had shorts on and a belly-button-cut tank top. It was May 28, just a few days after the murders.

The artist laughed. "Huh! Eat a few more cheeseburgers, honey. Look at you."

Erika smiled. She loved the comment.

BJ was sitting there beside Erika as she grimaced and bit her teeth while the artist inked the new tattoo.

"She's a fighter," BJ said. "She's tough. She can take a punch." He laughed.

"My husband has a new tat," Erika said. She explained the swastika on BJ's chest, but BJ would not show the man.

"You guys ever seen the movie *American History X*?"

Erika said she and BJ had seen the movie and loved it. BJ was in and out of the shop, always returning with a drink in his hand.

If nothing else, Case learned while interviewing the tattoo artist that Erika and BJ were like any other married couple, getting along, laughing, joking, having some fun while on vacation, and getting a tattoo. There was no indication that BJ was controlling his wife and making her do anything.

58

No More Tears

Arcky visited with Erika a few times throughout the month of June and into early July. When the time came to begin talking about the actual polygraph, Arcky felt fairly confident Erika was ready.

Joel Todd called Arcky one morning in early July.

"We need to sit down with Erika and we need to go over this thing in detail." Since their initial contact during the weekend of June 1, 2, and 3, detectives from the OCPD and/or Joel Todd had not spoken with Erika at any length. Everyone was waiting on the polygraph to see which road the case would take next.

"Sure," Arcky said.

After hanging up and taking care of a few issues in his office, Arcky took off to visit with Erika and explain that going in to speak with OCPD detectives and Joel Todd before she took the actual polygraph was more or less a requirement of the deal she had signed. She needed to sit down with them, in other words, and lay everything out. For the OCPD, it was a certainty that every time they uncovered something on their own and brought it to Erika, she kind of said, *"Oh yeah, I remember that now."*

"It was a game with her," Bernal later said. "She had selective memory."

Erika agreed to sit down and talk. She had no choice, really.

As he thought about it, something gnawed at Arcky. A gut instinct, perhaps. He had a feeling something was off. He was still concerned about the deal. Mitch and Cookie were continuously telling him that Erika would never lie, and never keep anything from him (or them). That she would stick to her end of the deal. Arcky had nothing to worry about.

Before they headed over to Joel Todd's office, Arcky explained to Erika that if there was any minor detail she had forgotten to tell him, she needed to come clean with it now.

Erika insisted, reaffirming her earlier position, that there was nothing to worry about.

A few hours later, Erika and Arcky sat in Joel Todd's office. Todd and OCPD detective Scott Bernal were on one side of the room. There was a tape recorder in the middle. Todd and Bernal wanted to question Erika again about everything to make sure her story was the same. It was, essentially, a *pre* pre-polygraph exam. Erika would be preinterviewed again by the polygraphist once she was inside the room where the actual test would be taken, but Todd wanted to be certain she wasn't wasting everyone's time.

Bernal questioned Erika as Arcky and Todd sat and listened. Things went well. She was stronger than she had been a month earlier. More together. She'd even put on a little weight and seemed to be adapting to prison life quite well.

As the interview went forward, Erika answered Bernal clearly. She was confident and seemingly open and willing to talk about everything. At one point, Bernal asked if BJ had any brothers and if Erika was scared of him or his family at all.

"No brothers," she said. "One sister."

"Does he have anybody that would carry out any deed he would want them to do, or do you know if there's any friends—"

"Yes! I'm actually a little scared about that," Erika interrupted. "He has SEAL friends that might . . . I don't, like, I definitely would not want him to know that I was here talking to you. And if I go up and testify, and for some reason you guys don't get him locked up, my family will end up like Joshua and Geney. So I hope that you guys know what you're doing. I seriously do. Because my family, my parents' home will be burned down, and my family will end up exactly like those people. Cut to pieces and him jerking off to the body parts. . . ."

This was the first time they had heard that BJ had masturbated on the body parts after cutting up Geney and Joshua.

Arcky shook his head at times, agreed with the questioning at others, and felt decently reassured that all would go well for his client with the polygraph. The entire story Erika had retold, which amounted to about three to four hours' worth of details, was full of new information and gruesome particulars Todd and Bernal had not yet heard. It was here where Erika talked for the first time about how BJ had wanted Erika to take a photograph of him holding up Joshua and Geney's heads and send it to his SEAL buddies.

As the interview went forward, Erika admitted that the story she had told of Geney and Joshua being murdered on the beach was nonsense. It happened inside the condo. In that bathroom upstairs. She was sleeping, she said, downstairs. She heard the shots. Woke up. Saw the bodies. Helped BJ get rid of them after he cut them up.

It was BJ's doing all the way. Erika said she had taken no part in any murder. Heck, she wasn't even there when the actual murders took place. He did it all. She was an accessory, sure.

But only *after* the fact.

After everyone ate lunch, they all met up again in Joel Todd's office to continue. They were almost done, Todd said. "Just a few more questions."

Erika continued to blow the trumpet of BJ being responsible for everything. Arcky watched Bernal. He felt Bernal wasn't so convinced Erika was being truthful. Arcky could tell by Bernal's tone and the questions he asked that he still had reservations regarding Erika's claim of total ignorance.

Arcky could understand. The guy was a seasoned detective. But enough with the continued badgering of his client! The polygraph would answer Bernal's concern.

And then Bernal came out with it: "What about the second couple?" he asked Erika.

Arcky was puzzled. *Second couple? What is he talking about?* Arcky had no idea what Bernal meant.

On the Wednesday after Geney and Joshua were murdered, Erika and BJ had invited that *second couple*—Todd Wright and Karen Wilson—up to the condo and it had apparently turned into a scene much like what had happened with Geney and Joshua—except for the murder and dismemberment part. BJ had gone berserk and accused them of stealing Erika's purse.

"What?" Arcky said, stopping the questioning for a moment.

"I'm sitting there thinking," Arcky recalled later, "'What's this all about?' It was the first time I had heard about another couple in a similar situation inside that condo. Also, how could this same conduct occur in that room a second time without anyone being killed? None of it made any sense to me as I sat there listening."

Bernal was interested in the fact that Erika had allowed this same situation to take place a second time, after knowing what BJ had done the first. Throughout the interview, Erika had repeated over and over that she was terrified of BJ all week after witnessing what he had done. She was scared that he'd kill her or her family and went along with everything he had done because of that fear. Sitting there, listening to her, Bernal knew it was all bullshit. He knew from his own investigation that Erika had gone along with BJ that week because she *wanted* to serve him. BJ hadn't threatened her.

"She was lying to us. I knew it. We all knew it."

If, in fact, she had *not* participated in the first crime, why was she involved in the second? Why hadn't she walked out? More important, knowing what she knew about the first couple, and how they ended up dead, why had she helped BJ lure this second couple back up to the condo? This second occurrence screamed of Erika's hands-on involvement.

"It told us," Bernal said, "that Erika was in on this as much as—if not more than—BJ ever was."

Moreover, as Bernal sat and listened to Erika put it all on BJ, he could see images from the photographs the OCPD had confiscated inside BJ and Erika's Rainbow condo. Erika playing miniature golf, smiling, eating shrimp and crabs, drinking beers, getting a tattoo, shopping at Home Depot, lying on the beach. Was this a woman being held captive by a domineering husband who had killed two people and made her help him dismember and dump the bodies? Or, Bernal wondered, was this a woman who had helped her husband murder one couple and had tried to again assist him in luring a second couple up to the room so they could engage them in their missing-purse game in order to do the same damn thing?

Hearing Erika mention the second couple, Arcky now knew for certain there were details Erika had not shared with him—and he felt slighted and used. Why wouldn't she admit to this second couple? Why would she keep it from him? He was there to protect her.

"Still," Arcky explained later, "I am sitting there, thinking, 'We're OK. We're not sunk yet.' Though I'm now worried what this 'new information' is going to do to the deal regarding her cooperation. I am confident that it won't have any effect on it at all."

On the other hand, no matter what, the state's attorney was bound by that deal—providing, that is, Erika passed the lie detector test. It all came back to that lie detector test she was scheduled to take.

As Erika talked about the second couple, Arcky allowed her to continue, thinking, *What else don't I know?* Which was more important to him than the information itself. How much had Erika kept from him?

"The fact that this situation took place a second time," Arcky said later, "was not something I wanted to hear. But, on the other hand, it doesn't preclude the deal, as long as they don't have some reason to think that she participated in the actual murder."

* * *

Leaving Joel Todd's office, Erika was confident she could pull off the polygraph. She had secrets, sure. But somewhere in her twisted mind, she believed she could contain them and get through that all-important polygraph.

59

The Right Button

Inside Erika and BJ's condo, detectives uncovered one of Erika's scrapbooks that proved to be quite telling in its own way. Being in the scrapbooking business, Erika had documented a better part of her life with BJ. It was as much her job to scrapbook as it was a hobby and something she enjoyed doing.

On one page of a book detectives took during the search, a few photographs of Erika and BJ struck them as particularly odd. BJ, for one, appeared younger and more boyish. He didn't have that gruff, military look to him. He was even smiling in several of the photos. Erika also looked content. She was a normal weight for her size, smiled genuinely, and looked comfortable next to her husband. You might even take a leap and suggest that they appeared to be in love.

Erika had titled the page in big bold letters at the top: **MARYLAND,** along with the subtitle *You are my sunshine.* It was a play on words, obviously. The "you" was Benjamin, of course. In her synopsis of the trip she and BJ had taken, Erika marked the date *May 2000,* and the reason for the trip to Ocean City that particular summer: to take a friend of hers she called "Becky," Erika's aunt, along with two of her aunt's friends, down to the seashore for a quiet getaway. They had all stayed at the Rainbow.

In reading this, the minutia of the trip didn't matter much to detectives. But it was what happened when Erika and BJ were in Ocean City that seemed to ring a familiar bell. Erika had documented on the page how she, BJ, and her aunt went shopping in Rehoboth at the outlet stores. After a long day of browsing through racks of overpriced sweaters and designer blue jeans, they all went out to eat. Where else? Hooters, of course, a favorite spot for Erika and BJ. After eating wings, they decided to walk around a muscle car show the restaurant was having in the parking lot.

It was a cold weekend, Erika wrote, which sent them looking for something to do indoors. The car show was boring, anyway, she added.

At a nearby tattoo parlor, BJ and Erika wanted to get some "new ink." Yet, once they got inside the parlor, Erika wrote, she had to back out. She didn't have any money. Nor did she have her wallet. In realizing this, she wrote, she *accused some girls [inside the tattoo parlor] of stealing my wallet when I really had left it at the Rainbow!*

It was a joke. Blaming the girls for thieving her purse when she knew where it was all along.

When Erika got back to the condo, she called her father. "I cannot find my purse." She was hysterical, her father later told me. She was convinced that someone had actually stolen the purse.

"Calm down," Mitch Grace told his daughter. "I'll check into it."

Mitch called condo management and had "everyone looking" for Erika's purse, he said.

After quite a spectacle of searching high and low, someone recovered the purse under a couch cushion inside the condo living room—now a familiar place for detectives. BJ had stayed in the background and watched the day unfold. He saw how obsessive Erika had become when she realized her purse was missing. She freaked out. According to some, this was when BJ began to understand that by the simple act of losing her purse, Erika had exposed herself. She had become unnerved to the point of mayhem. Losing something was one of Erika's many buttons BJ began to understand that he could push.

Another was the telephone. BJ would be in Memory Laine reading a magazine, Mitch Grace later said, or just hanging around, and the telephone would start ringing. Erika would be with a customer or just busy doing any one of the thousand things she had to do in the store every day.

Hearing the phone ringing in front of him, however, BJ would not budge.

"He could be sitting within arm's reach of the phone," said Mitch, "and he would just let it ring and ring and ring, because he knew it would get to Erika."

60

Training a SEAL

There was a time after BJ graduated from SEAL school, while living near Virginia Beach, when he and Erika weren't yet seeing each other regularly. Erika had met BJ by this point and had fallen for him—and had perhaps even become obsessed with him. But BJ had other plans: he was focused on SEAL training and his career. Erika wouldn't take no for an answer when BJ told her he really didn't want to get involved. They were out with a few other couples having some beers.

"Sorry," BJ said. "I want to focus on my training and military career."

Erika didn't say anything.

She refused to take no for an answer.

Before Erika met BJ, she had been dating another man. According to sources, the man had finally had enough of Erika's obsessive behaviors and possessive nature and told her to forget it. The relationship had run its course.

Erika wouldn't accept the breakup. She *couldn't* accept it.

So she got up, former friends said, walked over to a brick wall outside the bar, where they had all been hanging out, and began ramming her forehead into the wall.

"No, no, no, no . . . ," she kept saying.

Rejection was not easy for Erika Grace to swallow. She had left Pennsylvania as, essentially, the star of her hometown—a basketball superwoman.

Everybody's hero.

In college, however, rejection began: She wasn't the luminary anymore, but more of an average student and average ball player. In a sense, Erika didn't know how to react to rejection.

"Come on," the crowd said. "Stop that." She was beginning to bleed.

Erika continued.

And continued.

Until her head was bleeding profusely.

The cops were called.

According to witnesses, one of the officers asked, "What's going on here?" after rolling up to the scene outside the bar.

"She's upset," someone said.

According to law enforcement, this same scene played out again with BJ sometime later, when he decided after meeting Erika that they had no future. At first, seeing how badly bruised and bleeding Erika was, police thought BJ had been beating on her. But they split them up, asked some questions, and BJ was told to take Erika home.

They had known each other only a few days then.

As BJ's friends got to know Erika more intimately, she

began to express a part of herself that was quite odd, said one former acquaintance.

"Erika wanted what she wanted—and that was that."

She was possessive, yes indeed, but there was another side to Erika that shocked one friend. It began at the beach. They had all decided to go to the beach one day, to kind of accept Erika into the group as BJ's girl. After all, they were married. This same friend had dropped Erika off at the airport, in fact, to head off to Las Vegas.

"She mentioned nothing to me about going there to get married."

Anyway, they were at the beach one day and Erika told a story. She was partying down in Ocean City with some girlfriends a few years back, she said. They were drinking, doing pills, having a ball. "Yes," that friend said, "I knew Erika was into drugs before she met BJ."

"Listen," Erika said, "we're down there in Maryland and one of my friends gets into a car with this stranger, this guy she just meets, and takes off."

According to what Erika said, that friend was then raped by this guy.

What startled Erika's new friends—BJ's people, if you will—as they sat there on the beach, listening to Erika tell this story, was her reaction to the rape. "I guess that'll teach her not to get into the car with strangers again," Erika supposedly said, reacting to her friend's rape.

"It was very blasé the way she went about saying it."

One of the women there listening was a criminal defense attorney. The woman looked at the other friend as Erika spoke and they both popped their eyes out, like, *Huh? That's a bit weird—to have a reaction like that.*

"You'd think someone would tell a story like that with a bit more sympathy in their voice."

From then on, the former friend continued, Erika was "like psycho for BJ, crazy jealous."

BJ's sister came down to visit him once when they were living together in North Carolina with these friends.

Erika was jealous of BJ's sister and the time that he was spending with her.

There was one time when BJ hadn't seen his friends for six weeks; he was out on a training exercise with the SEAL team. When he returned, they all met up at a local bar.

"Hey, BJ," said his friend's wife. They gave each other a little hug. She kissed him on the cheek. "Welcome home, soldier!"

Erika was standing nearby.

She flipped out. "Never touch him. Never speak to him again."

61

Hide in Plain Sight

At one point, Erika had told Detective Scott Bernal that she had photographed BJ holding up Geney and Joshua's heads; his face was painted with blood, and he sported a throbbing, enormous erection. She said she had used a digital camera and mailed the card file back home with some of her other stuff. BJ wanted to send the photos to his SEAL buddies when they got back.

Bernal wasn't so sure if it was just a story, or if Erika was telling the truth. So Bernal and his boss, Richard Moreck, headed north to Pennsylvania to search Erika's apartment.

The Graces had put all of Erika's belongings into storage containers. They had emptied the apartment of everything and placed all of it, Bernal said later, into these containers and then into a storage shed in back of Erika's grandmother's property.

"Somebody knew what they were doing in storing that stuff there," Bernal said. "This became a nightmare for us to obtain a search warrant."

This story was worth checking out, however—no matter what the OCPD had to go through to get that search warrant.

After spending the day securing the search warrant, while going through one of the containers, looking for a digital camera or card file, Bernal noticed out of the corner of his eye that Mitch Grace, who was there watching their every move, had picked something up out of a container and had quickly put it in his pocket.

Bernal grabbed Mitch by the wrist harshly. "Hey, whatever you put in your pocket, if it's a weapon, move your hands back slowly."

Maybe it was the card file they were looking for?

Mitch had what Bernal described as a "kid caught with his hands in the cookie jar" look about him. He was scared. He took his hand out of his pocket and raised both arms.

"It's nothing," he said.

Bernal told him to put it on the table.

It was a marijuana pipe.

"What do you think . . . ," Bernal said. He was dumbfounded by what Mitch had done. "We're here, Mitch, searching for evidence of *murder*. Do you think we give a *shit* about some pipe with pot residue inside of it?"

Mitch didn't say anything.

"Mitch's mind-set," Bernal remarked later, "was always protect, protect, protect. That's where his mind was. He had no sense of where things began and where things ended. And to think, Erika did this to the poor guy. She destroyed that family."

62

The Test

Joel Todd called Arcky Tuminelli and made it perfectly clear that it was time to get on with the polygraph. It had been almost a month since that rather illuminating meeting and interview with Erika had taken place in Joel Todd's office. In order for what was officially now known as the "Memorandum of Understanding" agreement, which Arcky and Joel had drafted back in June at midnight in Todd's office, to be put into full effect, the polygraph needed to be completed.

"Let's go, Arcky," Todd said.

By now, the OCPD had forensically identified the torso, arms, and leg they had uncovered in that Delaware landfill as a match to Joshua Ford and Geney Crutchley. The state's attorney needed to get the case moving along. This had been a horrific crime, of which the media was buzzing around the periphery, wondering what was going on. Todd's community wanted answers, not to mention the family members on Joshua and Geney's sides. Beyond that, a preliminary ballistics report confirmed that the bullets recovered from Joshua's decomposed torso were fired from the gun Erika Sifrit had in her possession on the night she was arrested with BJ in the parking lot of Hooters.

If Detective Scott Bernal and Joel Todd were betting men, their money was on the fact that Erika was holding on to more secrets than she was willing to reveal. A polygraph, although not a legal means of truth-telling, was a good barometer to begin the process of where to take the investigation and prosecution next. But they needed to get Erika into that chair and get those wires strapped to her arms and chest.

Arcky met with Erika and her parents. It was showtime, he explained.

"Look, what happened is not something that's very helpful," Arcky said, referring to when Erika had withheld that information about the second couple from him, especially when it seemed so vital to her future defense. Not to mention why she would surprise Arcky with it. A *second* couple? Two people who actually lived to tell their story. Witnesses the state's attorney and OCPD detectives had already located and interviewed. "You're telling me I can trust you, and I didn't know about this?" Arcky explained later. He was upset that by withholding what was crucial information, Erika seemed to have deliberately tricked him.

What else was she withholding?

Addressing Mitch, Cookie, and Erika, Arcky was clear about where they now stood: "If there is anything *else* that you are not telling me, you need to explain to me now what it is. I cannot protect Erika if I don't know what the hell is out there." Arcky felt as if he'd had this conversation with Erika and her parents a hundred times already.

"OK," Erika replied. "I know. I understand." There was nothing else, she said.

It was July 24, 2002. Erika was driven in a white van over to where the polygraph was going to be conducted inside the OCPD. In the agreement Tuminelli had written with Todd, he made a point to insure that the polygraphist conducting the interview was to be an outside party, meaning someone from the federal end of law enforcement. An agency neutral to the case. Smartly, Arcky didn't want an OCPD detective to get Erika in the hot seat and begin to work on her. Erika had to feel comfortable. The questions, which Arcky had been given before the test, turned out to be more or less what he had expected. They were centered on the deaths of Geney and Joshua, but they also touched on the year 1999, before Erika had met BJ:

1. *Are the lights on in this room?*
2. *Concerning the deaths of Geney Crutchley and Joshua Ford, do you intend to answer each question truthfully?*
3. *Prior to 1999, did you spread lies or vicious rumors?*
4. *Did you shoot a gun at any of those people?*
5. *Prior to 1999, did you think about hurting anyone and not do it?*
6. *Did you cut on any of those people?*
7. *Are you now sitting down?*
8. *Prior to 1999, did you lie to a person in a position of authority?*
9. *Prior to 1999, did you threaten anyone with physical harm?*
10. *Are you in Ocean City, Maryland?*

Joel Todd had agreed to this stipulation. The FBI said it would never polygraph a witness if it wasn't involved in

the case. So Arcky went to someone he knew in the
Secret Service and asked if he could find an agent to do
the job.

The Secret Service provided the perfect agent, an un-
threatening female agent who was noticeably pregnant
at the time.

63

Door Problems

OCPD detectives were tracking down every possible lead. What impressed Joel Todd later was that the OCPD had located, at one time or another, just about every person in the background of every photograph Erika had taken over the course of her trip to Ocean City over that Memorial Day week. This had eaten up a lot of the OCPD's time, and some of the detectives were quite outspoken in their disagreement with being asked to do this by their boss. However, they did it without question.

Since one of the photos depicted BJ at Home Depot, detectives found customers in line with BJ and Erika. Clerks and managers. One woman distinctively remembered meeting Erika in line one day during the middle of that week. She said BJ was "carrying a money . . . like a deposit bag." He didn't say much while waiting in line. But the woman that BJ had been with—"Yup, that's her," the witness had said after looking at a photograph of Erika—had said plenty.

Erika was carrying a triangular-shaped piece of wood. The woman asked what it was for.

"You wouldn't believe it," Erika said, smiling, "that's all that's left of my door."

Erika and BJ had broken off a piece of the upstairs bathroom door in the condo to bring into the store so they could match paint colors.

"That must have been some party," the woman said to Erika.

BJ had walked off.

Erika had a good laugh after she heard the comment, adding, "I *guess* you could . . . call it that."

When the clerk didn't have the exact color BJ and Erika needed, Erika asked for a phone book. BJ had returned. He had a brand-new wooden door in his hands, but it needed to be painted.

"Hey, you know where this Lowe's is in Delaware?" Erika asked the woman. "Can you give us directions?"

"That's pretty far away. I don't know that you want to go there. It's over near the outlet stores in Rehoboth."

Erika beamed. Said it would not be a problem. "We were just in Rehoboth. . . ."

64

Truth or Dare

Having the Secret Service conduct the polygraph was something that gave Arcky Tuminelli a bit of comfort on a day that was filled with frayed nerves and anxiety, to begin with. Arcky felt that if Erika went into the interview and answered those questions just as they had talked about beforehand, all would turn out just fine. Joel Todd would be satisfied, the agreement would be consummated, and perhaps Arcky could begin to work on getting Erika out on bond and then structuring a solid defense.

Throughout the days leading up to the polygraph, Mitch Grace demanded constant feedback from Arcky regarding every nuance of the case. Both Mitch and Cookie were driven by the idea that once Erika passed the polygraph, she was coming home. It seemed they were under the impression—and Mitch later agreed with this—that once Erika passed that test, she was as good as out on bond.

After talking with Joel Todd and one of the Secret

Service agents, Arcky met with Erika and asked her one more time if there was *anything* that she hadn't told him. Now was the time to come out with it. Arcky made that perfectly clear, he later said.

Erika reassured him that she had nothing to hide. She was ready.

Arcky could renegotiate a deal for Erika at any time, essentially. The only time it would be too late to go back to the bargaining table would be *after* the polygraph—especially if Erika didn't do as well as she expected.

Erika and BJ had been in jail for nearly two months by this point. Just about every time Arcky met with Erika, she'd generally cry her way through the conversation. Here was a rich girl, if you will, from an upscale community in an extremely suburbanized part of Pennsylvania. Petite, fragile, and rather unassumingly shy and quiet, she was locked up with what were hardened criminals—of which, Joel Todd and the OCPD certainly believed, she was one. Erika herself had gone on and on in letters to a friend about the conditions she had faced in prison: not being let out of her cell, the rats, feces everywhere, vomit, the smells, the urine, the dirty showers.

It was not a nice place to be.

Many who spoke to Erika during this period, however, believed the crying and "poor me" aspect of Erika's demeanor had little to do with the situation she faced behind bars, but had more to do with the predicament she faced in a court of law. One of the stories Erika had told OCPD detectives included a desire on her part to stop the inevitable. There was a point during that awful night, Erika explained to the OCPD, when she, BJ, Joshua, and Geney were getting along rather well, but then BJ "flipped out," she claimed, "and accused [Geney] of stealing [my] pocketbook." Geney and Joshua were locked in the upstairs bathroom by that

point. BJ was standing outside the door, according to
Erika, pacing, stomping around, wondering what to do.
Erika told Bernal that she had run downstairs and had
searched the living-room area, hoping to find the pocketbook so she could calm BJ down. He was supposedly
incensed and getting violently angry. She knew how BJ
could get. She understood what he would do, so she des-
perately searched for the purse, fearing the worst if she
didn't find it.

"That was *one* story," Bernal said later. "We heard
so many versions of it, we had no idea what to believe
anymore."

Which was where the polygraph came into play.

"The bottom line," Arcky said later, referring to the
polygraph test, "was that if that test came out that she
was not being deceptive, Erika would not be prosecuted
for murder. It wouldn't matter what Joel Todd or the detectives believed. They wouldn't be able to prosecute her
under those charges. . . ."

It was as simple as that.

Joel Todd had made it clear that without a doubt he
believed that Erika had had more to do with these
crimes than she had been claiming. And although BJ was
the obvious muscle behind the crime spree the duo had
been engaged in for the past two years (burglaries and
now double murder), Erika was an important motivating
factor and a driving force behind the behavior.

It was just before 10:00 A.M. when Secret Service
agents Carri Campbell and Bill Doyle said they were
ready for Erika. They, of course, read Erika her Miranda
rights and asked if she understood that the polygraph
was voluntary. They were in a small interrogation room
at the OCPD. Arcky Tuminelli and Assistant State's At-

torney E. Scott Collins were waiting down the hall. It was going to take a while. Several hours, in fact. Joel Todd was in his office next door. Scott Bernal and the other detectives were in another part of the same building.

"Yes, I understand," Erika said. She appeared more confident and less dramatic than she had previously. She even showed poise. Arcky Tuminelli, Bill Doyle, Carri Campbell, Detective Bernal, and, from the Forensic Division, Jack Johnson, the Secret Service special agent in charge, had all been present when the forms were signed to conduct the test.

Carri Campbell was pregnant. It was most obvious. She would be asking the questions, while Doyle and Jack Johnson sat nearby and conducted the actual test. Erika took one look at Campbell and smiled. There was a built-in rapport there almost immediately. By 10:03 A.M., they were sitting down, comfortable, ready to begin. All Secret Service polygraphs start with a medical questionnaire, then proceed with a personal history questionnaire. Erika sat, pen in hand, and took her time answering each question. As she did this, she started to talk to Carri Campbell about her life before marrying BJ, and also her relationship with him afterward. Erika seemed forthcoming for some reason—as if she wanted to talk. No one had yet asked a question.

Campbell wasn't going to stop Erika from talking. Obviously, Erika felt at ease and needed (or wanted) to unload a few things before the actual polygraph started. *So be it,* Campbell thought.

After talking a bit about her mother and father's deep bond to each other and how it affected her upbringing (Erika said she often felt left out), Erika asked Campbell, "Have you seen my jewelry that the police had in their inventory room?" It was as if Erika felt she was going to walk out of the jail later on that same day and wanted the jewelry back as soon as she was finished with the test. She sounded almost cocky, like she'd had some sort of plan all along and it was almost completed.

"Yes," Campbell said, "I am aware of what is in inventory."

"Oh good!" Erika exclaimed happily. "I miss that shit and I really want my diamonds back."

It was odd that Erika was sitting, preparing to take a polygraph regarding a case where a double murder had been committed—and the bodies had been dismembered and tossed in a Dumpster like trash—and yet, she was concerned about her diamonds. If nothing else, the question told Campbell and the others where Erika's priorities were.

A pre-polygraph interview is an important aspect of any polygraph examination. It establishes a melodic, conversational tone between the examiner and the examinee. They begin to trust each other and develop a way to communicate that the machines begin to pick up on. It is extremely important for the examinee, being that a polygraph is based on the nervous system and blood pressure. As they spoke, Campbell and Erika became more appreciative of each other's lives. Erika began to talk about where she met BJ and how they had run off to Las Vegas together to get married, describing that first year of their marriage as "exciting" and full of partying "five days a week" with "cocaine and ecstasy." The way Erika described the drug abuse, it was as if it was a stage every marriage went through.

"It was the second year," Erika said at one point, "when I started to fear him."

"Oh, really?" Campbell responded. "How so?"

Erika talked about how BJ, a nonbeliever, dragged her kicking and screaming "away from God." She had grown up Lutheran, Mitch said later. They weren't ultrareligious, but they believed in God and Jesus Christ and had attended church at times.

"We didn't celebrate Christmas," Erika said, "because BJ didn't believe in Jesus."

As Erika opened up more about her marriage, she said, "Beej never gave me a present until April this year, when he bought me a Smith and Wesson .357."

In doing this, Erika had admitted to a government agent—perhaps without even realizing it—that the gun that killed Joshua and Geney was indeed hers.

"No kidding. Wow," Campbell said, encouraging Erika to continue.

"Yeah," Erika piped in, "it's the same weapon Beej used to shoot Josh."

"Really?"

"Yes. I never even fired the gun since I've owned it."

"Not once?"

"Beej was trying to frame me by using that gun, you know."

And so as the conversation continued, it seemed at first that Erika was laying the foundation for her defense. Sitting there, calmly talking to a Secret Service agent, she may have been thinking the entire time that she was getting one over on the agent. Maybe she could lay out her side of this story and push all the blame on BJ.

Yet, Erika was about to drop a bombshell—something that would stop the interview in its tracks.

65

Her (Latest) Story

There is no doubt that Erika Sifrit was the flame in the Grace household. As Erika was unable to accept magazines in the jail where she was being housed, her mother would sit in front of the wire mesh that separated them and hold up a current issue of *Vogue* or *Vanity Fair* and turn the pages slowly for Erika, several jailhouse sources said. She and her mother would not marvel at the articles, but rather at the jewelry ads. Erika was a jewelry addict; into and out of her college years, she could not go without expensive, over-the-top diamond rings, necklaces, and bracelets. Jewelry was one of those luxuries Erika *needed* to have. And the anecdote of Erika sitting with her mother, both of them staring at the magazine while Erika sat behind bars, is a metaphor, essentially, for how strong the attachment was between the Graces and their only child. And yet, Erika herself was about to jeopardize any chance the Graces had of saving their child.

As the pre-polygraph interview continued, after telling

Secret Service special agent Carri Campbell a story of how BJ had asked her to get pregnant, only to turn around and demand she abort the child or he would cut it out, Erika began to reflect on that night in Ocean City when she and BJ met Geney and Joshua.

Down the hall, like an expecting father, Arcky Tuminelli was staring at his watch, waiting and wondering. Arcky had no idea that as he sat and waited with E. Scott Collins, Erika was confessing to the entire crime, beginning with how and why she and BJ ended up going to Ocean City, Maryland, that week. Moreover, even if Arcky felt like walking in on the interview to see what was going on, he couldn't. If he barged into the interview and stopped it, Joel Todd could tear up the deal, which was what he probably wanted to do, anyway. And anything Erika had said during the time she was speaking with Carri Campbell would then be written into a report.

As Erika sat, talking to Campbell, a terrifying picture regarding her version of the events that took place in room 1101 emerged. As Campbell listened and her colleagues wrote down what Erika said, it seemed as though Erika was unleashing a great weight from her shoulders.

An enormous monkey.

She began with a breakdown of her criminal life with BJ. As Erika explained, she and BJ's crime spree had begun back on April 4, 2002. Erika said she started participating in what she called "B and E's" with her husband, seemingly against her better judgment and even will. Before she got involved, Erika said, BJ would "pick locks at ATMs and other locations" just for the fun of it. Some called BJ an expert lock picker. Erika was more concerned about her role in these crimes than their nature, however. For example, she said they were at a reptile show once and BJ broke into an LA Weight Loss Center while she was passed out drunk in the car. There was another time when, again, she claimed to be passed out in the car in Duncansville, close to where they lived at the time, when BJ robbed a Nextel store.

Still, that was the beginning. Over the course of several weeks after this, or the "next five B and E's," Erika said, she committed those herself. It was a rush. She got off on the notion of breaking into a building and robbing the store blind, then turning around and selling the items on eBay. The more she did it, the more she wanted to do it.

"He picked the locks and I ran in, making several trips inside the store, back to our Jeep Cherokee, until it was full," Erika said. BJ would be the lookout. They'd use extremely expensive walkie-talkie radios—which they stole, of course—to communicate while Erika was inside the establishment doing the job. It was as if they were living out some sort of wild Hollywood fantasy.

Bonnie and Clyde.

"Did you two have code words, or anything?" Campbell asked.

"'It is good,'" Erika explained. She'd be inside the business or store and BJ would be guarding the entrance, looking out for people. The all-clear sign was "It is good."

The look in her eyes as she talked about the crimes: Erika was transfixed by the way in which she and BJ had broken into so many different stores and never got caught. She ticked them off, as if talking about a tour they had gone on: Cost Cutters in Altoona; Sports Nutrition in the same Orchard Plaza strip mall, where her scrapbook store was located; the Top Ten Tanning Salon in Duncansville; and "two heavy-duty supply stores," but she had trouble recalling the names, one in the Blockbuster Plaza in Altoona and the other in Johnstown (both burgled on the same night).

Now, that was a real rush: two in one night.

The Sports Nutrition store was an interesting choice, seeing that, under BJ's direction, Erika stole cases of Yellow Jackets (over-the-counter speed pills). She said BJ had fed them to her "so I wouldn't eat."

The life of a prolific thief and scrapbooking business owner was getting to Erika, however, she admitted. She and BJ were getting tired. They worked all day at the store and then went out at night and stole things. The speed stopped working. They were burning a candle. BJ was even sleeping inside the scrapbook store during the day so he could rest up for a night of crime.

"I needed a vacation," Erika explained to Campbell.

The drugging and drinking weren't helping, either.

"Your dad can get us a room in Ocean City," BJ said one afternoon. It was close to the Memorial Day holiday. The thought perked Erika up a bit.

"Yeah—"

"We can do some serious B and E's there," BJ suggested. Murder wasn't part of the plan, Erika claimed. They had intended to go to Ocean City and steal as much as they could.

Erika smiled. She liked the idea.

They'd sold some goods on eBay recently and had a lot of cash lying around.

"We take cash with us," BJ said, "so we don't have to use credit cards and leave a trail."

"No one can trace us," Erika said.

66

Snakes
on a Plane

According to what Erika was now telling Carri Campbell, she, Joshua Ford, Geney Crutchley, and BJ sat around the living room of their condo after leaving Seacrets together and walking the beach back to room 1101. Geney and Joshua had stopped by their room on the way to the Rainbow to pick up their bathing suits, in case they decided to take a romp in the hot tub. Joshua had also, Erika claimed, picked up some marijuana. As Geney, BJ, and Joshua sat around the living room, Erika explained to Campbell, and "smoked some weed," she walked out onto the balcony of the condo and shut the door behind her. She needed a moment to herself. That Saturday, May 25, 2002, had been a long day of partying. All those drugs. All that booze. Up. Down. In and out of it. Erika was tired and burned out. On top of that, she wanted to make a phone call to a friend. It was either that, someone close to her later suggested, or she was setting up an alibi for herself, knowing exactly what she and BJ had planned for Geney and Joshua in the coming moments.

Erika's "friend" Brian (a pseudonym) lived in Florida. A popular exotic-reptile trader, with an upstanding reputation on the Internet, Brian would meet Erika and BJ at various reptile trade shows up and down the East Coast so Erika and BJ could pick up whichever reptile they had previously ordered. Brian later said that he and Erika communicated daily—by telephone and/or e-mail—for a spell of time when she was in a buying frenzy. Brian was well-liked by his customers. He'd taken photos with the likes of *Snakes on a Plane* movie star Samuel L. Jackson and successful film director Quentin Tarantino. If you wanted a crocodile, cobra, turtle, or any number of hard-to-find exotic reptiles, Brian was definitely the go-to guy.

In the scope of their relationship, however, Brian and Erika had met only two times, and BJ was present during both business meetings. Still, in a series of e-mails between them leading up to Memorial Day, it was clear that Erika had a crush on the guy, and he was not doing much to push her away. In fact, in one e-mail exchange, Erika had apologized to Brian for calling the previous night. She said she hadn't even recalled the phone call because she was so high. Apparently, Brian's wife answered a few times and there were some words exchanged. Erika had even told Brian at one point that she and BJ were at a bar they had just been kicked out of after she fell off a bar stool and her .357 Magnum slid out of her purse when she fell. After the incident, she called Brian and told him about it, adding that she and BJ were on their way to "do a specific heist."

It was 2:26 A.M. when Erika made the first call to Brian on that night when Geney and Joshua were in the other room with BJ. According to what Erika later said, she had called Brian to let him know that she was in Ocean City. It was late, she realized, but Brian was one of those guys she felt she could bother at any time of the night (although Brian said that their relationship was strictly professional), even if she hadn't spoken to him for a while. ("I had a little crush on him," Erika admitted to Carri Campbell, "even though I knew he was married.")

"Hi," Erika claimed she said when Brian picked up the phone. Although half asleep, Brian recognized who it was.

"It's late," Brian said groggily (according to Erika). "What are you doing?"

"I know . . . sorry."

"Call me back in the morning," Brian purportedly said.

As Erika started to talk, she could hear Brian's wife in the background saying something. Then the phone went dead, she claimed. ("[Brian's wife] had unplugged the line," Erika told Carri Campbell.)

According to Brian, however, the phone call went a little differently. He said his phone rang and he picked it up saying, "Hello? Hello?"

But nobody was there.

Phone records prove this call lasted five seconds.

A minute later, Brian's phone rang again. This time, he said, he knew who it was because his caller ID had picked up the number. "Hello . . . ?" he said again, but there was no one on the other end of the line.

That call, Brian said (and his phone records back it all up), lasted four seconds.

Why?

Because "I unplugged the phone," Brian later testified under oath.

Later in the week, Erika had called again. It was Wednesday night, Brian later told police, somewhere around midnight.

"I really need to talk to you. . . ."

"What?"

"I really need to talk to you," Erika said. "I met—BJ and I met—this guy at a bar. We went back to his place. BJ passed out. This guy . . . umm . . . he did some personal harm to me . . . and I really need to speak with someone about it."

"Call the police."

"I called 911. They called me a liar. They said I was drunk and fooling around. They didn't do anything."

"OK. You need to wake BJ up. Call the police and tell them what happened."

"Keep this between just us, OK? I don't want BJ to know."

The next day, Erika called Brian back. "I told BJ. We went looking for the guy. Thank God he left town. BJ was going to do something terrible to him."

"What do you mean?"

"He'd have killed him."

67

Déjà Vu

After the phone call to Brian, while Geney and Joshua were with BJ in the other room, Erika claimed she walked from the balcony to the kitchen to get "beers for everyone." Leaving the balcony, she closed the sliding glass door behind her, then passed by where BJ, Geney, and Joshua were sitting on the couch in the living room and smoking a joint.

"I wanted to be hospitable," she told Campbell, referring to making her guests feel comfortable by offering them a drink.

When they entered the Rainbow that night, Erika recalled to Campbell, she had placed her pocketbook on the kitchen table. She remembered this distinctly as she now walked back by that same table after making the phone call to her friend Brian. The only difference was that the pocketbook had been moved by someone (not her, she later claimed) and was now sitting on the backrest of the couch—which she thought was rather odd.

As she stood thinking about it for a moment in whatever drug-induced, cloud-of-alcohol haze she had been in after nearly twenty hours of drinking and drugging, the fact that someone had touched her purse without her knowledge began to bother Erika, she said.

So she picked it up and unsnapped the front flap.

"My jewelry and pills," she later explained to Campbell, "were missing."

And that, Erika now claimed, set off the beginning of the end of Joshua Ford and Geney Crutchley's lives.

68

"People with Diseases"

As they sat and listened to Erika describe what was a complete narrative account of the night, it was something Carri Campbell and, most certainly, Joel Todd, Arcky Tuminelli, and anyone else involved in the case had never expected to get out of a pre-polygraph examination. But Erika sat and talked openly about the details, as if she were reliving the night all over again.

As Campbell listened carefully, one thing became fairly obvious as Erika kept talking her way through the night: she hadn't yet made a connection between her and the murders. Thus far, she was putting all the blame on BJ, carefully telling a story that had BJ initiating the entire violent night—that is, until Erika spoke a few words that told Carri Campbell the lie detector test was never going to take place.

The comment came during a point in Erika's story in which she said Geney and Joshua were locked in the bathroom upstairs. BJ had walked over to Erika and asked, she recalled to Campbell, what to do now that they had two people locked in their bathroom—two people he had, in fact, just pulled a gun on. Erika had gone through and explained that BJ had pulled out his gun and threatened Geney and Joshua, asking them where Erika's jewelry was and why Erika's purse had been moved. It was after that, Erika explained, that Joshua and Geney ran into the bathroom and locked the door behind them to hide from BJ.

Now, according to what Erika was saying, BJ had gone to her and asked what she wanted him to do with Geney and Joshua. That it was entirely up to her.

Erika thought about it. Then, "Just fucking do it," Erika said, explaining to Campbell what she had told BJ that night.

"Huh?" Campbell responded.

"Now you have me on murder?" Erika asked as she sat there telling Campbell what happened.

"What do you mean by 'Just fucking do it' and 'just do it'?" Campbell asked. She wanted to be sure she understood exactly what Erika was saying.

Erika paused. Then, "I meant, 'Just *kill* them.'"

In other words, Erika was now claiming that she had given BJ the order to shoot Joshua and Geney. To murder them.

Campbell asked Erika the same question *ten times,* she later wrote in her report of the conversation, *and her answer was always the same.*

Except one time. Erika had changed it up a bit, saying, "I meant, 'Kill them.' I knew he wanted to."

"How could you know that?" Campbell asked.

Erika then proceeded to explain the remainder of the night.

"I knew he wanted to kill someone, because he asked me just two weeks ago if he could kill my family," Erika said to Campbell. "He wanted to kill my parents, both nannys and pappys (grandmothers and grandfathers), and even a wealthy aunt. He was going to do it in the middle of the night and leave for Argentina. Then I, being the sole heir to all the money, would fly over and meet him. . . ."

BJ was entertaining himself, Erika explained next, as she and Campbell got back into the actual narrative of what had happened inside the condo that night. Having two people locked in his bathroom turned BJ on. Because now, Erika said, BJ had Joshua and Geney right where he wanted: "Yelling and begging for their lives."

BJ got off on the fact that he had two people under his control, inside the bathroom, and, apparently, the green light from his wife to put a couple of bullets into their heads—something he had wanted to do to *somebody*, Erika suggested, for a long time.

And then as they both stood outside the bathroom door, Erika said something to BJ that rattled him.

"BJ . . . ," Erika said.

"What?"

"I called 911—"

BJ went ballistic at hearing the comment. "You did *what?*"

Erika said she started to cry. "I called 911."

"What the fuck are we supposed to do now? Am I supposed to—" And then he abruptly stopped talking.

He thought about it. Leaning with his back against the bathroom door, BJ seemed to have an epiphany, phrasing his next statement as a question to Erika, using what had become a familiar phrase: "I'm just going to fucking waste them, cool?" He smiled.

"Huh?"

He said the same thing again, phrasing it as a question: "I'm just going to fucking waste them, cool?"

It was a strange way to communicate. But when BJ said "Cool?" Erika knew he meant it as a question, or euphemism for "Is that OK with you?" It was BJ's way of once again asking for her approval.

Erika's stamp.

Joshua and Geney were "getting very loud," according to what Erika explained, "and I just wanted them to shut up."

Indeed, someone was going to hear the commotion.

"The people out on the beach," she said. (They might have figured out what was going on.) "I was worried about the police coming and the people out on the beach hearing us," she told Campbell.

Geney was screaming the loudest, banging on the door: "Help me, help me, help me." Then Geney went over to the glass window in the bathroom, which faced the beach. "Help me," she screamed again, banging on the window.

While Geney hammered on the glass, Joshua was thumping on the door with his fist, yelling, "Why are you doing this? Why are you doing this? Why are you doing this?"

BJ was on the opposite side of the door . . . thinking.

Erika was standing nearby. They were looking at each other. BJ had the gun in his hand.

"Just fucking do it," Erika said nonchalantly. "You got them fucking naked, you put a gun to their heads, just do it!"

The implication was that they were in big trouble by this point, anyway. Why not finish the job? Kill them. Get it over with.

"Why are you doing this?" Joshua yelled again. He was still thumping his fist against the door.

"Help me, help me," Geney was yelling.

BJ turned toward the door. Then he put the gun up against it. Eye level.

From looking at this situation, it's clear to see that BJ was playing a game. Considering his size and build—military SEAL training aside—he could have kicked that door in and shot both Geney and Joshua.

But he didn't—at least not at first.

As Joshua was beating on the door, BJ held the gun up and fired in the direction of the banging, then backed away from the door and, with all his might, kicked it open.

"The kick was so hard," Erika said, "that BJ fell backward."

The door flung open quickly with the force of the kick, and the door handle broke through the Sheetrock and lodged itself in the wall.

BJ was now inside the bathroom.

Geney was screaming. Joshua had gone quiet.

"I saw Joshua fall to the right side of the bathroom," Erika explained to Campbell, "against the closet."

Joshua had been shot. He was in great pain. Yet, he continued to scream at BJ, saying, "Why are you doing this?"

According to Erika, BJ walked over to Joshua at that moment and shot him in the head, silencing him. Shortly after BJ killed Joshua with that single gunshot to the head, Erika pissed in her pants. Then she walked out of the bathroom (she had been standing in back of BJ) and sat on the edge of the bed and "waited for it to be over."

With that comment, Carri Campbell asked, "What do you mean, 'Waited for it to be over'?"

"The killings," Erika answered.

The killings.

As Erika sat on the edge of the bed, she heard two more shots—and they startled her—in quick succession, "five seconds apart."

BJ walked out of the bathroom, flexing his muscles like a bodybuilder, yelling and laughing. He was covered with blood, Erika claimed. The blood, as she looked at

BJ, was smeared all over him. He had taken some of the blood and lathered himself up with it.

War paint.

"Come here," BJ said to Erika. He was pointing to the bathroom. He wanted Erika to see his work. Joshua's necklace had shattered when BJ shot him. There were little "black beads" from the necklace, Erika explained, all over the floor. Geney was in the corner of the room, underneath the vanity, crying, shaking, scared for her life.

He hadn't killed her yet.

BJ picked up several of the black beads and tossed them at Erika. "This is your cherry," he said mockingly. "Isn't it a beautiful sight?"

Geney had curled herself up into what Erika described as the "fetal position." There was a channel of blood around the vanity, Erika added, "so deep that it would splash" whenever one of them stepped in it. Joshua was leaning against the closet, his legs extended outward, blood all over the front of his body.

Dead.

Bill Doyle, the other Secret Service agent with Carri Campbell, stopped the interview for a moment and took out a photograph of Joshua and Geney and showed it to Erika, asking, "Is this the couple you're talking about that was killed?"

Erika smiled. "I took that picture," she said nonchalantly, as if she and Geney and Joshua were old friends. It was odd. She had just finished describing how scared she was and how violent Joshua's murder had been, and now she was smiling at the photograph of him. Then she added, "He's cute! I sort of hoped something did happen at Seacrets that night in the bathroom. . . . Do you think he was Jewish?"

"Did you and BJ *think* he was Jewish?" Campbell asked, searching for a motive.

"BJ was never able to tell, but he always asked if I thought someone we met was a Jew."

"Why is that?"

"BJ did not like niggers or Jews," Erika said, "or people with diseases. He believed mongoloids, retards, and cancer people polluted the gene pool."

69

The First Cut

What was clear as Agents Carri Campbell, Bill Doyle and Jack Johnson sat and listened to Erika Sifrit talk about how she and BJ murdered Geney and Joshua was that Erika was doing her best to paint BJ as a twisted sociopath who got off on murdering two people and, in turn, sucked her into his evil web. She made it clear that it had been all BJ's idea—that she only went along because she felt she had to; that she only said "Just fucking do it" to feed a desire he'd already had to kill a few people.

With Joshua dead and Geney about to die, it occurred to Erika as she stood inside the bathroom—blood all over the place, from the floor to the walls to the ceiling—that BJ had fired her gun several times and that the noise might arouse some sort of suspicion. More than that, she later told Carri Campbell, "I asked BJ, 'What about 911?'"

BJ looked at her. Surprised. Oh yeah, *that*.

"Where's my shit?" she then asked, talking about her jewelry.

"You need to run down to the Jeep, get the Motorolas, check the beach for our stuff, in case Geney and Joshua threw it over the balcony, and take a look around for the police," BJ said hurriedly.

Erika just stood there.

"You understand me?"

She nodded.

"What the fuck?" BJ asked. "What did you do, wet your fucking pants?"

Erika looked at herself.

BJ started laughing, mocking her once again.

Erika ran downstairs, found the Motorola radios, and quickly brought one back up to BJ and then ran back down to the beach to check for the jewelry BJ had claimed Joshua and Geney had stolen and maybe tossed over the balcony.

As she walked along the beach, scoping things out, Erika keyed the radio. "You there?"

"Go ahead," BJ said.

"I want to come back upstairs. . . . There are people out here on the beach. Are we good? Are you the only one up there?" It was the same language they had used when committing burglaries. Erika was asking if BJ had finished what he was doing: had he murdered Geney (who was still underneath the vanity) yet?

BJ didn't answer.

"I was paranoid," Erika later explained, "to say 'dead' or 'alive' on the radio in case someone heard me."

Erika ran back up to the penthouse when BJ failed to respond. He was still upstairs in the bathroom, she said, just staring at the vanity, where Geney was hiding. He had a look on his face, a crazy haze about him.

Erika stood beside him. "Baby," BJ said, "open your

knife like I taught you. Get down there and check to see if she's dead. Get down there and make sure."

"But I thought you said she . . ." Erika started to say, walking over to where Geney was hiding.

Kneeling down, Erika looked and saw Geney was still crouched in a fetal position. She claimed later that she didn't know, at this point, if Geney was alive or dead, but that she was under the impression BJ had shot and killed her.

"So I began to cut her body," Erika explained to Carri Campbell.

With that comment, Campbell moved into the same position she believed Geney might have been in at the time. But Erika said no, that wasn't it. And then she got up, crouched down, and curled up to show Campbell what she meant, saying, "Like this."

Back inside the bathroom, Erika explained, she got down on one knee and began "cutting" Geney. "Deep," she said. Geney started bleeding so profusely, Erika added, that the blood got all over her clothes as she continued. Interestingly enough, as Erika described this graphic, brutal scene, she showed no emotion. She never once said she felt forced to do it, or that it grossed her out having to cut up a fellow human being.

"Where did you cut her?" Campbell asked.

Erika explained it was the right side of Geney's abdomen, above her hip.

"I was surprised how much pressure it took to cut the skin, since I had never cut someone before. I cut her twice, like this," Erika said, and then proceeded to show Campbell how and where.

At one point, Erika paused, looked at Campbell, and said, "You have me on murder, don't you?"

Ignoring her, Campbell asked, "Was [Geney] alive or dead when you cut her?"

"I do not know for sure, but I thought she was probably dead."

"Did you check to see in any way before you cut her?"

"No."

70

My Girl

From about the time she was nine years old and playing Pee Wee League basketball outside Altoona, Pennsylvania, Mitch Grace stood along the sidelines—sometimes as her coach—cheering on his daughter, hanging on every move she made with that ball. In fact, in all those years, Mitch said later, right up until Erika left for the University of Mary Washington in Fredericksburg, Virginia, he'd never missed a game.

Not one.

The game Mitch recalled off the top of his head took place in New Orleans when Erika was twelve years old. It was during an AAU tournament. Erika's team had made it to the finals, but they faced elimination. Down by two points, with no time left on the clock, Erika, the best three-point shooter on the squad, hurled a bomb from her hip as the buzzer went off, but it slapped the backboard and failed to go in. It seemed there would be no Hollywood finish. No cutting down of the net. No hoisting Erika on their shoulders and parading her around the gymnasium floor. Their season, at least for the moment, was over.

Or was it?

As the shot flew through the air, Mitch Grace, sitting, watching every degree that orange-and-black ball arced toward the basket, thought he heard the faint rustlings of a whistle.

Erika had been fouled.

"Three shots," the ref yelled.

No one could believe it.

The team could not have asked for a better free throw shooter. Erika had spent countless days taking hundreds of foul shots. One obstacle she put on herself before she allowed herself to retire into the house after school, her father later explained, was she needed to hit a layup, a foul shot, and a three-foot jumper, all in a row, or she wouldn't eat dinner.

As much as she pushed to succeed on the court, Erika lived for the pressure. She reveled in the chance to take a free shot and move her team forward. Still, today the team needed her to be perfect: If she made all three, they won. If she missed one, overtime. Missed two, they were going back to Pennsylvania with their heads between their tails.

Not only did Erika Grace make all three shots, but the ball never rubbed against any metal: all three swished the net and the team won by a point.

Mitch Grace almost had a heart attack from the anxiety, but he nearly cried as his only child was heralded as a champion and hero.

That Disney moment seemed to embody the life Erika Grace would begin to lead after that game, setting a precedent for herself as she began to go through life, as a teenager and then into her early twenties. There seemed to always be that constant pressure to perform.

Constant pressure to *be* somebody. Constant fear that she would not live up to the expectations others had put on her. Even at home.

Mitch and Cookie, a former nurse, met in a hospital one afternoon while Mitch was working construction nearby and had injured himself. They dated. Then married. And, Mitch said later, they had never—"not for one night"—been apart since, some twenty-five years later.

As Erika grew up, she was a witness to the perfect life. The white picket fence. The cars. The money. A mom and a dad who truly loved each other.

Her idea of the perfect life, Erika later said, as she began to date and think about perhaps going to law school, became: Could she live up to what was expected of her, without failing? Erika Grace: the overachiever who, inside, was scared to death of disappointing and letting people down. Scared because, as Erika grew into a woman, she began to have these strange feelings guiding her—feelings of darkness and remorse, anger and resentment. Feelings that her mother and father cared more about their marriage than they did for their daughter. On paper, Erika had the ideal upbringing. In reality, underneath her transparent, thin skin, Erika suffered self-esteem issues that would lead her away from her goals and into a life Mitch and Cookie could never have imagined possible—even in a nightmare.

"It's such a horrible crime," Mitch Grace later told me, talking about what had happened to Geney and Joshua, "so it's hard to talk about it. I don't want to make light of it, implying that she (Erika) is more important than the poor thing that had happened to these good people."

Although Mitch was clear that he didn't want it to sound like his daughter was more important than the victims in this case, he was concerned that his daughter would be forever branded a monster for the fact that

Geney and Joshua were dismembered, admittedly, by Erika and BJ. Mitch, of course, didn't want to view his daughter—what father would—as some sort of barbarian who could cut another human being up in pieces.

"She has been portrayed as this horrible killer," Mitch continued, "but no one understands. . . . Because she's my daughter, I feel there's a huge difference between actually killing somebody and not knowing. Everybody in a situation has their own tragedy."

The implication was that Mitch believed Erika had had nothing to do with actually murdering Joshua and Geney—that it was all BJ's doing. And yet, as Erika herself continued to explain to Carri Campbell, she had participated willingly in these murders, ordered them, and then took part in dismembering their bodies.

71

Can It Be True?

Agent Carri Campbell noticed that Erika had what looked to be a fairly new snake tattoo on her right side, slightly above her hip. It was in the same location that she had just claimed to have made that first "cut" on Geney. "Is that the location you cut [Geney]?" Campbell asked, pointing to the tattoo.

"Yes," Erika answered without hesitating. "I got this tattoo two or three days later."

"Did you choose that particular location on your body for some reason?"

"Yes, I did." Erika seemed intrigued by the conversation. Even stimulated by it. Not in the least bit sorry or remorseful. "BJ told me to get it there! He loves it, too. He compliments me all the time on it."

This was important to Erika, because BJ, she claimed, had only made compliments to her about "two things. Before the murders he said I was a cool wife for going to strip clubs with him, and now he says he likes the tattoo because it is in the same location that I cut [Geney]."

Campbell noticed that Erika had a small scar above her thumb. "Is that from cutting yourself while cutting [Geney]?"

"No," Erika said. "That's a crocodile bite."

After she finished "cutting" Geney, Erika explained, she went downstairs to get some garbage bags. When she returned, she got her first view of the horror that had gone on inside the bathroom, and the additional horror, in fact, that was about to take place. Now there was blood covering just about every square inch of the floor, all over the walls, and even on the blinds. BJ was naked, as if participating in some sort of ritual, and completely covered in blood. By now he had moved the bodies into the hot tub.

BJ just sat there for a moment as Erika looked around the room. Still, seeing her husband naked and covered in blood didn't really have that much of a negative or even sinister effect on Erika. Because no sooner had she walked into the bathroom did she run back out into the bedroom, she later explained, "to look for my shit."

It was important for Erika to find her jewelry. After all, two people had lost their lives because of that jewelry.

"I just love my stuff," Erika explained to Campbell, as if they were two women out for a day of shopping, "and have about forty thousand dollars' worth of diamonds, including a two-inch carat canary diamond my grand-mother gave me."

According to Erika, as she was looking around the room, BJ came in and said, "Look underneath the bed."

She said she got on her stomach and lifted up the blanket hanging over the edge of the bed—and there it was: all her stuff.

"He put everything there," Erika said later, "to mess

with me. He probably did it so I would be upset with Geney and Joshua and want to kill them."

This part of Erika's story doesn't add up: the bed had only about a half-inch clearance underneath it.

Nonetheless, Erika said, she sat on the bed with her things, looking through them, to make sure everything was there.

Within a few moments, BJ sat next to her. Without warning, he said, "I masturbated over their bodies."

"What?"

He said it again.

Erika later explained that she didn't see him do it, "but he told me he did."

72

Horror Show

Erika explained to Carri Campbell that she was still wearing the same clothes she had wet herself in, which now had blood on them, when she went out to get those garbage bags for BJ, at 4:00 A.M.

When she returned about thirty minutes later, and ran immediately up to the bathroom, she said, "I saw BJ cutting a leg off one of the bodies."

"Do you know what that is?" BJ asked, pointing to another body part on the floor next to the tub.

"An arm?"

"Can we eat it?" BJ asked.

"No, Beej. We cannot eat it," she answered.

After he finished carving both bodies into six parts, BJ put all the body parts into garbage bags, tied them securely, then put the garbage bags into military duffel bags and loaded those bags into blue plastic tubs. Erika admitted that she helped him wrap up Joshua's torso with a "cream-colored blanket" she took from one of the closets in the condo (which was later confirmed).

She was detailed in describing, Campbell wrote of Erika's descriptions, *the way Josh's torso (with no arms, legs, or head attached) was balanced on the edge of the hot tub.*

Again, Erika showed no emotion or even cried as she talked about these graphic scenes of her husband dismembering two human beings. It was as if she was describing a dream, or some horror movie she had recently seen. There seemed to be no human or emotional connection whatsoever to what had transpired.

After disposing the bodies in Dumpsters behind a grocery store in Delaware, Erika explained, she and BJ "were both very tired and just slept downstairs for a few hours."

When they got up at noon that same day, Erika told BJ, "We need to clean up the bathroom."

"We used cleaning supplies, such as bleach and Drano," Erika explained to Campbell.

The following day, they went and made sure the Dumpsters had been emptied.

According to Erika, "Boy, what a number you did on [Geney's] throat," BJ said to her as they were driving. This was the first time Erika Sifrit had ever admitted—in not so many words—that she had actually slit Geney's throat.

73

Deal's Off

Arcky Tuminelli paced, drank coffee, and wondered what in the world was taking the Secret Service so damn long. He'd had some previous experience with polygraph tests, and they had never gone on for this duration of time.

Come on . . . what's the problem here?

Something was up.

Arcky went and got a drink of water, wondering if he should go in and interrupt the test. In truth, however, if he destroyed Erika's chances for taking the test, the deal would be taken off the table. There was no legal grounds on which he could barge into the interview to check and see if things were going all right.

In the interim of talking with Joel Todd about when to do the polygraph, Arcky had been presented with a second agreement, on top of that first agreement he and Todd had drafted late into the night in Joel Todd's office. This second agreement was actually a document designed to protect Erika. In it, under no condition or circumstance could anything Erika say during the *polygraph* be disclosed to anyone without her written consent.

It's important to note the word "polygraph" here.

So Erika had walked into that interview under the impression that whatever she said—no matter what—could not be used against her, even in a court of law, without her written consent. This test was simply a way for the state's attorney to feel more comfortable about granting Erika the deal.

One would have to wonder: Was this why Erika decided to open up to Carri Campbell? Was she displaying a hubris on her part that said, *"You people are so stupid . . . . I can say whatever I want to, and still walk out of here"*?

What was important about the wording of the second agreement, however, was that it covered the polygraph itself, *not* any of the preinterviews.

When Erika finished what had become an almost four-hour pre-polygraph interview and Campbell emerged from the room, Arcky took one look at the pregnant Secret Service agent and knew something was wrong. He had been sitting and waiting with the Assistant State's Attorney E. Scott Collins. The morning had dragged on. It was well into the afternoon.

Looking at Campbell, Arcky said, "What's going on? What's wrong?"

By now, Erika had been sent back to her holding cell. According to several witnesses who saw her later that day, Erika looked as if she had unburdened herself of a great weight. She had color in her face. A bounce in her step. A smile. She was either callously having some fun in describing such gruesome aspects of her crimes, or she was seriously trying to release an overwhelming amount of evil that had accumulated in her system.

The two Secret Service agents stood in front of Arcky Tuminelli and Scott Collins. Campbell spoke first. "We cannot use these questions," she said, holding a piece of paper.

Arcky looked concerned. "What do you mean? What's going on?"

For a polygraph to work properly, the relevant questions need to elicit a *negative* response from the interviewee. The test is set up in a way in which the answer that is *not* incriminating would have to be *no*. If it is a *yes*, then the entire test has to be reworked and new questions written to correspond with whatever new information has been accrued.

Arcky knew this. So when Campbell said she couldn't continue the test based on the questions they had all previously agreed to, his heart skipped a beat. He stood up. "*What* are you talking about?"

The surprises for Arcky just kept coming and coming.

The problem was that Erika had admitted to Carri Campbell that she had taken part in the crime itself. She said she was *there* at the moment of the murders and had even participated in the act and, in some respects, had commissioned the murders. One of the relevant questions on the polygraph was *Did you cut on any of those people?*

Erika had admitted that she had, in fact, "cut" Geney Crutchley.

Knowing what she now knew, Campbell understood that Erika would have to answer *yes* to that question when she asked it during the polygraph and, essentially, negate the polygraph test itself.

What did this do for the deal Arcky Tuminelli had drafted for Erika with Joel Todd? For starters, the examination was over. They could not continue.

According to a report drafted by Detective Scott Bernal, who was there during all of this legal madness now taking place, *It was decided that with the answers Erika Sifrit gave to Special Agents Doyle and Campbell that the relevant questions which were intended to be asked should no longer be asked. Mr. Todd [and] Mr. Collins discussed this with Mr. Tuminelli and he agreed . . . [that] the actual polygraph examination should not be administered.*

The other problem—which became larger as the day carried forward—was that Erika had made a claim that BJ told her to "cut up" Geney. Erika said she cut Geney on the side of her hip. This particular answer, of course, canceled out the other relevant question on the pretest regarding cutting any of the victims.

"We need to reformulate these questions," Carri Campbell announced.

Scott Collins nearly jumped out of the chair. Arcky Tuminelli felt as though he'd been burned once again by Erika.

"We don't need to reformulate anything," Collins said. "There's not going to be a polygraph. The deal's off!"

Rubbing his head, Arcky Tuminelli said, "Wait a minute . . . just wait a minute, Scott. Hold on. You were *not* there when we drafted the agreement. Hold on."

"No . . . the deal was that she didn't have anything to do with the murders."

It was clear that Erika had admitted to her involvement. The details of what she did, and how and when she did it, well, none of that really mattered as far as the agreement was concerned—at least from where Scott Collins and the state's attorney's office stood.

"Get Joel to come here," Arcky said. "We've got to talk about this."

"No. The deal is off." Collins didn't want to hear about it. "She *participated* in the murder, Arcky."

End of story.

74

Technicalities

Arcky found himself—and his client—in a terrible position. Why would Erika do such a thing? Why would she jeopardize the agreement by spending nearly four hours talking about her involvement in a double murder, without her attorney present?

"To place all the blame on Benjamin," said one source from the prosecution's side. "If you notice, everything during that interview with Carri Campbell she said was designed to implicate Benjamin and lessen her involvement."

It was a plan, in other words, on Erika's part, to walk into that interview and begin laying the foundation of her defense: it was all BJ.

Nevertheless, her freedom and subsequent charges were contingent upon Erika passing the polygraph.

"And if she cannot pass the polygraph," Arcky considered, "we're back to square one."

Erika had been told a number of times about the importance of being honest with her attorney. It was something she was made well aware of by several different people. On the eve of the polygraph, Arcky had met with Erika and reminded her of this very issue and its importance. According to several sources, Erika understood clearly what her lawyer meant.

Arcky Tuminelli and Scott Collins were listening to Carri Campbell, and at first, none of it registered for Arcky. But then Campbell explained things further, and now there was this problem of the deal being quashed by Erika's own words of admission.

After Campbell explained the most damning statements Erika had admitted to, Collins said, "That's it. There will *definitely* be no polygraph now."

It was Erika's "Just fucking do it" statement that had turned out to be the clincher. This statement made her an abettor. Therefore, Erika's own words proved her possible guilt. If that was so, there was no way she could take a polygraph and prove to Joel Todd that she'd had nothing to do with the murders.

To Arcky, however, the agreement he had written with Todd "wasn't that clear," he later said. "It simply said she had to *pass* the polygraph. It did not go into detail."

"Wait a minute," Arcky told Collins. "You have to get Joel down here. You weren't there when we drafted this agreement. I don't think it requires what you think it requires."

"Fine. I'll get him down here," Collins finally conceded.

An hour went by. Arcky was sitting by himself in a conference room, where he and Collins had tried working things out previously. Erika had been taken back to the jail.

Looking at his watch, tired of waiting, Arcky went over to Detective Scott Bernal, who was also there, and asked, "What's going on? Where is Joel Todd and Scott Collins?"

"They're here," Bernal said. "In that room over there."

Arcky walked down the hall and opened the door. Collins and Todd were waiting.

Bernal followed.

Later, Joel Todd would say that Arcky Tuminelli had a "deer in the headlights" look to him when he entered the room.

"They had this look on their faces," Arcky commented, "when I walked into the room, like the cat that swallowed the bird."

They were gloating. And yet, sure enough, they had plenty to smile about. It was obvious they had been briefed by Carri Campbell as to what, exactly, Erika had said.

Erika was in a heap of trouble. She was going to face first-degree murder charges, which was what Scott Bernal and Joel Todd had expected—and wanted—from day one.

Bernal wrote in his report of this meeting that Todd sat down with Arcky and began talking about the previous agreement Erika had signed. Todd was firm. No way. Erika had not fulfilled her obligations, and the deal was done.

Finished.

Off the table.

Arcky was in a jam. What could he do?

"Are you satisfied," Todd asked, which Bernal verified in his report of the meeting, "given the information that we got from Erika Sifrit, that [we] have fulfilled the conditions of the Memorandum of Understanding?"

According to Bernal's report, Arcky thought about it for a moment: "Absolutely, I agree."

"You do. Good," Todd responded.

There had always been serious concerns about Erika from the prosecution's side that she was more involved than she had wanted to admit. Now they had proof—in her own words: "You have me on murder, don't you?"

* * *

Arcky Tuminelli left the OCPD after speaking with Joel Todd and Scott Collins, realizing there were going to be major repercussions over what had happened. He drove back to his hotel in Rehoboth, and sat and thought about things.

What do I do now?

He awoke at four in the morning and started reading the "Memorandum of Understanding," which he and Joel Todd had drafted. He was looking for that loophole to get Erika out of what she had gotten herself into. It was his duty as her attorney. There had to be *something*.

"There was nothing in the agreement," Arcky said later, "that specifically said that she *had* to pass the polygraph and that it *had* to be related to questions that she in no way participated in the murders or encouraged [Benjamin] to do the murders."

It was a long shot, sure, but all that Arcky had at this point. Erika had created a vacuum. Her entire defense was being sucked into this one interview with Carri Campbell.

Arcky Tuminelli called Joel Todd later that morning. "Look, Joel, I have issues that this is concluded now and that you can go ahead and prosecute her for murder." The previous day, Todd had made Arcky well aware of the fact that he was likely going to be filing first-degree murder charges. "I'm looking at the agreement," Arcky continued on the phone to Todd, "and it doesn't say anything about what the questions need to be. It simply says that she has to *pass* the polygraph."

Erika, Arcky was arguing, had never been given an opportunity to take the polygraph, so how could she pass a test that she never had the opportunity to take?

"Come on," Todd said. He felt Arcky was reaching. It was ridiculous.

"Technically speaking, you have an obligation to give her that polygraph test," Arcky said.

After Arcky Tuminelli said it, he knew damn well it was a difficult argument, not to mention a stretch. The legal language was on his side, however.

"No way, Arcky. No way." Todd was getting annoyed that Arcky would even try such a thing. "Come on—"

"You do what you have to do, but I think you need to give her a polygraph."

That was the position Arcky said he was taking. End of argument.

Joel Todd was under the impression that Arcky Tuminelli clearly understood that taking the polygraph was for the sole purpose of proving Erika wasn't involved in the murders.

Hanging up, they both knew that, in due time, the decision would be in the hands of a judge. For now, there was nothing else to talk about.

Part IV

He Said, She Said

75

Judgment Day

As promised, Joel Todd tossed out the agreement and filed first-degree murder charges against Erika. It took a few months, but a judge finally sat and heard evidence from both sides regarding a motion Arcky Tuminelli had filed to have the charges dismissed in light of the agreement he and Joel Todd had drafted and signed.

Now Joel Todd and Arcky Tuminelli were witnesses. Testifying, telling their versions of what was now being called the "midnight deal."

During a hearing on September 30, 2002, from Arcky Tuminelli's viewpoint, the charges against Erika were supposed to be dropped in exchange for her helping authorities locate the victims' bodies, and also for her potential testimony against her husband, BJ. It was, Arcky said, as simple as that: Erika helped the OCPD; now it was their turn to help her.

Arcky insisted that Scott Collins and Joel Todd had violated the arrangement. "The breach," he said rather vehemently, "occurred when they refused to allow my client to carry through with a polygraph examination, terminating a pretest interview after she incriminated herself."

"She maintained that [Benjamin] was the murderer and she was the obedient spouse," Todd testified. "She contradicted herself so many times, I wasn't sure she had any value as a witness. She was *not* innocent! And therefore, well, she needed to be prosecuted for murder."

Plans for BJ's trial had moved quickly. He was scheduled to face a jury on December 9, 2002. Arcky described Erika as "too distraught at the prospect of not being allowed to testify against her husband."

When Erika was asked whether she remained willing to take a polygraph and testify against BJ, she said, "Most definitely. Yes. Of course."

In rejecting the motion, which Arcky expected, circuit court judge Theodore R. Eschenburg Sr. said, "In early interviews, Erika Sifrit told authorities she had been on the first floor of the two-story Ocean City condominium and heard shots as her husband killed Ms. Crutchley and Mr. Ford in an upstairs bathroom. Her statements, July twenty-third, however, show otherwise."

Erika had changed her story. Not once, but time and again.

Erika's trial was scheduled for December 2, but Arcky told reporters outside the courthouse after the motions hearing that he was seeking a postponement based on the "extensive publicity" surrounding both cases. More than that, Arcky said, "I'll be asking that my client's trial be moved outside Worcester County." There was no way, Arcky maintained, that Erika could get a fair trial in any courtroom near Ocean City, seeing that the case had generated so much publicity—most of which pointed a guilty finger at BJ and Erika.

Regardless of what happened during the hearing, many were now well aware of the fact that innocent little Erika Grace Sifrit, who had been paraded in various news stories surrounding the case, up until this point, as some sort of golden child, whose family and friends could not ever place her in the role of a potential killer, had had a much more significant part in the murders and dismemberment than she had originally admitted.

The tide had changed.

76

The PI

Mitch and Cookie Grace were beside themselves with pain, dread, and disappointment. They had expected at some point that their daughter would be released on bond and back home working on a defense for what would be the fight of her life.

But that never happened. Erika was denied bond and her trial date was postponed until June 2003.

And to their credit, Mitch and Cookie, every week, drove the eight hours down to Maryland from Pennsylvania, stayed in a hotel, and visited with Erika. Meanwhile, however, as Arcky began to build a case for Erika, Mitch hired a private investigator without, according to Arcky, telling him. Arcky didn't find out until the guy was running around interviewing people and doing nothing more than eating up—some close to the case later said—Mitch's money.

"Look," Mitch later said, "Arcky told me that at some point we would need private investigators, and so I hired them and sent them to see Arcky to see what needed [to be] done."

Arcky saw this differently, saying, "That's bullshit. Of course, Erika, Mitch, and I understood that if a plea agreement could not be worked out, we would eventually need an investigator. If I had been involved in hiring an investigator, it would have been someone I was familiar with in the Maryland area. Without any knowledge or input on my part, Mitch announced to me that he hired [this guy] and a former police officer as investigators. After my initial introduction to [this guy], a short time later he called me. He advised me that after talking to Mitch, he would be traveling to Virginia to conduct some interviews. I told him it might make sense to wait to see, if after the polygraph was done, we got a plea agreement from Joel Todd. I mentioned that it did not make sense to spend Mitch's money on interviews in Virginia, if there would not be a trial. [This guy's] response was 'You're on my dime. It's none of your fucking business how Mitch spends his money.' With that, he hung up on me. He later called me back after speaking to Mitch and told me he was going to Virginia to conduct the interviews. [This guy] later suggested that Mitch hire a DC lawyer (an acquaintance of his) to take over Erika's case. Mitch informed me of this, since he was considering hiring a lawyer to work with me. . . . [This private investigator] remained part of Mitch's team until [he] was barred from visiting Erika after she and [this guy] were observed fondling each other in the visiting room."

According to reports, the PI was kicked out of Worcester County Jail when guards caught him and Erika in an awkward position. Sure, this spoke to how inadequate, perhaps, the PI was as an investigator. But what did it say about Erika? She had claimed she couldn't live without BJ, that her entire life had revolved around the guy. She even said that BJ had controlled her and that she could do nothing without his order. But here she was, not six months after being arrested, caught in a compromising position with a private investigator her father had hired.

"What was clear with Erika and her family," one source told me, "is that the legal system is not a system where culpable people get punished. It's a system where, they believe, if you have a good enough attorney and you pay him or her enough money, that no matter what the case is about, or what the hearing is about, you can *always* win."

It's not about justice; it's about winning at any cost.

"We would do everything we can to help our daughter," Mitch Grace told me more than once.

Part of Erika's downfall was that she expressed a sense of hubris in that she believed, said one source close to her during this period, that "all she had to do was walk in there and pass that polygraph."

As time and the courts had proven, however, that just wasn't the case.

Mitch and Arcky ran into each other outside the Worcester County Jail one day after a brief hearing on Erika's behalf. Mitch looked distressed. Everything that could have gone wrong, it seemed, had. Mitch had no more answers. He wasn't ready for a trial, but what else could he do? His daughter was facing the rest of her life behind bars. If nothing else, he could feel good in knowing that Arcky had at least gotten the death penalty taken off the table. Nothing could change that. With a case like this, Arcky knew, considering all of the gruesome aspects of it, if it had been a death penalty case, a jury would likely have no trouble sentencing Erika to death after understanding what she had taken part in—suffice it to say that the OCPD crime lab had photographs depicting the horror Erika and BJ had purportedly perpetrated.

"Look, Arcky," Mitch said, smoking a cigarette outside near a tree. "I think this is all my fault and your fault that it happened the way it did."

Someone needed to be blamed.

Arcky was overwhelmed with confusion and dismayed by the comment. "What's my fault and your fault, Mitch?" He didn't understand. Had he misunderstood the guy?

"We didn't do a good enough job making Erika understand that she had to tell you the truth."

There was a pause. Arcky looked up in the air and sighed. "Mitch, that's crazy. Erika's not a child. She *knew.* It's not your fault. And it's not my fault. We both impressed upon her as much as we could the necessity to tell the truth to us, and she didn't. Don't tell me it's *my* fault."

"Well . . . ," Mitch started to say.

"Hey, I'm not done talking here. I don't know what the hell else I could have done."

By the end of the conversation, Mitch and Arcky agreed to disagree on the issue of who was to blame for Erika's downfall. What else could they do? Arguing about it would not ease the situation or help Erika.

Water under the bridge.

77

Letters

Erika couldn't simply sit, accept the idea that she had to prepare for the fight of her life, and wait for the chance to speak her truth during trial. Instead, she had to go and get herself involved in a maelstrom of controversy once again. As the date for BJ's trial drew closer, Erika began writing— and once she started, she had a hard time letting up.

Letter after letter after letter.

Erika had been receiving fan letters from around the country: other inmates in prisons and pen pals. Friends and family also wrote to her. For the most part, Erika didn't answer the letters, especially those from admirers and criminals.

One of the first letters Erika answered during that first summer she spent behind bars was full of an obvious "poor me, poor me" rhetoric she had seemingly spent some time working out. Erika was writing to an old friend from high school she had stayed in contact with, but with whom she had recently lost touch. She viewed the old friend, she said in her first letter, as always more "popular and pretty" than Erika believed she herself ever was. She claimed it was BJ who changed her and that God would somehow, someday, show the world the truth about what had happened inside room 1101.

She was confident in what Jesus Christ was going to do for her.

It was as if each letter was designed to lay a further foundation for Erika's future defense. Erika seemed to be grooming potential character witnesses, not realizing, perhaps, that Detective Scott Bernal was monitoring each letter that went in and out of the prison. Bernal would get Moreck, his boss, and Brett Case together and read each letter aloud.

In the next letter to the same friend (whom we'll call "Laurie"), who was now receiving calls from Erika, too, Erika wrote, *I had nothing but the most love [for BJ] . . . and now he's framed me.* She wondered if *God had put [me in prison] to get me away from BJ.* Had it been some sort of universal master plan she had no control over?

In August, Erika explained to Laurie, she was receiving letters from guys all over the country, but that she never wrote back. Instead, she read the letters and "laughed." She claimed every one of them wanted something from her, namely, "paper sex—no joke!"

From there, Erika wrote about her living conditions: *I stink, my cell stinks.* She wrote how there was *shit & boogers & food on the walls.* Her mattress was full of holes, and *with about 18 million other people's hairs . . . it is so gross.*

I did not kill them, she wrote, regarding Geney and Joshua. And never fired her gun. It was a setup on BJ's part from the moment they met Geney and Joshua.

Erika said she was sure of it.

Throughout the summer, the letters were a way for Erika to ladle on as much self-imposed sympathy as she could. Every topic she wrote about turned out to be about her. The letters had very little to do with Laurie's life. If it wasn't about the medication Erika was "forced" to take, it was the food she could no longer stand to eat, or the "Miller Lite" beers she couldn't drink. In every letter, Erika began with how much weight she had lost since writing the previous letter: *Down to 95 pounds. . . .* Then *90.* As she carried on and on about how much she had learned from being part of the judicial system as a prisoner, not once did Erika ever say she felt sorry for the victims. She claimed not to have had anything to do with the homicides; yet she showed absolutely no emotional connection to Geney or Joshua, other than to put them into the predicament she faced or the context of her prison life.

And then, by the fourth letter to Laurie that summer, Erika was laying it on with a fervency that was so obvious it's hard to imagine how Laurie didn't see through the transparency of it all. Erika was now ending her letters: *Well, I'm off now to go read the Bible and pray to God. . . . Love always, your sister forever, Gracey.*

Erika explained that BJ had promised that if she ever thought about betraying him, she had better think twice, because he would "bury me alive after torturing me." But he was in prison now, she was assured, and couldn't hurt her anymore—that is, of course, besides framing her for double murder.

It was after about a half-dozen letters when Erika began to tell Laurie that it was probably best if Laurie "flushed the letters" down the toilet after reading them.

You know, just in case.

And then, when she felt confident she could trust Laurie completely, Erika began to open up about what was going on in her head regarding the murders. Erika said she had totally given up on BJ and stopped writing to him. She wanted to think of BJ as her loving husband and remember him through the trips they had taken down to Chile. They had climbed volcanoes and drove for hours listening to Bon Jovi, Erika explained. It was an easy image to digest, she wrote, as opposed to seeing BJ *covered in blood with a knife in one hand and a limb in the other.*

Regarding that "trip" to Chile, this author asked detectives if they believed BJ and Erika might have gone down there to begin some sort of killing spree. In Erika's writings about that period, she was preoccupied with the feeling of how free they were there, to do whatever it was they wanted. She seemed to view the trip as a period in her and BJ's marriage when they truly bonded.

"We thought the same thing," one detective told me. "That they had maybe committed murder in Chile. We did some checking, but it was difficult. We didn't get too much assistance from the Chileans. I'll say this, however, I still think BJ killed a homosexual male in Pennsylvania."

That case was closed. There's another man in prison serving time for it.

78

Flashbacks

According to Erika, the most vivid flashbacks she'd ever had—when the murders began to haunt her dreams—began in late summer or early fall 2002. She had been experiencing daydreams, as she called it, for about a week, she explained to Laurie.

It was Joshua.

In one flashback, Joshua was "very handsome," Erika explained: *Dressed well, great body—black belt [in] karate, 30 years old*. Joshua wasn't dead in Erika's dream. He and Erika, as sick as it sounded, were together, boyfriend and girlfriend, she envisioned. They were at a "club"; Geney and BJ were not even in the picture. *There was no concept of them at all*. So she didn't feel as if she was cheating on BJ. Everything was OK. Life was great. She said she didn't "understand the feelings" she was having for Joshua: *I feel like I am in love with him & want to be with him*. She was fixated on the fact that in her dreams Joshua thought she was beautiful, and that BJ had never looked at her the way Joshua did. She dreamed of Joshua putting his hands all over her (BJ never did that, she said) and dancing with her (unlike BJ), and telling her how pretty she was and how much she meant to him.

While in prison for the possible murders of Joshua and Geney, as well as taking part in dismembering their bodies, Erika Sifrit was having dreams about one of the victims taking her and riding off into the sunset into a fairy-tale life.

For some, it was nearly incredible to think that this was the same mind claiming not to have had anything to do with these horrible crimes.

79

Love (Jail) Birds

Erika wrote to Laurie and told her about a "pen pal" in a nearby prison who had written to her. She said she had received about "twenty letters" from the guy, but had answered only one—so far. This man, whom she described as a *6'5", lanky and handsome black guy,* had played college basketball and was not interested in her life of crime (like everyone else), but rather in her basketball career.

Jimmy (a pseudonym) hit at the core of Erika's ego: her famed basketball career. He knew exactly how to approach her. For Erika, Jimmy was the first inmate she had heard from who could actually spell, she explained to Laurie: *Unlike 99% of inmates, he has a college education. . . .*

This impressed Erika immensely. She wrote that the guy was a genuine gentleman who *never spelled a word wrong*.

Between June and late November 2002, collected all together into one neat package, the letters Erika had written to Jimmy—stacked up, about two inches' worth—

became a manifesto describing a fantasy life Erika now wanted to share with Jimmy.

Over the course of the first few letters, Erika talked about her likes and dislikes; it sounded like they were out on some sort of a blind date. She carried on about her reptiles. Jimmy had shared with her that he had a child, and Erika said "my kids" are snakes and crocs. She said she had even walked her two crocs, Clarence and Alabama, whom she had named after her *favorite* characters in her *favorite* movie of all time, *True Romance*. This film is a 1993 violent saga, written by Quentin Tarantino, that starred Christian Slater as a comic book lover who falls for a prostitute (Patricia Arquette) and "rescues" her from her pimp, steals five million dollars' worth of cocaine, then runs off on a violence-fueled rampage cross-country. Much like Erika's life with BJ, the film is an unconventional love story revolving around drugs and murder, as two people seem to be taken in by how exhilarating violence and lust can be when mixed together.

After talking about her reptiles, Erika moved on to her love of tattoos and the beach and being "as tan as I can be." All of her tattoos meant something, Erika said, but she didn't go into what, exactly.

Within a month, using her best gangsta grammar, Erika was calling Jimmy her "luv-a." And, in one letter, she told him that she was going to spend an entire Saturday night writing to him.

Erika told Jimmy she wanted to wear a "belly shirt" for him so he could put his hands all over her "tummy and back." She liked to wear backless shirts, she wrote, because the *back . . . is the sexiest part of the female body.*

She claimed that she had "made love" to only BJ, but she wrote that she had *been with around 25 guys. . . .* And she was scared of not being able to satisfy Jimmy because, she believed, he said he had slept with at least two thousand women over the course of his life, and had probably done everything there was to do. Still, Erika was never one to back down from a challenge and became determined to get it started, even from behind bars, promising Jimmy that she would soon write him "paper sex." She signed off, *I love you.*

After describing how tight her vagina was, she wrote how she was going to do *everything and anything* Jimmy wanted when they got that *house on the beach and did it 5–6 times a day.* Erika told Jimmy she was disappointed that her mother couldn't send him anything. Apparently, Erika and her mother had sat during a visit that weekend and discussed all the different items they were going to send Jimmy for his birthday in a "care package." The prison had said no. Mitch even called and asked, but he was turned down.

Yes, I have a beautiful plump [vagina], Erika wrote. It was *sickening,* she added, *how I fantasize about you all day.* . . . She explained how her *huge [vagina] lips for you to suck on . . . then open with your fingers . . . always shaven clean, fresh pussy.* She wanted to know if Jimmy got "hard" reading her letters. In her cell while writing them, Erika wrote, she had to *squeeze my thighs together + feel my pussy throbbing.* . . .

Clarifying what was truly important to Erika, even as she sat in prison facing life, she wrote page after page on the topics of diamonds and clothes: her likes and dislikes in those areas. She was obsessed with jewelry, sure, but it was clear from these letters that expensive diamonds satisfied and even fed a part of her soul.

By the next letter, Erika was calling herself "your wifey," signing off the letters by saying that Jimmy could have her for the rest of his life if he wanted. She wrote that he could stick his *chocolate cock in and out of me* anytime he pleased. Then, in another letter, she talked about how she had taken on two guys at the same time before, and even once had two women: *Only did it that one night . . . I had double penetration. . . . It was awesome.*

Erika's handwriting varied from perfect printing to scribbled cursive; large letters to small; absolutely fine penmanship, with flawless margins, to chicken scratch that was hardly legible. From reading these letters and studying the context and motivation, and the telltale signs her handwriting leaves, it could be presumed that Erika Grace Sifrit was, at best, totally on board with the notion that she had screwed her life up and knew it; and, at worst, that she honestly believed she had done nothing wrong other than marry BJ Sifrit and love him.

It was odd that Erika continued on and on about how ignorant and gullible she was for falling for a "pretty face" and navy SEAL, so taken by the uniform and title, and yet she was telling Jimmy how much she had loved him and adored him and would spend the rest of her life with him, but she hadn't yet seen or met him. All she knew was the guy on the page sending her these incredibly well-written love letters.

Her language, too, was beginning to show signs of her environment. She explained to Jimmy how she and BJ had run a business and sold stolen Hooters merchandise on eBay and were making upward of $1,500 a week, with that gig alone, *but of course the shit was hot hot hot hot—feel me?* In the same breath, she mentioned that she was convinced there was still *about $300g worth out there . . . I don't know where it is no longer . . . feel me?!?!* She was finished stealing, she wrote, . . . *even though the cash was sweet.*

She said her parents were going to be broke by the time all was said and done. The "total tab" would be "about half mil." At the same rate, however, she wrote Jimmy: *If you need cash . . . my parents [will send it].*

By September, Erika was concerned that Jimmy's parents in New Orleans would not accept her because she was white. She worried how they would react to a "white chick" Jimmy brought home, adding, "I'm no ho."

According to Erika, her dad was now sending Jimmy $50 money orders. Sometimes $40. But they were being sent pretty regularly, and Erika was promising Jimmy that more were on the way.

Heading into November, Erika had written Jimmy fifty-nine letters, all of which she numbered. There were letters in which all she talked about was her OCD; others that she went on and on about how much of a "snob" her mother was, and how she didn't want to come across that way but probably did; and still others in which she went into graphic detail about what she was going to do to Jimmy during the first opportunity she was alone with him. She'd write what she called "sex stories," in which she'd make up a scenario—a favorite was returning to a fictional locker room after a ball game, because she forgot something, only to run into Jimmy, who would be taking a shower—the sexual innuendo and promises in these letters were graphic and vile.

As the letters progressed, Erika wrote, she was falling deeper and deeper for Jimmy and it scared her *shitless. Every letter, every word . . . every thought . . . I fall more in love. . . .* To Erika, there was no doubt about it, she had finally found her "soul mate." There was only one other man she had viewed in that respect: a friend of the family her father had hired.

She was now calling Jimmy's penis "Mr. Chocolate," writing she would *attend to him 24/7 @ his request . . . if he waits for me. . . . Don't break my heart.*

What was interesting became how Erika referred to BJ in one of her later letters as her "serial killer ex." Did this mean there were other murders she knew about? Was it a slip? Why would Erika call her husband a serial killer if he killed only two people, both at the same time, essentially?

In October, Erika was promising Jimmy a "steamy" Halloween letter. On the other hand, in another letter that month, she wrote how she was upset because two television shows she had just watched, *CSI* and *JAG,* had portrayed SEALs as good guys. Seeing the show brought it all back for Erika. She said she was sick and tired of people treating SEALs like heroes. None of them were honorable, she ranted. She got so "pissed," she claimed to have shattered the pay phone outside her cell. She wrote she was livid that her *crazy f-ing lock-picking "honorable" Navy SEAL is going to kill more innocent people when he walks away laughing at Joel Todd*. . . . The only thing that had calmed her down that night, she said, was dreaming of Jimmy and *Days of Our Lives* character Nick Fallon "double-teaming" her.

From there, she carried on for two pages about perhaps getting a boob job when she was released. She wanted to know how Jimmy felt about it.

One of the guards had come up on Erika as she was writing one night near Halloween and "raided" her cell. The guard ended up finding "a stash of pills," according to Erika. This translated into twenty-plus pills, according to police.

Jimmy gave Erika a good solid tongue-lashing in one letter, letting Erika know that he could see right through her "snobbish" veneer. He was upset that she had lied to him—this time about being sober. The raid on her cell told Jimmy she wasn't.

Erika answered back, saying she couldn't "help" being "spoiled" all her life. If she had those pills in her cell right at the moment she was reading Jimmy's angry response, she said, she would have taken all of them. No one knew, she insisted, how tough she had it. Jail was the easy part of her life, she explained. It was living with the notion that her husband was framing her for murder that was tough. That and the horror she had witnessed. *Do you think I feel good . . .* , she wrote, *that he . . . fucked a headless, lifeless woman . . .* and then said it was *better than me?*

Prison time was getting to her. She was having panic attacks over her upcoming court dates and potential sentence. She couldn't do life, she said. No way. It was too much. But not because of the time, or the idea of spending the rest of her life behind bars; instead, Erika wrote, she was worried about losing her figure, her youth, *my body,* [and] *. . . 99% of the fear* was that she had *found the perfect man of my dreams and I'm facing life.*

By Monday, October 21, 2002, Erika was sleeping during the day and staying up all night writing long, tedious letters to Jimmy about everything from the fashion magazines the guards were sneaking into her cell for her, to the fact that she didn't like the idea of being videotaped having sex. However, being in the middle of a room, during a party or gathering of some sort, while she and Jimmy went at it like bunnies, didn't bother her one bit.

It was her mom's fifty-fourth birthday, she wrote, which meant that it was BJ's twenty-fifth; they shared the same birthday. Erika had just gotten word that her trial was supposed to begin on December 2. Erika had had a visit with her parents earlier that same day—and as she was leaving the visit, she got up and turned, and there was BJ. She wrote, *He somehow knew I was coming. . . .*

BJ was apparently waiting by a window (both jails are connected), staring at her with that wide-eyed face, she wrote, *when he's all jacked up + grits his teeth. . . .* This was fighting mode for BJ, she knew. She was sure he was trying to intimidate her.

She was scared of BJ even more than she had ever been. Erika told Jimmy she spent that entire day and night underneath the covers. Seeing his face, that stare, those steely eyes, she considered that he was going to get out and kill her family. She said she couldn't even think about it anymore without having anxiety. It was his *face and his eye + his disgusting erection while he committed these crimes. . . .*

After describing how terrified she was after seeing BJ, and thinking of what he might do to her family when he got out of prison—and, she was certain, if BJ made up his mind that he was getting out . . . well, he had a plan—and would be looking for payback. Next, Erika started in about her reptiles again. She went on and on about how "awesome" they were and how "crazy" she was about her snakes and crocs and couldn't understand how people were scared of them.

In another letter, as Erika started meeting with her attorneys—Arcky Tuminelli and Tom Ceraso, an attorney Mitch had recently hired to help Arcky out—Erika told Jimmy she felt her parents had "deceived" her: . . . *they taught me marriage was the one guarantee in life. . . .*

It was the first time she had met with Ceraso. He got *2 thumbs up,* she wrote later that night.

Before they had even sat down to talk, Erika asked him, "Who killed the two victims?"

Ceraso's "immediate response," Erika said, was "Your husband, of course."

"Let's talk," Erika said after that, sitting down.

Jimmy had convinced Erika to keep a notebook of "details" pertaining to the murders—everything she could recall. Erika gave that notebook to Ceraso.

What was clear from the meeting, Erika wrote, was that her best defense was a good offense: abused wife.

If there was one common theme throughout all the letters Erika wrote to Jimmy, it was that she was certain BJ would, in her words, "get off." She felt the system was a rotten organization of prosecutors out to get her and allow BJ to skate.

Ceraso had returned to tell Erika they were motioning the court for a postponement of her trial and a change of venue. Either way, Ceraso said, he was hopeful that the court would allow Erika bond.

As the new year dawned, Erika's letters to Jimmy were more conservative and pointless, really. They centered again on television and likes and dislikes. Her lawyers must have told Erika to lay off talking about the case, because she rarely mentioned it. But then, Erika was never one to take on an authoritative slap in the face with any humility. She knew damn well what was best for her, but she insisted on doing things her way, perhaps taking the position that she was going to walk because she had, as she explained to Jimmy, God on her side, and BJ didn't. She began to feel that everyone—the press, the prosecutor, her own lawyers, and anyone else who didn't believe her—was against her and with BJ. "Why?" became one of Erika's favorite questions to bounce off Jimmy. *Why me? Why now? Why not look into BJ's "past"?* The answers would be quite obvious.

She said repeatedly that she did not kill those people. He did.

I have less hope everyday. . . .

Later, *I've already disgraced my entire family. . . . They* can't *save me this time.*

80

Mind Games

According to several people close to BJ Sifrit, his favorite book was Niccolò Machiavelli's *The Prince,* a centuries-old treatise about the art of how "a ruler can retain control of his realm." In other words, BJ was good to his SEAL training in that he believed in—or at least studied and was fascinated by—mind control, manipulation, and total supremacy over another human being. *The Prince* was just one more way for BJ to feed what several later said had become a Communist-slanted way of thinking he had developed over the years.

Two additional books detectives later found in BJ's possession were *Explosion of Hate: The Growing Danger of the National Alliance* (the *X* in the title is depicted as a swastika) and *The Anarchist Cookbook. Explosion* has section titles that explain perfectly where BJ's head was at, if this was bedside reading: "Thriving on Hate," "Bonds with Other Bigots," "Exploiting the Internet."

The Anarchist Cookbook was no different. With section

titles along the lines of "Drugs," "Electronics, Sabotage, and Surveillance," "Natural, Nonlethal, and Lethal Weapons," and "Explosives and Booby Traps," the book outlined recipes to make bombs and start drug factories; how to scramble electronics and broadcast free radio and build natural weapons and gelatin dynamite; how to make homemade hand grenades, conduct successful bridge destruction, time delay devices; and so on and so forth. This is something a terrorist might have in his library as a user's manual.

Another book BJ favored was *Masterpieces of World Philosophy,* a compilation of essays from the likes of Tao Te Ching and Karl Marx, with titles that, again, spoke to how interested BJ had become in things like "Human Nature and Conduct." This coincided with pages upon pages of humans keeping their fellows in bondage—of which, a former friend of BJ's later told a *Baltimore Sun* newspaper reporter, BJ had highlighted many passages detailing the most violent behavior known to man. What was interesting about BJ's copy of the book was that those passages he underlined and highlighted regarded the treatment of females. In one, the author had called women "half human," which was apparently a point of view BJ favored.

BJ envied the manner, he told another friend, of snakes and other reptiles, including crocodiles—so much so, he bought both and would spend hours sitting and watching their movements and behaviors. He was particularly interested in their "savagery," an acquaintance of BJ and Erika's told the *Baltimore Sun.* Moreover, it was well-known inside BJ's close circle of in-laws and friends of Erika's that he was taken by Hitler "for the power he amassed."

BJ was into mind manipulation. He once asked Mitch Grace if Mitch would hire a friend of his. Mitch's construction company was always looking for good help. BJ said he had somebody in mind.

"Send him over to the store," Mitch told BJ.

A day later, BJ and his friend showed up at Memory Laine. BJ's friend, Mitch noticed, had parked outside the store by the curb in an area not zoned for parking. It was clearly marked by a yellow line. This tiny detail told Mitch "two things," he later said. One was that the guy obviously had "no respect for right and wrong."

After BJ's friend left, BJ asked Mitch if he was going to hire the guy.

"I don't think so," Mitch said.

BJ had that cocky, almost "I knew it," look on his face. "Why not?"

"Well," Mitch explained, "your friend parked in that no parking zone, which told me a lot about his ability to follow rules."

BJ smiled coyly. "No kidding . . ."

"It also showed me that he's probably lazy, too, because he didn't want to walk from the parking lot into the store."

BJ walked away.

As the next week unfolded, it was clear to Mitch that BJ had derived something from the conversation. Because for every day he showed up at the store afterward, BJ parked on that same yellow line, in the no parking zone. He never said anything. He just parked his car and went into the store as a normal course of his day. Mitch noticed it immediately, but didn't say anything—that is, until he couldn't take it anymore.

"BJ, can you stop parking there!" Mitch said one day after about two weeks. Then Mitch grabbed BJ's keys and moved the car.

BJ never said a word. He was testing Mitch. Seeing how far he could push him. Seeing how Mitch would react.

There was another time, Erika later explained to a pen pal, when BJ was outside the store looking in through the window. Erika was busy doing something and hadn't noticed two customers in the store. As BJ watched, he apparently spied them shoplifting several small items.

Finishing up what he was doing outside, BJ walked into the store, locked them all inside, and then pulled out his gun.

Walking around, waving the weapon, he told the couple, who were pushing a stroller with a child, to put everything on the counter.

They were terrified.

"Put it on the counter and pay for it all," BJ insisted, Erika later said.

"What?"

"You wanted it—well, you're going to buy it all now."

Erika further explained that the couple was down to "pennies" in the bottom of the woman's purse to pay for it all.

81

Dead Serious Talk

Erika was in a terrible spot—being in prison and not being able to control her life outside the barbed wire. She had put so much trust in her lawyers, and they were doing all they could, but now she apparently felt that the only way out of this mess was to take control of things herself.

Writing once again to Laurie, her friend from high school, Erika began a letter with **DEAD SERIOUS TALK,** written in bold letters at the top of the page. Erika was livid. It was *time,* she wrote, *to start fighting fire with fire.*

In her nondescript, wink-wink type of tone, she wrote to Laurie that she *never wrote this letter. . . .* She asked Laurie to "memorize" and then "tear" it up. *Flush it down the toilet,* she penned, whatever Laurie had to do to get rid of it. A trash bin wouldn't work, Erika said. Then, *You're my girl.*

The letter was an outline and reminder of *the activity that* [Laurie] *had seen BJ do.*

Again, wink-wink.

Erika was royally pissed off that she had nothing to

show for bringing the cops to the bodies, and here she was sitting in jail—the nerve of those people—and BJ was not five hundred yards away in the same jail, and *Guess what . . . I got nothing for all the info I gave them,* she wrote.

Well, now she was taking her life back. She was going to explain what Laurie needed to say *and* when she needed to say it, along with whom she needed to say it to.

Home-court advantage . . . , she authored.

Judges, prosecutors, and the politics of the system were all the same: out to get Erika.

But, like I said, you never got this letter . . . , she wrote.

From there, Erika spent page after page, even bulleted and numbered sections, explaining to Laurie what Laurie knew, how Laurie was supposed to phrase it, and how Laurie was going to help Erika get out of prison.

Once again, it was all BJ's fault. He was the abusive husband: *Remember?*

You didn't hear it from me.

BJ was the racist.

Not me.

Remember?

BJ was the one who caused *me to get an abortion.*

Remember?

BJ was the one who could kill people.

Not me.

Remember?

Erika also told Laurie a story that she claimed happened a few weeks before they had left for Ocean City. BJ had suggested that they try to have another baby.

Already tried that, Erika said she told him.

No, have the baby, BJ supposedly suggested, get an insurance policy of $1 million, and then, according to what Erika was telling Laurie to remember, BJ would kill the child so they could collect on the insurance.

Remember when he said he would kill his mother if he ever saw her again? . . .

Erika asked questions. Regarding a penchant for anxiety in high school, she wanted to know if Laurie remembered her having it.

Of course not.

Then there were a series of other questions painting BJ as the abusive husband who had pushed Erika into a life of crime. Erika, of course, gave Laurie the answer to all of the questions: yes.

Near the end of the letter, Erika launched a "poor me" diatribe regarding how she didn't deserve to be in prison, and how they were best friends now and that Laurie could help her if only she followed these felonious directions.

You can't get into trouble . . . , Erika promised in writing. She admitted that she *could spend the rest* of her life in jail and that *this letter is not exactly legal.*

In her next letter, Laurie was angry. She didn't want anything to do with being given directions to testify in court.

Sorry, Erika wrote later, *my life is over and I just need help.*

82

Brutally Honest

In March 2003, Detective Scott Bernal took a phone call from Joel Todd regarding a conversation Todd had recently had with Mitch Grace.

"Mitch wants to turn over some military items BJ left at the house."

Bernal explained that he and Detective Richard Moreck were heading to Altoona the following day to interview former Sifrit friends and neighbors. They'd stop by and pick it all up. Apparently, there were some explosives involved.

While in Altoona, Bernal and Moreck met up with Lisa Campfield (a pseudonym), one of Erika's former childhood friends. Lisa was a bit frightened of the police presence.

"No need to be afraid," Bernal assured her. They just wanted to talk.

"Have you visited with Erika since her arrest?" Moreck asked.

"No . . . ," Lisa said, but it was clear she had something on her mind—something was bothering her.

"Have you spoken with her on the telephone?"

Lisa hesitated. "Yes, I have."

"Tell us about what she's been saying," Bernal suggested comfortingly.

"Well, I'm going to be brutally honest with you," Lisa began.

Bernal and Moreck looked at each other. "Go ahead, of course."

"Erika told me during our phone conversation that BJ made her cut Crutchley's head off."

Silence.

"Continue," Bernal said.

"BJ also made her watch as he masturbated over her body."

"What did you say?"

Lisa went quiet.

Bernal said, "Did I hear you correctly: are you telling us that Erika cut off Crutchley's head?"

"No, I said that BJ made her watch as *he* cut off Crutchley's head."

"What else?"

Lisa confirmed the "rat in sulfuric acid" story. She said she was there that day, in back of the LA Weight Loss Center, next door to Memory Laine, when she saw smoke coming from a little bucket. "What's that?" she asked BJ. The bucket had a horrible smell to it.

"I put a live rat in the bucket of acid to see if it would dissolve its bones."

83

Break These Chains

There had been a legal argument over whether BJ was going to be allowed to sit in court with or without being bound by shackles and handcuffs. During a motions hearing, Joel Todd and E. Scott Collins brought out the fact that BJ had tried—rather successfully—to pick the lock of his cell.

BJ had been put in a holding tank one afternoon and the actual lock on the cell was broken, so guards put a chain and sturdy padlock on the door. Well, as the guards were busy doing whatever it is guards do, BJ went to work on the lock, picked it, took the chain off, opened the door, and went back to lying down on his cot.

"What BJ was saying," someone close to the case later told me, "was 'Hey, show me a little bit more respect than that. I can get out of here if I want to.'"

This episode, Todd and Collins argued, was a good indication that BJ Sifrit was a risk and had a tendency to want to "get away." And yet, as jury selection began on

March 31, 2003, in Montgomery County Circuit Court, in Rockville, Maryland, there sat BJ, up front, in his plush dark suit, neatly pressed, *without* handcuffs.

By the day's conclusion, twelve jurors and four alternates had been picked from a small pool of 243 potentials. In the end, it wasn't as hard as everyone had at first expected to find good men and women to hear BJ's case.

State's Attorney Joel Todd had an uncanny way about him, which spoke of a more Southern, hard-nosed prosecutor. Yet, he was also a gentle man with an enthusiastic eye, not to mention brawny passion, for justice. For Todd, the blame for Geney and Joshua's gruesome deaths could be spread equally between Erika and BJ. He didn't necessarily see one as being more guilty than the other. "It was, somehow," Todd told me later, "just a bad combination. I suspect if she'd never met him, she'd [have] been fine; and if he'd never met her, he'd be fine. But somehow the combination of the two of them was just"—and he stopped for a moment and thought about how to phrase it, searching for just the right words, finally settling on—". . . just awful."

Todd was born and raised in Worcester County. He ended up in Florida at Nova Southeastern University (NSU) doing his law school undergraduate work, but he quickly fell back into his roots in Maryland when he graduated from law school.

"My first job after law school," Todd said, "was for the Worcester County Circuit Court as a law clerk." The same court where he was now preparing to go after BJ Sifrit, along with the help of E. Scott Collins. Still, becoming a prosecutor in a busy district was not necessarily Todd's ambition as a young legal grad. "I had envisioned myself as becoming a real estate lawyer, doing real estate settlements and land development work—that kind of stuff."

Working for the circuit court as a law clerk, however, sitting in on trials, changed Todd's mind rather quickly, and showed him, essentially, where the action was. Pushing real estate documents and counting beans in an office all day soon took a backseat to a more dramatic, animated life of arguing felony cases in front of a jury. It just seemed to suit his personality a little more.

And so Todd went into private practice and learned rather quickly after his first wife had triplets that paying the bills was going to be tough on his meager private-practice salary. But as luck would have it, a job as a deputy state's attorney opened up in Worcester County, and it was paying more than Todd had yet made in the private sector. The job also offered health benefits for his young family. So he applied, and as he humbly put it, "I was fortunate enough to get the job."

Nine years later, when the seat for state's attorney of Worcester County was vacated, Todd ran for office and was elected.

That was 1995.

Any career has bumps, any profession has its ups and downs. For Joel Todd, anytime you go into court, you run the risk of losing. "As a prosecutor, I have never [seen] myself as someone in the business of getting convictions, but as someone who is in the business of doing justice. If I have a defendant that I have doubts about whether he is guilty or not, I drop those charges. The last thing I want is to have somebody behind bars and I am not sure if he's innocent or guilty."

On the other hand, when Todd felt he was going after someone who was, beyond a doubt, guilty: "I'm going after that person full steam ahead."

84

A SEAL Finally Squeaks

Opening statements took up most of Tuesday morning, April Fool's Day, 2003. Joel Todd stood and, addressing the jury, promised to bring in a star witness to explain how BJ "confessed" to putting bullet holes in a bathroom door, which eventually led to the murder of a couple.

BJ's attorneys told jurors the state had no such evidence—that the case against their client was, at best, circumstantial. No jury was going to buy the notion that BJ Sifrit killed these two people. It was Erika all the way. *Yes!* She was the mastermind. This guy here, this former navy SEAL who had finished at the top of his class, went along with the cover-up of this terrible tragedy only at the behest of—and to protect—his wife.

But BJ Sifrit was no killer.

On April 2, the state put on ballistics and DNA experts, who tied the weapon used in the murders to the Sifrits, and the blood and tissue on the bullets found on the kitchen table, along with all the blood in the bathroom, to BJ and Erika Sifrit and Martha "Geney" Crutchley and Joshua Ford.

The following day, April 3, Joel Todd questioned his "star witness," Karen Wilson, who told her story of having gone through what she called "a living nightmare." She was terrified and feared for her life that night. She believed BJ when he said he was "ridding the earth of bad people." He had brandished a gun. He had walked around the condo like a drunken cowboy looking to kill someone. He had threatened her.

Wilson's story was compelling, if not chilling. No one could deny her that. But BJ's attorneys pointed out rather emphatically—trying to trip her up on details—that when the rubber hit the road, jurors were either going to believe that BJ confessed to Wilson or not. Going back and forth. Restating the obvious, trying to shake the woman was going to do nothing but delay justice. It was yes or no. There was no variable. No middle ground.

Most of Thursday and Friday were eaten up by the state concluding its case with Charles Atwood, a former navy SEAL friend of BJ's, who described how he and BJ were buddies who liked to meet up at bars and take a little man time together. Yes, they talked about how to kill, and then dispose of a body. Yes, they joked about murder for hire. But it was over beers and watching strippers. How many guys talked about vile and violent things while drinking beers and handing out dollar bills to naked women? In the real world, men called this blowing off steam. How was a good time at a strip joint part of such a diabolically violent murder plot?

With their questioning of Atwood, BJ's lawyers seemed to insinuate it wasn't.

After the weekend, on Monday, April 7, Burton Anderson, BJ's court-appointed attorney, made it clear that his client *was* going to take the stand to explain to jurors his version of what had transpired that night. The newspapers had had their opportunity to tell the story. Joel Todd his. Erika hers.

Now it was BJ's turn.

Before the former SEAL took the stand, however, his mother, Elizabeth, reluctantly walked forward, her head bowed, tissues ready, there to retrieve a bit of BJ's humanity back from the vultures who had been pecking away at it. The media had turned the guy into a monster. Some sort of vicious, bloodthirsty killer who had absolutely no value for human life. Elizabeth needed to give her son an identity beyond being accused of such a hideously gruesome crime.

Answering those first few standard questions, Elizabeth came across as sincere and entirely credible. Her tone was obvious. What had happened? How had her boy's life turned into a made-for-TV movie of the week?

With genuine tears and anguish in her tired voice, Elizabeth went on to speak of a boy she watched grow into the perfect young adult, achieving goals the other kids around him rarely even thought about. When BJ left for SEAL training, his parents were, of course, proud of him. BJ would make it. She was certain of his abilities and never doubted for a minute he would graduate with honors. After he left, BJ stayed in touch with the family as much as the navy allowed, which turned out to be almost every other day. It wasn't until Erika came along, Elizabeth Sifrit testified, that BJ started to drift away and soon stopped calling home altogether.

Elizabeth and Erika did not like each other—that much was evident from Elizabeth's tone on the stand, and also in the letters Erika wrote to Laurie and Jimmy. There was never a time when the two of them went out shopping together and "did lunch" and talked like a mother- and daughter-in-law. And that relationship they shared—however brief it was, Elizabeth made clear—indicated the instability of the woman, who had become ever more obsessive and hard to deal with as time went on.

When it was his turn, BJ sat next to the Sixth Judicial Circuit Court judge Paul H. Weinstein and held up his hand; then he recited the "nothing but the truth" oath.

BJ sat calmly and, in his surprisingly soft and almost effeminate inflection, began to tell his story. You'd think a man of BJ's caliber would speak deeply and aggressively, but BJ spoke warmly, with affection and poise.

"He had a squeaky voice," one detective later observed. "It was striking the first time we heard it, because you'd expect a manly tone out of such a person."

Detective Scott Bernal sat next to Collins and Todd and watched every move that every witness made. Taking notes, in big bold letters on white notebook paper, he wrote out questions and comments for the lawyers to consider.

As Burton Anderson questioned BJ, the young former SEAL talked about growing up in Iowa and Minnesota, and then moving to Texas at age fifteen. He recalled being the big brother to a sister he loved. After high school, BJ didn't stick around town and kick beer bottles into the curb and work at the local hardware store. Instead, BJ left for the navy immediately, answering an inner call to serve his great nation and fellow countrymen. It was the SEALs from day one, BJ said. He had an "ambition," he explained, to become a military man. A drive. A great desire he couldn't really explain. He knew the twenty-five-week training, including seven days referred to as "hell week," would test his emotional and physical reserve, strength, and abilities. But he had been bred from tough genes and was confident, even back then, that he could endure anything he was faced with.

As his testimony steered into the training part of his naval service beyond SEAL school, BJ began to lay the foundation for an argument of a delicate man being put through some of the most taxing emotional training the military had to offer—forever on the verge of collapsing into a robotic human being capable of just about anything. It was a good frame of reference for the jury to mull over: *The navy had screwed me up and I snapped.* He never said it, but it was the SEAL training that had a profound effect on the way his mind worked later on. It was almost as if he was apologizing for the gruesome nature of the crimes he was being accused of, saying that he had been trained not to feel (and definitely not to think) about the horror men could do to one another.

And then came this new woman in his life, Erika Grace—and everything changed the moment he met and—three weeks later—married her.

"How would you describe your relationship with your family . . . during the first three years of your naval career?" Burton Anderson asked his client about fifteen minutes into BJ's direct testimony.

"Very close," the former SEAL said, sounding confident and believable.

"This three-week relationship before you got married, are you able to tell us what the attraction was?"

"I guess, I don't know . . . Every relationship starts out good."

It was a sound point.

A few questions later: "Did Erika's obsessive-compulsive anxiety disorders have an impact on your naval career?"

"Yes . . ."

"Tell the ladies and gentlemen of the jury how that impacted your naval career."

"She couldn't handle me being away, and that was made clear right from the beginning."

From there, BJ and his attorney discussed where BJ was stationed with Erika, and how often she made mention of him going away to places he couldn't tell her about. Typical for a SEAL, he was away three hundred or more days per year—and it could be anywhere—in training.

All that SEALs did was train. And when they were finished, they trained some more.

Burton Anderson asked BJ how Erika reacted when he went away and she didn't know what he was doing or where he had gone. BJ wasn't allowed to tell her where he was going for training.

"She had emotional breakdowns," BJ explained. "She'd stop eating. Not be able to function. Not be able to go anywhere [or] do anything."

It had always been rumored that BJ had been the one to "make" Erika watch her weight. Erika maintained that it was BJ who forced her to starve herself in order to stay rail thin. This was abuse perpetrated by BJ, she claimed, that had turned into an eating disorder, bulimia. But here was BJ giving his version of those same stories: it wasn't him, after all, he claimed, but Erika herself who had refused to eat when he was away.

And then she started taking speed pills to curb her appetite. Incidentally, in her letters to Jimmy, Erika goes on for page after page regarding being fat. She talked about how she had no tolerance for fat people. That she couldn't understand how fat people could stand all that extra weight, and she would never allow herself to get that way. Not once while telling Jimmy about her feelings regarding overweight people did she *ever* say that BJ had forced her not to eat.

"It got to the point," BJ told the jury, "where she would follow me to these places of training." He said it was not something that the navy was happy about; spouses weren't supposed to follow SEALs around the country. Rather, they were supposed to show support by staying home and accepting that this was the life they had chosen.

But Erika could never do that.

There was one time in 2000 when BJ was sent to Alaska for mountain training. On the day he was slated to leave for the mountains, Erika showed up unexpectedly at his room, he said, on the Alaskan base.

Basically, according to BJ, before he met Erika, his "life was the navy SEALs." But after he married her, "I ended it."

If what BJ said on the stand was true, he had "acted out" in the SEALs in order to get discharged more quickly because Erika was acting so crazy. When the lawyer she hired for BJ had made it clear that an administrative discharge would take four to five months, Erika went ballistic and had an "episode." (You can assume this included the day she pulled a handgun on Elizabeth Sifrit, BJ's mother.)

"After you got married . . . ," Burton Anderson continued, "how did it affect your relationship with your family?"

"Get ready to object," Joel Todd whispered to his co-counsel, Collins.

"Were any restrictions placed on the contact you had with your mother, father, and family?"

"Yes."

No objection yet . . .

"Tell us about that."

"I wasn't allowed . . . My family welcomed Erika, but she didn't get along with them."

Without an objection, they then discussed BJ and Erika's scrapbooking business and how BJ had obtained his weapons under legal permits. General stuff. Nothing earth-shattering. BJ's lawyers were laying out his life. However, as his testimony continued, it became clear that BJ was pushing the entire blame—for his own social and psychological meltdown—on Erika, placing the complete context of his life spiraling out of control on an obsessive-compulsive wife who couldn't stand being without him.

As BJ sat and described for the jury his life with Erika, he managed to begin talking about "that night" in Ocean City, which had landed him on the witness stand. In not so many words, he described a wife who was totally out of control from the moment they arrived in Ocean City.

Xanax.

Booze.

More Xanax.

More booze.

She had walked away from him with another man while they were waiting in line to get into Seacrets, BJ said.

Then he talked about meeting Martha "Geney" Crutchley and Joshua Ford.

From there, BJ described how they all left Seacrets together—which would become the one major difference in their stories: BJ said he went to the Rainbow while Erika, Geney, and Joshua stopped at the Atlantis. It was then that BJ said he arrived at the Rainbow by himself, only to realize he was locked out of the room. Because he had no key, BJ testified, he said he "pass[ed] out in the Jeep downstairs in the parking lot."

85

The Blame Game

Sitting nimbly on the witness stand, telling his version of the story, BJ Sifrit was fairly believable and certainly sure of what he was saying. As he was "passed out" in the Jeep downstairs in the parking lot of the Rainbow, waiting for Erika to arrive with Geney and Joshua, BJ told jurors, he was startled awake by Erika.

She was frantic. Banging on the window. Yelling.

BJ hadn't realized it, but he had been asleep for hours.

"What . . . what is it?" BJ said, coming to, waking up from what he described as nothing short of an alcohol-induced coma. He'd had countless "Long Island Ice Teas" that night, he said. How many was anybody's guess, but surely in the double digits. BJ couldn't recall what time Erika had woken him, "but it was still dark outside." The sun hadn't yet come up.

"We have to get out of here," Erika supposedly said.

"What?" BJ was still trying to figure out what was going on.

"We have to leave," Erika said again, forcefully this time, demanding.

Surprising to BJ, Erika was not overly emotional. She wasn't calm and collected, either. But unlike what would be a normal routine he had come to know when she started panicking, she wasn't acting crazy and out of it. "She was upset," BJ explained, "but she *wasn't* hysterical."

"Come on, get up," she said.

"Why? What's wrong?" He was rubbing sleep from his eyes.

"We have a problem." Erika started mumbling at this point. Saying all sorts of things that didn't make any sense whatsoever to BJ, who could tell that something terrible was wrong; he just didn't know what. He had never seen Erika act this way.

"Why? Why do we need to leave?"

Erika was making it clear that she wanted to get out of town. Not just leave the condo. Leave the state. Get the hell out of Ocean City as fast as they could.

Erika said something that BJ had a hard time registering. "I didn't believe her," he testified. "I didn't know what to believe. I was still half asleep."

"Why weren't you there for me . . . ?" Erika started screaming. "Why, Beej? Where were you?"

"What?"

"Why, why, why, Beej? Why weren't you *there* for me? I needed you! Where were you?" Erika was getting more animated and excited by the moment.

Then she started talking so fast, and making so many different accusations, that BJ hardly had a chance, he explained, to get a question or comment in.

So he got out of the Jeep. "Let's go upstairs," he said.

Erika hesitated at first.

Then she followed behind him.

"What is it?" he asked.

Nothing.

They took the elevator.

BJ walked into the condo first. Erika was in back of him. He went upstairs and into the bathroom. Looked down on the floor.

"There were two dead people in the bathroom," BJ told jurors. "The people we met on the bus."

Joshua Ford and Martha "Geney" Crutchley.

BJ said he bent down and checked both their pulses as he had been trained by the navy.

"Joshua Ford looked like he had been shot in the head," BJ explained. "I don't know . . . about Martha Crutchley . . . but they were both covered in blood."

If you are to believe what BJ testified to in court, he then walked out of the bathroom and went into the bedroom nearby and sat on the edge of the bed, dropped his head into his hands, and began thinking: *What do we do now? Two dead people. My wife obviously responsible for these deaths. What is the right thing to do?*

Beyond that, *What in the world had happened up here while I was passed out downstairs in the Jeep?*

Had Erika snapped? Had she just shot the two of them in cold blood without rhyme or reason? What the heck had happened?

In what seemed like thirty minutes of pure silence, BJ said he sat and contemplated what he could do, calculating the options he believed he had in front of him.

I can either help, or not help, my wife. Abandon her and not go to the police, or just go to the police.

In helping her, BJ knew, he understood that meant "covering up the murders."

BJ stood up and walked around the bedroom for a moment, and then, after sitting and thinking it through, he decided on the best way out of it all. During this entire time, Erika sat near him without saying a word.

And so a husband had made a decision to help his wife cover up two murders.

The only way in which BJ had known to dispose of dead bodies was what he had been taught. Standing over Geney and Joshua, wanting to help his wife in whatever way he possibly could, BJ said later, he decided to do the only thing he knew how.

Dismember them.

After disposing of the bodies in trash bags and tossing them in several different Dumpsters in Delaware, Erika and BJ went back to the condo to begin the process of cleaning up the scene and enjoying the remainder of their vacation.

86

Whose Idea Was It?

As BJ sat on the witness stand after explaining to the jury that his wife had killed Geney and Joshua, his attorney asked whose idea it was to dismember the bodies. The idea was for the jury to hear from BJ how that entire scenario played out—regardless of how much it would likely alienate each juror. Yes, BJ Sifrit was culpable. Yes, BJ had made a decision to help his wife cover up two murders. And yes, BJ had deliberately and callously taken a knife, cut those bodies up, and placed them in bags and disposed of them in Dumpsters.

But no, BJ Sifrit was adamant, he did not kill those people. His wife did.

"It was my idea," BJ told the jury, to help his wife try to get away with murder.

"Were the bodies placed in trash bags?" his lawyer asked.

"Yes."

"What'd you do with the body parts after you put them in trash bags?"

Save for a cough here, and a throat clear—*ahem*—there, a silence had overtaken the courtroom during this exchange. This quietness had not been present since the start of BJ's trial. People were dumbfounded and in shock. *How could you? How dare you? How awful!*

BJ's voice sounded scratchy and torn. "I threw them away," he said, referring to what he had done with the body parts. There was a touch of remorse present in his inflection: Was it genuine? Real? Or was BJ very good at what he did?

Beyond that, there was a certain sincerity in BJ's voice as he testified under direct examination, which was hard to dismiss.

BJ's attorney showed the jury several photographs of BJ and Erika taken throughout the week in Ocean City after the murders. In all the photos, Erika appeared happy-go-lucky, smiling, partying, just having a ball. On the other hand, in the photos BJ's lawyers presented, BJ looked dark and torn up and totally out of it. His face was sunken and morose. He wore sunglasses in many of the photos, hiding the true nature of what he had done.

Showing BJ a photo of himself and Erika from that week, his lawyer asked BJ to explain.

BJ said, "That's me, but I was not happy that week."

"The person standing there (in that photo) is the same person in this courtroom today?"

"No," BJ said softly, in almost a whisper, looking down toward the floor.

"Why not?"

He paused. Thought about his answer. "Because I shouldn't have done it. I should not . . . should not have *helped* her."

Near the conclusion of BJ's direct examination, his lawyer led him down a path of questioning that seemed to answer some of the questions the jury might have when they began to deliberate. One included the testimony of Karen Wilson, which seemed to prove BJ had bragged to her in some respects about killing "those people."

"Now," his lawyer asked, "did you confess to [Karen Wilson] on that Wednesday night that you had killed two people in that condominium apartment?"

"No, I didn't," BJ said stoically, without reservation.

A few questions later, "What was your plan with Erika in respect to . . . she'd killed two people, BJ, what were you going to do?"

"Well, I was trying to get through the week. I was drinking a lot. Umm . . . I realized that things were going to have to change when we got back to Pennsylvania."

"When [and if] you got back [home], what changes, what plans, were going to be made, BJ?"

"Well, I had tried for three years to make things work between us, but it just wasn't working. There was just no way I was going to stay married to Erika."

"Your involvement in this dismemberment, the accessory after the fact (one of the charges), why did that occur, BJ?"

"It was a bad decision."

"Did you kill Joshua Ford?"

"No, I didn't."

"Did you kill Martha Crutchley?"

"No, I didn't."

After asking BJ several more questions, most of which centered around common things he and Erika had shared—cell phones, cars, etc.—his lawyer asked, "Were there any colors not allowed in your house, BJ?"

"Yes."

"Objection, Your Honor . . . relevance?" E. Scott Collins said sharply.

A brief sidebar was called. Judge Weinstein put his

hand over the microphone and asked BJ's lawyer in a whisper, "Is this a racial thing?"

"Huh?" the lawyer said, surprised by the judge's question.

"Are we getting into a racial thing here?" the judge asked.

"No, no, no," the lawyer said. "The color purple wasn't allowed in the house because it was the favorite color of BJ's ex-girlfriend."

The judge laughed. "Oh, go ahead and ask it."

When BJ was finished explaining how Erika would not allow the color purple in their apartment, his lawyer said he had no further questions.

With that, E. Scott Collins stood up, flattened out the front of his suit coat, checked his tie, cleared his throat, and said, "This is going to take a while, Judge. . . ." It was a pleasant way to suggest a break for lunch now, so he wouldn't have to stop once he got started.

"Well, let's get going, you have fifty minutes [until lunch]," the judge said, sitting back, waiting for Collins to begin.

87

Showdown

Going into BJ Sifrit's case, Scott Collins and Joel Todd knew that convicting BJ was going to be an uphill battle. After all, BJ hadn't said a word to police. As soon as the cuffs were squeezing his wrists after he and Erika were pinched at Hooters, BJ went into prisoner-of-war mode and clammed up.

Name, rank and serial number.

"We had him dead to rights on the burglary," Joel Todd later told me, "and probably the accessory after the fact—there was no way those bodies could be removed without him knowing or participating—but that's it. Everything else was her (Erika)."

The other obstacle the prosecution faced was Secret Service agent Carri Campbell's interview with Erika and the statement Erika had made during her pre-polygraph interview, which had not been allowed into the trial. "Everything she said about him would be considered hearsay," Todd said.

The one thing the prosecution had to get across during the cross-examination of BJ Sifrit was that he not only helped his wife dispose of the bodies, but he also helped his wife kill Geney and Joshua. Part of it was a game that either Erika, BJ, or the both of them, had played on people: hide the purse and make an accusation of theft.

And the penalty for losing that game?

Your life.

Karen Wilson had made that perfectly clear already with her testimony.

BJ didn't look so comfortable up there, now that Scott Collins, who spoke with a deep Southern drawl that echoed throughout the small courtroom, was facing him. It was 11:42 A.M. when Collins began. Detective Bernal sat next to Collins, his trusty white pad in front of him, ready to remind Collins of those little details that only a detective who had investigated the case could.

"Mr. Sifrit," Collins asked, "when you married Erika Grace . . . where were your parents, your family, living?"

"The Midwest."

"Iowa?"

"Wisconsin . . . I think."

"You think? Are you sure?"

"No, they move a lot."

Next, Collins pecked away at how Erika reacted to, as he put it, "married life." It was clear from BJ's earlier testimony that Erika hadn't taken to married life all that well. In fact, it was easy to prove that Erika's psychological behavior seemed to spiral out of control once she and BJ, three weeks after meeting, got married.

BJ agreed.

Then Collins moved into BJ's training as a SEAL. He made the jury aware that BJ had been expertly trained to "blow up things." More than that, he brought out BJ's qualifications as a skilled marksman.

"Expert shot, is that right?" Collins asked, flipping through his notes. His voice varied from sarcastic to sentimental. Facetious is probably too strong—but Collins made no secret about his loathsome feelings for BJ Sifrit and his understanding that BJ was on that witness stand for one reason: to save his own ass.

"Yes, yes," BJ said hurriedly, referring to his marksmanship abilities.

"Now, you said you came to view the body as a machine—is that correct?" BJ had testified on direct that while training to save his military fellows out in the field, he was told to view humans as machines he was there to fix so "it" could go back out into the field and continue to fight.

"Yes, yes."

"And, per your training, as a trained . . . as battlefield experience, if a person is injured or has a gunshot wound, what is the first thing you do?"

"It depends on the situation," BJ said after some confusion, and an objection by one of his lawyers. "If you're on a battlefield, you're probably going to want to return fire. After that, if you can get to the person without getting injured, then you'd assess your situation."

"You assess their condition, which means you check them for injuries, bullet holes . . ."

"Yes."

"You look them over real carefully, correct?"

"If you want to save their life, you'd need to, yes."

Over the course of the next few minutes, Collins had BJ establish that he also had hands-on experience in New York City training with EMTs during real-life trauma situations.

The point of it all from Collins's view was to show how BJ had run up to that bathroom, and, as a trained medic with the navy, did absolutely nothing to try to save their lives or even check to see if they were still alive.

As they continued, BJ talked about his marriage to Erika at its earliest stage, where they lived, and who was, essentially, wearing the pants. BJ had made a point during his direct to say Erika called most of the shots and he went along like some sort of trained minion. Collins was interested in this.

"Now, you stated that Erika had emotional problems. She worried a lot, she was anxious, and she had what you described as obsessive-compulsive disorder."

"Yes."

"And did you realize this *before* you got married?"

"No."

"Didn't notice *any* obsessive-compulsive anxiety prior to your marriage?"

"Zero."

BJ seemed comfortable in the witness chair. It's generally rare for juries to get an opportunity to hear from a defendant; most defendants never take the stand in their own defense. BJ was that exception, however—the guy who believed, beyond anything else, he could do whatever it was he put his mind to. And here he was, faring pretty well, as the assistant state prosecutor threw him what were, at this point, softballs.

BJ had an answer for every question. He was speaking his truth and it appeared genuine. Collins asked about Erika's compulsion to contact him whenever he went out on SEAL temporary training duty and how that affected his performance. BJ described one time in Alaska when Erika showed up unannounced as he was out in the mountains, and she had called his platoon leader back in Virginia Beach and demanded that BJ be pulled out of the mountains because of an emergency.

"Was it an emergency?" Collins asked.

"No, it wasn't," BJ answered sincerely.

Collins was certainly setting the stage for something momentous, but he never seemed to get there, at least not within the first ten minutes of his cross. It was more of just pointing out what BJ had already testified to, and hopefully making the jury keenly aware that there were two sides to every story.

At one point, Collins asked, "I wrote this down—You testified, you said something like, 'I wasn't allowed to contact my family.' That what you testified to earlier?"

"Yes."

"And . . . did you have a telephone?"

"Yes."

"OK, could you have picked up the phone and called your family?"

"I could have, yes."

For any prosecutor worth his or her salt, the beginning of any great cross consists of pointing out the obvious, so there's no confusion with the jury later on when the hammer drops.

"I mean, Erika wasn't handcuffed to you, was she?"

"No," BJ said, his voice beginning to crack.

Then Collins went through several times when BJ was away from Erika and how he undoubtedly had access to a computer, telephone, pencil and paper, and BJ admitted, well, yes, of course he could have contacted his family.

But he never did.

"Did you allow Erika to control you to that extent?" Collins asked more forcefully.

"I was just trying to make her happy," BJ answered.

"I understand, you know, I try to make my wife happy, too," Collins said humorously, "but, come on, you're a young man, in seemingly excellent health and condition. You had just gone through what we all have to know is some of the most strenuous training that our military can dish out—that SEAL training. And *you* graduated number *one* in your class. Is that correct?"

"Yes . . ."

"You're the top man! And yet, I believe Erika is described as five foot six, one hundred pounds, and this woman could *control* you to that extent that she wouldn't let you even *call* your mother?"

Bernal sat there, waiting for BJ to answer: *Come on, do you expect us to believe that shit?*

BJ was sweating. He was shifting in his seat. "Yes," he said quietly.

"What were you afraid she was going to do?"

"She wasn't going to be happy. I was trying to make her happy. It was extreme."

Collins had BJ describe how the anxiety Erika experienced and supposedly suffered from had this hazardously corrosive effect on the relationship. Through that period of the marriage, she had become addicted, essentially, to Xanax, according to BJ, and she would go through her prescriptions to the point where she needed to order more drugs over the Internet.

But then, as things seemed to be going smoothly for BJ as he talked about Erika's digression and the hell he went through living with her, Collins asked an important question—one that spoke of a man who was obviously not too worried at all about his wife's behavior.

"And it was during this time," Collins said, slowly walking his way toward what was sure to be a climactic punchline, "when she's having these *anxiety* problems, as you described them, these 'mental problems,' that you, *sir*, you went out and you bought her a .357 Magnum revolver." He paused for a moment. "Is that correct?"

"Yes," was all BJ said.

"Now, you're quite familiar with guns, are you not?"

"More than most, I guess."

Collins made a point to say that a .357 is a powerful handgun. Certainly not a weapon for a novice. And generally not the first weapon of choice for a female to begin a love affair with.

For the next several moments, Collins questioned BJ about the photographs he and Erika took while they were in Ocean City. It was apparent from Collins's tone that he was leading BJ somewhere else now. He showed a photo of Erika and BJ on the beach, both of them smiling, sunning themselves. It was merely hours after she had purportedly murdered the couple and he had dismembered them. It was a photo BJ's lawyers had not shown the jury.

"That was Sunday, correct?" Collins asked.

"Yes."

"Right *there*," Collins said in his deep voice as the next photo moved onto the screen, quite evidently meaning to emphasize the word as a photo of the victims' remains appeared, "is the homicide of Martha Crutchley and Joshua Ford. How long after the murder of Martha Crutchley and Joshua Ford do you, *sir*, do you begin to dismember these bodies?"

88

On the Ropes

The feeling in the courtroom after Scott Collins brought up the issue of dismemberment was shock and silence. BJ and Erika's vacation went from the two of them having a grand old time, to some type of wild, ghoulish party of knives and blood and body parts. The juxtaposition of reality and what seemed like scenes out of a summer Hollywood slasher film was entirely apparent as jurors and courtroom watchers sat and, in their minds, went through Geney and Joshua's final moments of life.

They had been emotionally tortured.

Threatened.

They had been abused.

Died painful deaths.

They had plenty of time to think about the fact that they were likely never going to make it out of that bathroom.

And their bodies—after death, the temple of their beings—had been appallingly mistreated and deformed.

How could anybody put a bow on that part of this crime and try to minimize it?

For all intents and purposes, BJ kept his responses to one plain level of emotion: he never broke down, got excited, or, for that matter, seemed at all remorseful. To BJ, in other words, those grisly murders were just part of another day in the life of living with Erika. And a major aspect of that sick life had included cleaning up a mess Erika had created.

He was wrong to do it. He'd cop to that, BJ insisted.

But he never killed anybody—that was his story, and he was sticking to it.

When he finally spoke, BJ answered Collins's question regarding how long he waited after the couple was murdered before dismembering them, saying, "I don't know exactly when they were murdered."

Bernal was eagerly scratching out questions for Collins to ask and calling the prosecutor over: *No blood on the carpet* . . . Bernal kept writing down and sliding the paper toward the prosecutor. Then he'd underline the "no blood" portion of the page, tapping on it with the tip of his pen.

Collins never said anything about it.

"What I was trying to get across to Scott Collins," Bernal said later, "was that, in my opinion, from looking at all the evidence, the bathroom door had been kicked in and then Josh was shot in the head. That door had been kicked in so hard that the doorknob hit the corner of the wall when it opened. It hit it so hard that the knob dented the corner bead in about an inch to an inch and one half. The corner bead is a thin L-shaped metal strip that protects the integrity of the corner. There was no way Erika kicked that door in. BJ had to have done it, and if Josh was alive while that door was closed, BJ had to have been there when Josh was shot and killed. I kept writing notes to Scott Collins and telling him to talk about the door and the force needed to generate the type of damage caused by the doorknob. I know. There is not a *doubt* in my mind, that if that information had been presented to the jury, BJ would have been convicted of murdering Joshua . . . [but] for some reason, he just wouldn't ask the question."

"Well" was all Collins said to BJ, going through a timeline of the night again, asking BJ a series of questions pertaining to times and places, where and when they were, and where they ended up. At one point, Collins changed his focus of the question and asked BJ why, if Erika had had such a tough time being separated from him, did she voluntarily get off the bus with Joshua and Geney—*strangers*—while BJ continued on to the Rainbow supposedly by himself? Without saying it, Collins was making a play that the state was not buying the story that BJ knew nothing about the murders.

"I guess she was OK with the separation this time," BJ said.

"You *guess* she was *OK* with it?" He paused. "Oh . . . *kay*," Collins said sarcastically, moving on to another topic.

Collins next had BJ go through his complete story again. There was a lot of back-and-forth: yes, no, yes, no, maybe, I guess, if you say so. Most of it was on BJ's part. He tried to come across as if he was holding his own, but Collins was chipping away at his story, piece by piece, with every question, not necessarily the answers BJ was giving.

"So you go into the condo—" Collins said, describing how Erika had woken BJ up in the Jeep and told him there was a major problem upstairs.

"Yes."

"—and you see what *you* describe as two dead people on the floor of the bathroom. Is that the upstairs bathroom?"

"Yes. Yes."

"And where were these two dead people lying?"

Details were important now. Every minor detail was a possible point to argue. In fact, something else Collins never brought up was that Erika—all one hundred pounds of her—had managed to kill a black belt in karate and his girlfriend. And she had walked away with absolutely no possible defense wounds of any type.

"They were to the right, as you walk in."

Collins put a diagram of the bathroom up on an easel in front of the jury, facing BJ. He had BJ take a laser pointer and point out where, exactly, Geney and Joshua were lying on the floor.

"OK, and how were they dressed?"

"It was either their bathing suits or under garments—they were in shorts," BJ said.

"OK . . . and as a medic, an emergency medic corpsman, did you immediately go over to these people to check them to see if they were injured?"

"I checked to see if they were alive, yes," BJ said.

"Did you look at them to see where their injuries were?"

"No. They were both . . . obviously dead."

Collins wanted to know how BJ could be so sure.

BJ said he just knew. There was blood in every nook and cranny of that bathroom. The floor. All over their bodies. The walls. The blinds.

Everywhere.

This—mind you—before they were cut.

"Well, how can you be so sure? Why don't you describe what you saw?"

There was an objection.

"Describe Joshua for us," Collins spurted out, ignoring the objection.

The judge allowed him to continue.

BJ went quiet. "Um . . . uh . . . right here," he said, using the laser pointer to show where Joshua was lying, "there were some drawers, and he was half slouched over with his back against these drawers."

But with all that blood? Bernal seethed inside, scribbling again on his notepad in big bold letters for Collins to see: *BJ checked for life, walked through all the blood, yet tracked NO blood on the carpet or on the bed where he said he sat for 30 to 60 minutes <u>before</u> making his decision to help his wife?*

Why wasn't Collins calling BJ on this point? Bernal wondered. The forensic team had not found one trace of blood on the carpets *or* the bed. What in the world was going on? Why wasn't Collins taking his lead? Bernal was livid. *He's lying . . . ,* Bernal wrote out, again sliding the pad over to where Collins could see.

"Was he sitting on the floor?" Collins asked, referring to Joshua.

"Yes."

"Legs out in front of him?"

"Yes."

"Any obvious signs of injuries on his body?"

"Yes, his head was very bloody."

"His head was *very* bloody. OK . . ."

Bernal started writing again: *We know Martha wasn't shot; she was killed after Josh, but we don't know how she was killed!!!*

Why wasn't Collins asking these questions?

"Yes," BJ said.

"And how did you ascertain that he was alive—did you check his pulse?"

"Yes. They weren't breathing, and they didn't have a pulse."

Collins and BJ continued this rapid back-and-forth succession of questions and answers for a few more moments. Intensity was building.

Then Collins wanted to know if BJ examined Joshua's body for any wounds.

"There was blood everywhere," BJ said again.

Come on, Bernal thought, *perfect opportunity to ask about the absence of blood on the carpet.*

But Collins didn't. Instead, as he tried to back BJ into a corner, pressuring him to answer more quickly, in a more detailed manner, maybe beginning to trip BJ up, the judge interrupted, "Is this a good time to break for lunch?"

It was almost 12:30 P.M.

Writing again, Bernal threw his pen down on the table.

Lunch? No one had paid much attention to the time. Collins had mentioned at the start of his cross if this would happen, and bingo: he had BJ on the ropes, ready, he felt, to crack, and the judge was forced to break for lunch.

"Yes," Collins said reluctantly.

89

The Details of a Crime

When they returned after lunch, BJ took the stand once again, and Collins tried to get back to where he had left off. But it was clear something had been lost in the disruption. Collins could spend the rest of the day and still not get that spark back, that natural tempo created by the facts emerging and momentum building on its own.

Bernal and Collins talked it over during the break, and it was clear they viewed the way in which Collins should ask BJ questions much differently.

What could Bernal do?

A few questions into his postlunch cross, Collins showed BJ a series of photos of the lock picks he had used to break into Hooters. He asked BJ if those same lock picks were always inside the Jeep.

"Yes," BJ answered quickly, without thinking about his answer.

"Are you a trained locksmith?" Collins asked.

"No," BJ said, almost laughing, "but I can pick locks,"

he added braggingly. Some claimed BJ could pick any padlock made.

Smartly, Collins pointed out the fact that inside the Jeep on the same night BJ said he had waited for Erika and eventually passed out—because he had been *locked out* of the condo: Erika supposedly had the keys and she was with Geney and Joshua—were three sets of lock picks. The implication was fairly apparent, without Collins having to say it: *Why hadn't BJ, an expert lock picker by his own admission, picked the lock at the Rainbow?*

More than that: how had BJ gotten into the Jeep without keys? (There's not a chance he had left that Jeep open, not with several weapons and other personal items stored inside.)

But Collins didn't ask. Even after Bernal suggested it.

Collins went back to the line of questioning he had left off with, before lunch. A short while in: "You testified that you dismembered them, correct?"

"Yes."

"Now, on the pieces of the bodies we *did* find, they were found disrobed. Did you also *disrobe* them?"

"Yes."

"And they were also found with no jewelry. Did you also take the jewelry off them?"

"No."

"You did not?"

"No."

"OK. Did anyone help you dismember them?"

"Erika."

"Erika helped you dismember them. OK."

"Yes."

"Tell me," Collins said in a rather demanding tone, "how do you dismember a body, sir?"

BJ's attorney objected.

"Which part do you cut off first?" Collins continued after the objection was overruled by the judge.

Bernal wanted the jury to understand what was an old trick that sociopaths often tried to use when they testified. Bernal knew because he had seen it countless times in an interrogation room, but also in a court of law. "There's a thing called 'limiting your involvement.' Admit to the lesser crime to try and get away with the major crime." He wanted Collins to walk along those lines with his questioning and stamp it into the jury's minds: BJ was willing and able to admit his involvement so he could skate on the more serious charges.

There was an awkward, eerie silence in the room at the moment Collins brought up the idea of dismemberment and how BJ had actually gone about it. No one wanted to hear it, and yet it was entirely relevant. The reality of the crime was that BJ and Erika, maybe one or both, had cut these two people up into twelve pieces. The jury deserved to hear from BJ the gruesome facts surrounding this particular part of the crime.

"I used a knife," BJ said.

"You used a knife," Collins remarked, shaking his head. "What *kind* of knife?"

"A silver one."

"A silver one. Are we talking about a butcher knife twelve inches long, or a pocketknife four inches long?"

"Somewhere in between."

"Somewhere. In. Between."

They argued over which knife BJ used, finally deciding on a knife that BJ had brought with him to Ocean City from home.

Collins flipped a page of his notes and asked, "Let's start—which one did you dismember first?"

"I don't remember."

"You *don't* remember?"

BJ shook his head. It seemed to Collins that a person should recall effortlessly which body he cut up first. It was such an unimaginable horror—how could a man forget such a thing?

"OK, do you remember which *limb* you took off first?"

BJ's lawyer objected.

"He's got a right to ask these questions," the judge said reluctantly.

"No," BJ answered.

"Where, exactly, did you dismember these people?"

"Right where they were."

"*Right* where they were?" Collins asked. "Well, right next to where they were was a hot tub, wasn't there?"

"Yes."

"Did you dismember them in the hot tub?"

"No."

"You didn't? You dismembered them right there on the floor?"

"Yes."

A few questions later, Collins asked, "Did you go out and buy Drano the next day?"

"Yes."

"OK, why did you go out and buy Drano?"

"I . . . I . . . There was blood in the hot tub."

"Oh, I see, OK," Collins said with a sarcastic effect, "there was *blood* in the hot tub. Now, how did the blood get into the hot tub?"

"I don't know *how* it got there."

(In her statement to the Secret Service, Erika had claimed BJ was standing in the hot tub, his naked body painted with the victims' blood, like some sort of warrior. After having masturbated on them, he cut the bodies up inside the hot tub. Erika had recalled seeing Joshua's torso on the edge of the hot tub as BJ stood by watching, asking for her help to get it into a duffel bag.)

It got to the point where whatever Collins asked, no matter how hard he pushed, BJ kept to his story. At one point, despite the objections from BJ's attorneys, Collins put up a full-color image of Joshua Ford's severed arm, which was sitting on a medical examiner's metal table. Then Collins asked, "What is that?"

BJ's lawyer interrupted. "Your Honor, I object. This is ghoulish and unnecessary."

"Overruled."

"What is that?" Collins asked a second time.

"Joshua Ford's arm," BJ said.

The arm had been removed with a clean slice near the shoulder. There was no residual cartilage, skin, or bone hanging from it.

"Did you remove that arm?"

"Objection!"

"Overruled."

"Yes," BJ said.

"Now, there are a bunch of other cuts on that arm, did you do those, too?"

BJ thought about it. "No."

Collins put up a photo of another arm. "Whose arm is that?"

"Joshua Ford's."

This arm had obviously taken a bit more might to be removed, as if BJ had a tough time cutting it off, gave up, and, bracing himself by putting his foot on Joshua's shoulder, pulled (or ripped) the arm off, instead. It looked as though it had been torn from the shoulder instead of cut; there was tissue and cartilage and tendons hanging from it.

"You see a difference in the two?" Collins wondered aloud.

The judge finally sustained one of the objections from Burton Anderson.

Collins showed a series of additional photos depicting the dismembered bodies. When he arrived at Joshua's torso, he asked BJ, "Did you cut Joshua's head off?"

"Yes."

"Did you cut Martha Crutchley's head off?"

"Yes."

After BJ established that he had, all by himself, dismembered the bodies, Collins asked him where Joshua's head had been placed after it was decapitated from his body. (Both heads were never found.) "What did you do with it?" Collins asked.

"I put it in the same place as everything else."

90

Closing One Door

Near the end of the afternoon on Tuesday, April 8, 2003, both sides were given the opportunity to address the jury one final time. In his closing argument, as BJ sat and looked on with little or no emotion, Joel Todd came out of the box strong, stating emphatically, "These victims were killed by a heartless, mindless, cold-blooded, calculated couple—and one member of that couple is here today."

Todd painted BJ as a sadistic, violent, "trained killer," based on the time BJ had spent in the SEALs, as it were, graduating honor man at the top of his class. He said BJ had selective memory, recalling only what he wanted to, regarding the night Geney and Joshua were so brutally murdered for no good reason other than they met up with a couple whose lot in life was to play a game of "catch and release" with pocketbooks. A sick and twisted amusement at that: one that BJ and Erika, Todd suggested, had devised as a way to entertain themselves.

"This defendant could only remember what had *helped* him. He has *no* credibility whatsoever," Todd asserted.

Todd talked about the state's star witness, Karen Wilson, and her devastating testimony, which included a confession from BJ that he was indeed involved in the killings. Jurors had to consider Karen's vulnerable state that night and the fact that she had no real reason to walk into a courtroom and lie about such a traumatic event in her life. "He told her he was ridding the earth of those bad people," Todd said quite convincingly. When it came down to it, jurors would either believe Karen Wilson or not.

BJ's attorney Burton Anderson had some help. William Brennan stood and began his closing after Joel Todd finished, and the judge announced to the jury that the trial was nearly concluded.

Hang tight. Almost there.

Brennan figuratively pointed a finger directly at Erika, saying how manipulative and controlling the woman was, and how BJ was basically led down a path to these murders by an overbearing wife ever since leaving the SEALs. When push came to shove, and he was roused out of a stupor in that Jeep that night, BJ faced a terrible dilemma: turn his wife in to the authorities, or help her clean up two murders and (try to) get away with the crimes.

BJ had said he felt an obligation to help his wife, whom he loved.

"The woman who cannot control herself," Brennan raged loudly, "that is the same person who committed these murders."

More than once, Brennan claimed Erika was crazy. In one example, he put up a photo of Erika. She was smiling, wearing Joshua's ring on a chain around her neck. "A trophy," Brennan suggested. The woman was wearing a piece of her victim because she was sick and twisted and got off on the fact that she had killed two people. Then, a short while later, "I asked Benjamin what happened that night. The state's attorneys didn't want you to know. They want to talk to you about everything *except* what happened in *that* apartment, and which of those two people is going to go nuts when the purse is missing? What possible motive could there be for Benjamin Sifrit to kill two people? What *possible* motive?"

Brennan made a great point, saying that the only reason why Karen Wilson was alive and able to walk in and testify was the simple *fact* that BJ wasn't passed out in a Jeep downstairs on the night when Erika started that "missing purse" game for a second time that week. The fact was, BJ was standing there inside the condo to "control his wife," Brennan told jurors, who seemed to take note of such an important observation.

Wrapping up that observation neatly, Brennan concluded, "When Benjamin Sifrit is there, people don't die." There was passion and fervor in his voice. Brennan clearly believed what he was saying.

On the flip side of that argument, Brennan shouted, "When Benjamin is *not* around, well, ladies and gentlemen, Erika is *not* kept under control."

In his rebuttal, Joel Todd said the defense was simply trying to push all the blame on Erika Sifrit. "When the facts are in your favor, you argue the facts. When the law is in your favor," Todd added before pausing a moment, "you argue the law. When *neither* is in your favor, you get *angry* and point the finger."

Regarding whether Karen Wilson was making up things that simply didn't happen, which was the notion that Brennan was suggesting in his closing, Todd said,

"Who in this case has more of a motive *not* to tell the truth? Benjamin is *not* telling the truth, because he doesn't want you to *hear* it."

Most important, Todd wanted to impress, if the jury was not entirely convinced BJ had actually pulled the trigger, they could still find him guilty of first-degree murder if they believed—and Todd cautiously and persuasively pointed this out—that BJ had "aided and abetted in the homicides."

If BJ was there, in other words, in that condo when Erika killed Geney and Joshua, and did nothing to stop it, he could still be found guilty of first-degree murder. Jurors needed to be aware of that option.

Sitting down, looking over at jurors, Todd was a bit apprehensive and guarded. He knew BJ was guilty. He knew Erika and BJ were equally responsible for the murders of Geney and Joshua. But he also knew how juries could react to testimony and lack of evidence. Because when it came down to it, Joel Todd had no smoking gun. There was nothing tying BJ Sifrit directly to the murders of Geney and Joshua.

91

Shock and Awe

"BJ's was the weaker of the two cases," Joel Todd told me later. In fact, as they prepared for BJ's trial, Todd and Collins were "not convinced," Todd said, "that we would not get anything out of BJ's case other than burglary convictions, and possibly an accessory after that fact."

Why?

"BJ had lawyered up from the moment he was arrested. And all of the evidence that we had," Todd explained, "pointed to Erika. She was the collector and she was the one that had the IDs, the gun. . . . BJ certainly knew about it all. He couldn't have been there and not known about it. But the most we could show was that BJ probably helped clean up the mess . . . but technically that wouldn't even make him an aider and abettor."

Erika had an uncanny knack, Todd said, to tell the police only what they knew at the time. And when she figured out what the police knew, she would add to it— but again, only what they knew. Never what they *didn't* know. In that respect, Erika had probably made up her mind early on what she was going to do and say in order to make her case stronger. For BJ, he had simply refused to talk at all, which was one of the best things he could have ever done. As it deliberated into its second day, the jury didn't have a statement from BJ to look back on and compare to any new facts in the case. The jury had to base its verdict solely on the state's *case* against BJ and the *evidence* against him—which wasn't much.

On Wednesday, April 9, 2003, the jury returned to the Montgomery County courtroom where it had heard the state's case against BJ, and the judge announced there was a verdict.

Joel Todd and Scott Collins weren't feeling it. The room had an uncomfortable feel to it, and the jury's posture and movement reflected what was certain to be a surprising—and disappointing—decision.

Indeed, BJ was ultimately convicted of second-degree murder in the death of Geney. Shockingly, he was cleared of all murder charges in the killing of Joshua.

A collective gasp seemed to hiccup throughout the courtroom.

Mark Ford, Joshua's brother, was beside himself, as was Deborah, his wife, Joshua's sister-in-law.

No one could believe it—except, maybe, for Joel Todd and Scott Collins, who looked disheartened, but not all that surprised.

Scott Bernal's heart dropped. He was devastated, and began, at that moment, to blame himself—he could have done more to get his points across to Scott Collins, who questioned BJ.

"Look," Bernal said later, "this jury believed that Geney, who was not killed first, according to BJ, just stayed still for the ten to fifteen minutes it took Erika to supposedly run eleven floors down into the parking lot, wake her extremely intoxicated husband up, make this drunk coherent enough to understand what she was telling him, get him out of the car, go up to the eleventh floor, then up an additional floor, once inside the unit, and see what Erika had done (according to BJ). All this, while Geney just waited around to be killed. If Scott Collins would have addressed the door being kicked in, the jury would have seen right through that sadistic prick's (BJ's) bullshit. It still bothers me today. Throughout that trial, I wrote several other notes to Collins to address other issues. He brought up a couple, not all. . . . The one thing I've learned in my career is that you never have enough evidence. Confidence in oneself is necessary in any investigation. Ego is not. . . ."

BJ sat, sullen and stiff; it was almost as if he didn't really realize what had just happened.

The jury also convicted BJ of being an accessory after the fact for dismembering the bodies and discarding them in a Dumpster to help cover up the crimes.

The jury took all of fourteen hours to come to its decision. Mark Ford told the Associated Press afterward, *"I'm totally disgusted. He took away a good brother. He's walking on my brother!"*

Judge Weinstein addressed the court after the complete verdict was read, saying he was delaying BJ's sentencing until a trial date could be set for what amounted to a burglary charge against him. But most people sitting there knew BJ was not going to be sentenced until Erika's trial was concluded.

From where Collins and Todd sat in the front row, the trial had gone better than expected. It seemed every decision, every motion, every objection, and every little nuance that makes up a criminal murder trial had gone their way. Because of that, Todd said later, they had expected maybe a better outcome, but they were pleased nonetheless that BJ had been convicted of at least *one* murder. He could have walked altogether, which would have been a disaster.

Heading out of the courtroom, Todd and Collins showed the disappointment on their long faces. Whether they expected it, or whether they ended up with more than they had expected, it really didn't matter. What mattered was that Joshua Ford's brutal death had not been redeemed by a court of law.

They had all been staying at the same hotel: Todd, Collins, and many of the family members of the victims, all of whom had attended the trial.

Todd expected to have to sit down and meet with them and talk about what had happened, and where they were taking the case against Erika. As he was in his hotel room, however, figuring out how to go about consoling the families, Deborah Ford knocked on the door.

"I just wanted to make sure you were OK," Deborah said comfortingly. "We all did."

The families were concerned that Todd and Collins would be depressed and broken by what had happened.

"Thank you," Todd said, and they sat and talked.

"That is the type of people the Ford and Crutchley family members are," Todd later told me. "Within all of their pain, here they were worried about Scott and [me]. They wanted to comfort *me*. That really showed me something."

92

Stealing the Spotlight

With BJ's trial out of the way, Joel Todd and Scott Collins focused on the one person they believed was more responsible for the murders of Joshua Ford and Martha Crutchley than BJ. And yet, from the moment Todd awoke on May 22, 2003, he knew it was going to be an uphill battle all the way to get that conviction. To his stunning surprise, the *Baltimore Sun* had interviewed Mitch and Cookie Grace, along with several of Erika's supporters, in what turned out to be a five-thousand-word article—two full pages and one-half page of the newspaper, which is a lot of real estate for a daily newspaper to devote to *any* story—running under the banner headline LIFE INTERRUPTED.

"What is this?" Todd said aloud as he opened the morning paper. "I was furious," he later added. "I immediately felt that somehow Mitch Grace had used his wealth or influence to get that article planted . . . hoping that it would have an impact on the trial."

There, sitting in front of the seasoned prosecutor on

his kitchen table, was a photo of Mitch Grace looking down, sullen and stone-cold in shock; Cookie's head on his shoulder, his arm around her. Mitch looked as though he had just stopped crying. Below the rather large photo of Mitch and Cookie was a snapshot of Erika on the basketball court, and below that was another photo of Erika with Benjamin, both of them smiling, sitting in a restaurant, somewhere, with a draft beer in front of them.

"There was no good reason for that article to be printed!" Todd said.

He couldn't believe it. Here was a seemingly sympathetic portrait of a family that, according to the article, had been turned inside out (rightly so) by the charges against Erika.

As Todd turned the page after reading the lead, which was about Erika's "charmed existence" in Altoona, growing up under the umbra of a wealthy father and loving parents, there, staring back up at him, was a photo of Erika from high school. The photo had taken up almost a quarter of the entire second page. The strange part about it, Todd considered, was the photo of the victims, Joshua and Geney (one quarter the size of Erika's), tucked underneath. Erika had upstaged two murder victims who had been "butchered," Todd said later, and "dismembered. . . . It was a disgrace. I couldn't believe what I was looking at."

It wasn't until the third—and final—page of the article that Erika was presented as a criminal, in handcuffs, walking into the courthouse in between an armed officer and a prison guard; her head was bowed, her skinny arms skeletal and brittle. Yet, the headline accompanying the photo said it all: LIVES ON HOLD FOR ONLY CHILD.

Near the end of the article, Mitch told the reporter, *"It's awful to lose somebody and not be able to even say goodbye."* Mitch was referring to the victims' families and their

suffering, but part of the statement was no doubt meant
to support his own feelings of not being able to hold his
daughter, or even touch her since she had been arrested. Chiming in on Mitch's comment, Cookie said
that it would have been easier in some ways for them if
Erika was gone completely.

And so Todd and Collins were hoping that their potential group of jurors would not be intimidated or
swayed in any way by the obvious attempt Mitch, Cookie,
and Erika's camp had made to portray Erika as a non-
threatening college grad who had made some bad
choices in life, but was, well, just an innocent little drama
queen fighting for her freedom and identity back. After
reading the long article, in which Erika's entire academic career and sports life were chronicled, a person
would think that Erika had gotten mixed up with the
wrong guy in marrying BJ—and that alone had led to
her troubles.

Because of such news coverage, Todd argued (and
Arcky Tuminelli subsequently agreed) that the trial
should be held in an out-of-the-way location, where a potential jury pool would not be tainted one way or another. And so the judge eventually moved Erika's trial to
Frederick County Circuit Court, in Frederick, Maryland,
about 180 miles, or three and a half hours, away from
the scene of the crime.

93

Her Turn—Again

Erika's trial began on June 3, 2003. In his opening statement, Joel Todd attacked her character first, saying he and Scott Collins, "together, will be presenting the evidence against the defendant in this case, Erika Sifrit, who is accused of murdering, dismembering, and covering up the murder of Joshua Ford and Martha 'Geney' Crutchley, as well as the burglary of Hooters in Ocean City."

Todd then went into an apology he believed the state needed to make, considering that the evidence and photographs he was going to present throughout the state's case were going to be graphic and horrific in nature. Or, as Todd put it, "gruesome and grotesque." But it had to be done in the great order of justice. It was important for the jury to see the horror this woman had perpetrated.

From there, Todd went through the case in chronological order, painting Erika as the diabolical, evil, twisted murderer he believed her to be. He spoke of how the state's theory centered around a game Erika and BJ liked to play with couples they met, where the loss of Erika's purse set in motion events that were beyond the realm of what any sane human being could imagine. Then he talked up an important point—something the jury would, Todd knew, take great pride in looking at closely and judging: how scared was Erika of her husband, truly, as she was likely going to undoubtedly argue?

"Tuesday [after the murders] was a fun day for the defendant," Todd said patronizingly, leaning on that aspect of his argument. "With little or no thought to the condition of the victims, our happy defendant plays miniature golf . . . and later she goes to Ocean City's famous boardwalk. . . . Later that same day, in Lewes, Delaware, the defendant gets a tattoo . . . and that evening, she goes to Hooters, where she shows off her new tattoo and poses with the Hooters girls."

In all of these photos, in fact, the woman is smiling.

Laughing.

Drinking.

Eating.

Enjoying her life.

They were devastating accusations. How could Erika claim BJ had made her participate in the crimes, and that he controlled her every move and she was terrified of him, if she was photographed hamming it up all over town after the murders? In fact, in many of the photos, Erika and BJ are holding each other, smiling, kissing, just happy to be alive.

"On Wednesday," Todd argued, "while our victims continue to decay, the defendant returns for fun to the boardwalk . . . followed by another feast of crabs . . . then another trip to Hooters . . . and another trip to Seacrets nightclub."

Todd explained Karen Wilson and her friend Todd Wright's story of meeting up with Erika and BJ. It was a night that started out with a flat tire and ended in some sort of bizarre hunt—a gun pointed in their faces—for Erika's belongings. And the entire time, Erika was supporting her husband. Why?

Because she was the instigator of this deadly game.

Watching from her seat in front of the judge, Erika sat comfortably and looked on with interest. Mitch and Cookie were sitting in back of their daughter, listening to every word carefully, holding hands, heads bowed at times, a grimacing look of disgrace and disgust on their ashen, tired faces.

Todd used a computer-assisted slide show at times to support his argument, which his office had spent a considerable amount of time putting together. Against a magenta background, Todd cued photos of the gun and items found in Erika's purse. He described their importance, implying sternly, with a tinge of sarcasm and anger, that some of the items were "morbid souvenirs" Erika had kept of the killings—especially Joshua and Geney's driver's licenses, which Erika—not BJ—had in her possession.

"Her hobby," Todd said, "was that she liked to *collect* things—anything, actually, to help the defendant look back and remember significant events in her life."

And these items, belonging to the victims, were relics to remind her of the night she and her husband had murdered and dismembered two human beings.

Concluding his short opening a few minutes later, Todd said, "The bullets fired into the body of Joshua Ford, which took his life, were fired from a weapon removed from the possession of the defendant. At the conclusion of this case, I will ask you to return a verdict of guilty to all of the charges."

Tom Ceraso had been brought into the case as Arcky Tuminelli's co-counsel. Now Ceraso stood and began to tell jurors that they shouldn't take whatever the state's attorney says as gospel. Think about BJ's involvement. Think about the powerful and strenuous psychological training BJ went through as a SEAL. Think about how he had *access* to Erika's gun and knife. Don't just assume, because some *prosecutor* says so, that Erika is guilty based on what amounts to *circumstantial* evidence.

Ceraso said he and Tuminelli would prove by the end of the trial that BJ killed Ford and Crutchley, using as evidence the statements BJ himself had made to others, as well as testimony from his trial.

"We have this confession," Ceraso hammered, "an absolute confession and concession on the part of Benjamin Sifrit."

There was a pause.

Then, "He killed them. He *butchered* them."

Ceraso promised he would allow Karen Wilson to tell her disturbing story of BJ threatening her and her friend Todd with the same gun that killed Joshua Ford, and yet failed to explain how he and Tuminelli would prove such an accusation. Moreover, some of the defense's most detrimental evidence, Ceraso said, would be BJ's own testimony from his trial, in which he acknowledged and talked about cutting up the bodies of Ford and Crutchley. What more evidence did a jury need? Here was a man admitting how he had butchered these two people. In fact, Ceraso said, when asked under cross-examination about his role, the question framed as, "You did it, didn't you?" BJ responded with a resounding "Yes." Reading aloud from a transcript of BJ's trial, before throwing it down on the table in front of him, Ceraso stared at jurors with a "can you believe this?" look.

The questions on everyone's mind as any murder trial begins are: Will the defendant take the stand? Will she raise her right hand and tell her story? All juries want to hear from defendants. They want to understand through the defendant's eyes, responses, and body language what role—if any—she played, or didn't play, in the purported crime.

Either way, juries want answers.

Ceraso hinted that Erika would possibly take the stand, although Arcky Tuminelli told reporters later that same day, referring to the same question, "I refuse to say yes or no."

94

Pathology

Joel Todd's first witness was Dr. Adrienne Perlman, Delaware's deputy state medical examiner (ME), who testified—same as she did during BJ's trial—how she removed two bullets from Joshua Ford's torso: one from the neck and one from the right side of his chest.

Both wounds, the doctor said, "were fatal."

Crutchley's death, Perlman told jurors, was a bit more complicated to theorize, and the method of murder was almost impossible to prove. The doctor couldn't determine how Geney had actually died, since the only body part authorities uncovered was her left leg, the ME said with a touch of disappointment in her academic-sounding voice.

Erika sat and acted as if this gruesome discussion of body parts was routine and unaffecting, like maybe she was indifferent to it all. And this was, possibly, part of Tuminelli and Ceraso's strategy: Erika should perhaps act as though she was emotionally immune to everything, emotionally uninvolved, and not invested in any part of it. BJ had warped her mind so badly, controlled her every move so tightly, and wound up her anxieties so profoundly, nothing shocked her anymore. She was a shell of a human being. She had turned into a robot, detached from society.

On the other hand, Erika was running back to her cell writing salacious letters to her paper lover, Jimmy, depicting sexual fantasies and plans for the future.

Two different people.

It was a good way for Erika to approach the jury—the only problem, Todd had effectively argued in his opening, was that this was the way Erika acted, only when it suited her needs. Like now. In front of the jury.

All other evidence available proved otherwise: Erika Grace Sifrit was a manipulator and chronic drug user, who, when she was married to BJ, thrived on good times, dark thrills, and obsessive behavior, which drove him out of the military.

In any event, Erika sat stiffly, not showing much emotion one way or another, knowing that she faced a maximum penalty of life in prison with the possibility of parole on first-degree murder charges—not to mention a litany of additional charges, including theft, burglary, carrying a concealed handgun, and being an accessory after the fact. As Todd sat there next to Erika and her attorneys, doing battle against them, the state prosecutor was contemplating dropping these charges—even though the charges could add the potential of an extra twenty or more years behind bars for Erika.

After Dr. Adrienne Perlman left the stand, Todd put on a few witnesses who were on the bus Geney and Joshua had gotten on in Ocean City on the day they met Erika and BJ. It was a good way for Todd to chronologically set up the narrative that ended Joshua and Geney's lives.

With lunch over, Todd had a friend of Geney's explain to jurors how she began to be consumed with worry over Geney, when Geney failed to show up for work on that Tuesday after Memorial Day. This was a good way to begin to bring in the state's parade of law enforcement witnesses to explain how it was that Erika and BJ Sifrit met up with Geney and Joshua—and eventually murdered them.

95

Pain and Loss

Mark and Deborah Ford had lost a daughter to a supposed serial murderer in Cape Cod, who had allegedly beheaded the young woman and, some claimed, removed her heart. Eight months later, they got a call explaining that another family member, Joshua, had been the victim of a brutally savage crime, which seemed to be motivated by nothing more than the sheer thrill of the kill. This trial, at least to Mark and Deborah Ford, was a formality. They needed to see it all end. And being a part of it, in any capacity, was one way to accomplish that task and, with any grace, move on.

As the afternoon wore on during this first day of the trial, Mark Ford was brought in—but not to carry on about how much tragedy had infested his life and how much he missed his brother and daughter. Sure, that was all true, and also part of his and Deb's daily life story. It was there when they woke up, and there when they went to sleep. And the jury certainly knew it, just from looking at Mark's face. The sadness and loss and compounded nature of the heartbreak he and his family had endured was evident there. But instead of talking about Joshua, and recalling memories of a lifetime, and imagining future memories that would never be, Joel Todd had Mark talk about the ring Erika had in *her* purse—with Joshua Ford's blood on it—on the night she and BJ were arrested at Hooters. It was the same ring, in fact, that Erika wore in a few of those after-the-murder photos.

During Mark Ford's testimony, Todd projected a photo of the ring, asking Mark if he recognized it.

"It's my brother's dragon ring," Mark said.

"Have you ever seen your brother wearing that ring?"

"Many times." The look on his face seemed to remind everyone that Mark would never see his brother wearing that ring again.

After Todd asked Mark a few more questions—one about Geney and one about a photograph of Joshua and Geney, in which Joshua was wearing the dragon ring—Todd turned Mark over to Tom Ceraso.

Ceraso didn't move from his seat. "No questions, Your Honor."

Why attack a guy who had managed to go on in life after such devastating losses? What could be gained by such a thing?

Rounding out the day for Joel Todd were three police officers who had been at the scene of the Hooters burglary. All three set the stage for BJ and Erika's arrests.

Throughout the day, it wasn't the witnesses and testimony that caused the most watercooler discussion; it was the state's exhibits Joel Todd and Scott Collins had presented to the jury. Todd had warned the gallery and the jury during his opening statement that it would be subjected to graphic photographs—and those images did not disappoint. The most ominous of the bunch was a shot of Joshua's arm, cut off from the shoulder, sitting deftly on a medical examiner's steel bench. It had been cleaned by the ME. Present in the photo were the remains—the results—of what Erika was being accused of, so graphic and sobering, Joshua's tattoo so perfectly centered on the cusp of his bicep, his fingernails still intact and manicured. The image was so surreal it didn't even look authentic. To sit and think that one human being had actually done this to another was stupefying and repulsive. The arm appeared to have been cut almost surgically off, whereas Joshua's other arm, which jurors had also seen photos of, looked as though it had been cut and torn off like a chicken leg, with bits and pieces of flesh hanging from the shoulder area. Either way, the photos injected an amount of surrealism into the trial.

Additional photos, which were not quite as shocking but carried their own weight as well, were of Joshua's torso, which did not look human. It had started to decompose, and having been buried underneath garbage for most of the week, it took on a look of having been taken from a fire, which, of course, it hadn't.

Then there were the photos of how each body part had been uncovered in the landfill. Here were photos of the body parts just sitting, blending in with the garbage around them, as if they were props placed there by a key grip, or special-effects expert. Jurors could no longer look over at Erika and see an innocent bystander, someone whom BJ had *forced* to take part in such a crime. Because when you took these autopsy and crime scene and landfill photos and put them into the context of what transpired *after* the murders, you had to conclude that the same couple responsible for this terrifying tragedy of unspeakable proportions was the same couple photographed a day later playing miniature golf and eating hot wings and drinking beers, smiling and laughing and enjoying themselves. The juxtaposition of the unreal and the real was strikingly evident, some sort of lingering aroma in the air inside that stuffy courtroom.

Indeed, no moral person there could deny how evil the people responsible for the remains of these crimes, seen in those photos, had to be.

96

The Setup

The morning of June 4, 2003, began much in the same manner as the previous day had left off. Law enforcement witnesses came in and described how they had arrested BJ and Erika at Hooters, and through that seemingly routine collar, they made a discovery that had turned what was a common burglary case upside down. In fact, it was the discovery of the IDs that led the OCPD to believe Joshua and Geney were being held hostage at the Rainbow Condominiums. This seemingly routine arrest of two rather sloppy burglars turned out to be the beginning of the most horrifying case many of the detectives working it had ever investigated.

As the trial moved forward, Erika took notes and conversed with Tuminelli and Ceraso as certain witnesses said things that she obviously disagreed with. And for what was the first time in almost two full days, Erika displayed a bit of emotion. Instead of it having been generated by graphic images, or testimony about the horror, it turned out that Erika's emotional display occurred only when she turned and stared at her parents, who were deeply moved by the proceedings, and mouthed, "I love you."

Erika and her parents were so close, and yet she couldn't run into their arms and be coddled and comforted. According to one witness there in the courtroom sitting near her, Cookie bowed her head and wept softly, saying, "Why, why, why . . ." to herself. She couldn't understand how this had happened to her baby.

After six police officers took the stand and described how the investigation into a burglary turned into suspicion of murder, Todd called a bouncer from Seacrets who happened to be working on the night Erika and BJ showed up *after* the murders. The witness quickly identified a photograph of Erika and BJ in which Erika was supposedly wearing Joshua's dragon ring. Then he testified how Erika had waved a gun willy-nilly and threatened to shoot him after he caught BJ trying to pick the lock on an automated teller machine (ATM) inside the bar.

Tuminelli and Ceraso made a point to let the jury know (through cross) that there was no way anyone could tell for certain if it was actually Joshua's ring in those photos, but the bell had been rung—and there was little Erika's team could do to lessen the severity of the implication. Not to mention that the bouncer put the gun that killed Joshua in Erika's hands, and describing her demeanor and aggressiveness, he made the assumption that this was one woman unafraid to wield or use a deadly weapon.

Todd next called the tattoo artist who had inked the snake tattoo on Erika's hip, allegedly on the spot where she had made the first cut on Geney, which BJ seemed to be so proud of. Todd used a photograph to show that Erika had a knife in her pocket on the day she got the tattoo, which was about forty-eight hours after the murders.

It was that same knife, Todd was going to prove, Erika had in her pocket on the night she was arrested.

The same knife used to cut up Geney and Joshua.

Near the end of the day, OCPD detective Clinton Chamberlain talked about some of the hard evidence the OCPD had collected. For Tuminelli and Ceraso, it was one thing to have the brother of a murder victim identify a ring owned by the victim, which the perpetrator had been allegedly carrying, and then later wore around her neck. But it was quite another to have an opinion of the same piece of evidence given by a law enforcement official.

"You can't say that the ring that is shown here," Ceraso asked, pointing to one of the photos in which Erika had the ring supposedly around her neck, attached to a cross, "is *that* ring, can you?"

"Not positively," Chamberlain replied.

97

Subtlety

The following morning, June 5, a Thursday, went pretty much along the same pace for Joel Todd. He presented a series of crime scene techs first, who came in and explained how they had collected evidence and what they had found. Throughout this, Todd had to be careful. Crime scene evidence wasn't the glorified, dramatic, state-of-art science portrayed on television. Crime scene investigators (CSIs) didn't bombard a crime scene with high-tech gadgets out of the future: they still did things, in many instances, the old-fashioned way—on their hands and knees.

To bore a jury and to bog down a trial with all of the mumbo jumbo that goes along with the scientific study of evidence under a microscope, and collecting it from doorknobs and carpets and grout lines, might slow the state's momentum considerably. The way in which Todd called these witnesses, however, perfectly outlined how monotonous a process crime scene investigation truly was in the real world: There were fingerprint specialists and serology techs and fiber and hair analysis experts. All of whom, however, came in and sat for no longer than ten minutes each, focusing their testimony on one specific aspect of their job, rather than every little shade and tone each had sketched during his or her part of the investigation.

It was a brilliant move on Todd's part.

When Todd was finished with his science experts, he called Detective Scott Bernal, who was, Todd himself later said, the one detective who had led the charge against Erika and BJ from the moment Geney and Joshua were reported missing. Surprisingly, though, Todd didn't have much for the veteran detective, other than having Bernal testify that he believed it was Erika's voice on the tape of the 911 call made that night from the Rainbow suite.

Ceraso stood when Todd finished and asked, quite simply, "I think . . . you've never heard Erika Sifrit's voice over the phone, am I right? Other than on the tape?"

"That's correct."

A few questions later, "I have nothing further."

OCPD detective Brett Case came in next and talked about his adventure on Monday, June 3, 2002, as he and scores of other officers went to the landfill in Delaware to begin the search for Joshua and Geney.

"We all routed there at seven A.M.," Case said, referring to the landfill. "We went over some preliminary instructions, safety concerns, certain things like that, and got the troops up to the top, top of the landfill, and we began to search with some heavy machinery and personnel." He said they started to actually begin digging through the tons and tons of garbage around 9:30 A.M., which was, looking at it from the scope of the ground, no different than searching for one specific pebble in a pile of topsoil. The landfill was immense, some 571 acres of timbered wetland. Each "cell" of the landfill was about forty to fifty acres in size. A cell is one small segment of land that makes up the whole. Laying it out like a grid, they searched certain cells, one at a time.

That search, Brett Case said, went on for twelve hours.

In what must have been divine intervention, Bernal and Case later said, within only a short period of time, an excavator picked up a bucket load. "The third scoop of trash," Case added with the same shock he had experienced on that day, "[had] unearthed what appeared to be a human leg."

Todd showed a photo of the leg.

"OK, and what was the next item you located?"

"We located a large duffel bag, dark-colored duffel bag, and this zippered-type duffel bag. Contained in that was a yellow hotel-style blanket and a torso of a human being."

Todd was smart to present "facts" of the case, which could not really be disputed. These were aspects of an investigation that added up to murder when put together.

Utter silence filled the room as Todd presented this disturbing image of what was left to Joshua Ford's torso.

The next item, Case said, was an arm.

Then another arm.

The graphic images kept coming.

And coming.

One after the other.

Various shots of body parts in different positions, from the dump site to the medical examiner's office, back to the dump site.

Flashes of horror. Like a slide show depicting some sort of ghastly scientific experiment gone wrong.

In what seemed more like a conversation between a state's attorney and one of his detectives—as opposed to a witness being questioned during a trial—Detective Brett Case described what had been one of the more macabre discoveries from a day filled with just about every grisly image one could imagine. In a plastic garbage bag, which had an Ocean City bus pass inside, alongside an arm, Case found what at first "appeared to us to be a rubber glove." It was located on the palm of a hand of an arm. But it wasn't a glove, after all, Case explained. "Ultimately we determined it to be the actual skin of the hand, which had fallen off and was resting in the palm." And from that sheath of skin, Case said, they were able to obtain fingerprints.

With that, and a few more insignificant questions and answers, Brett Case was finished.

Over the next few witnesses, the state went through the items Erika and BJ had purchased at Home Depot and Ace Hardware. It was important testimony, subtly telling jurors that Erika and BJ had no good reason, while on vacation, to replace a door and paint a bathroom, if they hadn't dismembered two people inside the bathroom, shooting one of them through the door, and making a terrible mess of things.

Then a pizza restaurant waitress testified how she remembered meeting Erika and BJ on Memorial Day, Monday, May 27, 2002. "They were the only people at the bar," she said.

Todd put up two photographs of BJ and Erika—together—inside a restaurant. The waitress said she took both photos.

Standing and staring at the photographs, which were still displayed, Tom Ceraso saw an opening. "Ma'am," he asked, ". . . this was Memorial Day, the twenty-seventh of May, 2002, correct?"

"Correct," she answered.

"I want you to look at Erika."

"OK."

"In that photograph, tell me if she has something around her neck."

"She has a necklace."

"And what's at the end of the necklace?"

"A cross."

"Is there anything else?"

"No."

"Thank you," Ceraso said smartly. "That's all I have."

98

Daddy's Turn

Late into that same day, Scott Collins called Mitch Grace. Mitch looked tired and turned over by this process of testifying at his daughter's murder trial. At this point in their lives, Mitch and Cookie should have been bouncing grandchildren off their knees, showering little pink gurgling babies with love and charm, spending their latter days enjoying the fruits of a wonderful life lived.

Obviously, it hadn't turned out that way. Here was Mitch, nervous and scared for his only child, sitting in front of her in a court of law, as she fought for her freedom. Erika faced charges so horrific, Mitch had a hard time facing up to how his daughter's life had turned out so dreadfully wrong.

There was some trouble hearing Mitch, and he was asked several times to speak up. When he did, Mitch talked about Memory Laine and what type of store it was, and how Erika loved nothing more than making scrapbooks and playing basketball. "Things like that."

Mitch admitted that he had indeed arranged for BJ and Erika to stay at the Rainbow through a friend of his who owned the condominium complex.

"Did there come a time when a present was purchased for your daughter by Benjamin, which upset you a little bit?" Collins asked.

This riled Mitch. He seemed unnerved by the question. "I don't know if he purchased it or not. He upset me when he told me that he was planning on buying *my* daughter a gun, and that *really* upset me, yes."

"And was that gun a .357 Smith and—"

Mitch didn't let him finish. "I don't even . . ."

"—Wesson," Collins tried to get in.

"I have no idea, sir!" Mitch raged. He was clearly taken aback by the question. "I told you he told me that he was planning on buying it. We had a big—we were—I was very upset with him for doing it. I didn't think he should do it and I told him that."

Collins asked, "Now, sir, do you recall giving an interview to the *Baltimore Sun*?"

"Uh, yes . . . ," Mitch said, and then Ceraso asked the judge for a sidebar conference.

Arcky Tuminelli approached the bench with Ceraso and Collins and told the judge he expected Mitch to be impeached by a statement he had made to the *Sun*. Collins was going to use the article—or a particular quote from Mitch in that article—to show the jury how Mitch had developed selective memory since the case had moved forward.

The judge thought about it for a moment, and allowed it.

"Sir, do you recall the interview for this article?" Collins asked.

"Ah, I recall it. It was sometime last summer, so—"

"Sometime. Would it be fair to say your recollection is not perfect?"

"Well, I mean, I'd say it's pretty good. I mean, that's, I didn't—"

Someone shouted, *"Really?"*

Mitch countered sarcastically, *"Really!"*

Arcky Tuminelli spoke up, "No recollection?"

"Would you feel it would be helpful if you reviewed a portion of this [article] to refresh your recollection?" Collins offered.

"On what?" The conversation seemed to be getting confusing.

"Yes, sir."

"But see, I remembered the exact conversation with Benjamin Sifrit," Mitch said, then explained how he wanted to relate *that* specific conversation, not what he had told the reporter from the *Sun,* which was exactly what Collins was trying to make clear. It got to the point where no one knew what the other was talking about because so many people were talking over one another. Collins wasn't talking about a conversation Mitch and BJ had; he was referring to the conversation Mitch talked about in the newspaper article.

Mitch picked up on Tuminelli's original objection, understood where Collins was going, and replied, "Well, but if I remember my conversation with Benjamin Sifrit and that's . . . and I related that to the newspaper, I don't know if they printed what I told 'em or not."

Collins rolled his eyes. Paused. "Well—" he started to say, but Mitch interrupted.

"I know. I know."

Then there was a heated, quick exchange between the two, beginning with Collins asking, "Can I show you what—"

"Benjamin Sifrit," Mitch blurted out.

". . . they . . ." Collins said, trying to finish.

"Told me," Mitch said over him, confusing matters more.

". . . printed . . ." Collins finally finished.

Ceraso objected.

After the judge sustained the objection, Collins asked what he probably should have asked to begin with: "Sir, did you ever see the weapon?"

Bottom line.

"No, I did not," Mitch answered.

"You did not?"

An uncomfortable silence.

After two more questions, Collins searched his notes for a moment. "No further questions."

The state brought in yet another ballistics expert after Mitch finished answering a few of Ceraso's questions on cross, and the day's proceedings concluded.

99

The Ring

Breaking news on the morning of June 6 wasn't that the case of *Erika Sifrit* v. *The State of Maryland* was likely headed into its final few days of testimony, but rather an uncommon seismographic event had occurred throughout the southern Midwest. "I was in my house," one man told CNN. "It felt like it was going to come off the foundation. It went three times and I thought that was it." Some other people said their vehicles were shimmying, and another woman with a four-poster bed said the posts were vibrating.

The earthquake measured a magnitude of 4.5 and had been the first of its size to strike the region in nearly one hundred years. No one was hurt badly, but people were reminded of how fragile life was, and how things that might appear to be moving along at a normal, methodical pace could often change in an instant. This became an apropos metaphor for what was about to take place in what had been Erika Sifrit's pampered life of running, drugging, drinking, and committing crimes with her former husband.

Since it was a Friday, most people in the courtroom were anticipating the weekend. It was spring. A beautiful day dawned outside the courtroom. Inside, however, Arcky Tuminelli got to work rather quickly on his defense, calling a series of witnesses to refute the state's contention that Erika was the main reason why Joshua and Geney had ended up dead and dismembered. Luckily for Erika, that statement she gave to Agent Carri Campbell, of the Secret Service, had not come into the trial. The judge had ruled it inadmissible, of course, based on the deal Erika had signed with the state. Still, Tuminelli and Ceraso were walking on eggshells—even if they didn't want to admit it—where that statement was concerned. Part of their defense strategy had to be built around the fact that if that statement became part of the trial, Erika Sifrit was finished. The bottom line was, if Erika took the stand, there was a good chance that statement would enter into the trial. And if that happened, Tuminelli knew, Erika would have to throw up her hands and take whatever the state offered.

In recalling OCPD detective Brett Case, Arcky Tuminelli had hoped to trip up the detective. In supporting a position Tuminelli and Ceraso were trying to advance, they wanted to remind jurors that although Case had testified that he believed the ring Erika was wearing around her neck in those photos, taken after the murders, was Joshua's, there was no way the detective could actually prove it.

"There was a question about the quality of the photographs," Arcky Tuminelli said later. "By recalling Brett Case, we wanted to point that out."

Still, Joshua's blood had been found on the ring. It was his ring, that much was not in dispute. And Erika had it in her possession when she was arrested. But as far as wearing it after the murders, no one could say that definitively.

"Look, it was one thing for my client to have that item," Tuminelli recalled, "but quite another to be running around that week wearing it around her neck." Arcky Tuminelli wanted to prove that although the photos might have depicted his client wearing the ring, there was no positive proof that it was the ring in question.

Tuminelli then asked Case about his experience, hoping to imply that he was somehow unqualified to make the assumptions he and Scott Bernal had made about Erika. Both detectives had made no bones about Erika's guilt. It was clear in their mannerisms, inflections, and tone: Erika was the mastermind, BJ the muscle.

None of it worked, however. Case was sharp and on his toes when answering any question Tuminelli put to him.

For the most part, the defense focused on Case's and Bernal's interviews with Charles Atwood, BJ's former SEAL buddy who had described the way in which BJ had talked about dismembering a human being, and what he would do with those dismembered body parts. Tuminelli knew this was damaging testimony. It pointed to guilt—but guilt on BJ's part.

Not Erika's.

Atwood had testified before Case, telling jurors the same story he had told the jury in BJ's trial: he and BJ had had beers one day at a strip club, and BJ talked about dissecting a human being into six separate pieces (same as Geney and Joshua). Tuminelli's strategy was to make the jury well aware of the fact that it was BJ's plan all along to kill and dismember these people, and Erika was just going along with her controlling husband, feeling pressured and even scared into participating. Atwood was the conduit into that innocent bystander defense.

"Now, Detective Case, as a detective, if you believe that a witness made a statement that you believed was simply a joke, that statement, would you travel—how many hours did it take you to get to Virginia (where Atwood was at the time)?"

Tuminelli was implying in the question that Case and Bernal took what was a casual beer-buddy conversation between two military colleagues drinking at a strip club and blew it way out of proportion.

But Case said he and Bernal went to interview Atwood for a "number of reasons."

Tuminelli marched on, focusing on the joke aspect of the conversation, wondering if Case and Bernal would have traveled all that way if the information was said to be nothing more than a joke.

Case kept saying he didn't understand the question. Repeat.

They went back and forth for a time, and then Tuminelli, frustrated and unable to get anywhere, relieved Case from his duties.

Tuminelli and Ceraso called a gun store owner next. The man testified that BJ had purchased the gun that ultimately killed Joshua—which was no surprise to anyone, as Collins and Todd had made it clear that BJ had bought the gun for Erika as a gift.

By the end of the day, Karen Wilson had taken the stand and, once again, told her story, recounting what had been a harrowing night with two seemingly mental cases she would much rather forget about. In the end, Wilson's testimony meant little to the scope of Erika's case. The jury was either going to believe that Erika played a part in the murders, or that she was coerced by a controlling husband.

Wilson's testimony could fit into either argument.

The jury was not going to hear from Erika. The major concern for Erika's camp was that if she sat on the witness stand and supported the main theory Tuminelli and Ceraso had been laying out for the jury—that Erika had assisted BJ *after* the murders—there was the great potential the statement Erika had made to Carri Campbell was going to be introduced. In order for that statement *not* to become part of the case, Erika would have to, essentially, lie on the witness stand. And once she perjured herself, and the state knew it and could prove it, the statement was up for grabs.

There was no way Erika's camp could take that chance. But what hurt them even more, perhaps, was not being able to explain to the jury why Erika wasn't going to testify. Because, in the end, most juries want to hear from a defendant.

It had worked for BJ.

With Erika's defense finished, the judge released everyone for the weekend and announced that closing arguments would begin promptly on Monday morning.

Without saying anything, Erika looked at her parents and was handcuffed and led back to her holding cell for the weekend.

100

"Miss Scrapbook"

Before closing arguments began on Monday, June 9, Detective Brett Case was called back to the witness stand to answer a few questions Tuminelli had most likely thought about over the weekend. And yet, nothing new came out of the exchange.

All Joel Todd had to do in his closing was simply point out the fact that there was no evidence supporting a theory that the murders had been all BJ's doing. If anything, the evidence pointed directly at Erika—and the jury's decision in BJ's trial supported that theory. So, like any good trial attorney, Todd keyed on this single issue as he began explaining to the jury how he had proved the state's case. "The gun which you've seen in the box here," Todd said, "the gun which was passed around and you had a chance to hold. That gun, we know, killed Joshua Ford."

It wasn't just a trial prop anymore. *That* gun, *that* weapon that started this nightmare. It was *hers. That* woman. The one sitting there. *She* owned it. *She* had it on her when she was arrested. *She* threatened a bouncer with it. *She* bragged to people about owning it.

It was the gun that had killed Geney and Joshua.

Todd reminded jurors that Erika's own father had testified and "admitted" that BJ "had told him that he, Benjamin, was buying a gun for Erika. . . ." There could be no confusion over whose gun it was that killed those two people.

All told, however, this was pure circumstantial evidence. The truth of the matter was, it was Erika's gun. That fact went undisputed. But that in itself had not proved she pulled the trigger; it only proved that her gun had been used in the homicides.

"What if," Mitch Grace remarked later, "BJ set it all up this way? What if BJ made sure his gun wasn't around because he wanted to frame Erika for this crime?"

As he found his rhythm, Todd focused on Erika's habit of collecting things, including Joshua's ring and what were the last photographs taken of Joshua and Geney, which Erika had snapped herself with her own camera. Interestingly enough, Todd said, Erika and BJ had met plenty of other couples that week, and yet the only "couples" photographs police found were of Geney and Joshua, who ended up dead, as if Erika and BJ had chosen them and Erika was documenting their final days as some sort of reminder or souvenir from that week.

Todd called Erika "Miss Scrapbook," who took "photographs of the ones (couples) that gave her a rush, the ones that gave her the excitement."

Geney and Joshua.

Another factor that Todd saw as significant became how there were only two bullets found on the kitchen table in the Rainbow condo suite where Erika and BJ were staying. Why was this? Todd wondered aloud. "We know there were more than two bullets fired, but there's only two bullets saved. . . . The state would submit, ladies and gentlemen, that it would have been easy to take that bullet . . . after the head was chopped off. That bullet was visible with the naked eye. But that bullet wasn't recovered. There was another bullet in the chest area, right under the arm. That bullet wasn't recovered. Two bullets were kept because the souvenir hunter only fired two of the shots! She had to keep *her* two bullets," Todd snapped, getting louder as he continued. "She's the *collector*. She's got to have the trophy." He paused and looked toward Erika. "*She's* got to have the *souvenir*."

As the gallery sat and listened attentively, that comment drew a collective breath. Todd had framed the motive and the thrill of the kill around Erika's own business and her desire to *collect* things. And, whether true or not, he had done a superb job of it.

In a second vein of the same accusation, Todd spoke of Erika having the IDs of the victims and Joshua's ring on her when she was arrested. What more evidence did anybody need to prove she was the collector? BJ had nothing on him. He didn't care about collecting things. In many ways, it was implied—not through actual words but subtle pronouncements—that BJ had lost everything when he got himself discharged from the navy and had little reason left to feel good about life. He was perhpas just going along with whatever thrill-seeking adventure his crazy wife wanted to do next.

"Isn't it ironic," Mitch Grace said later, playing devil's advocate, making some great points, "that all of those items were found on Erika? Isn't it a bit suspicious that BJ didn't have any of it on him?"

The one piece of evidence that didn't get much play during the trial, but certainly meant a lot in the scope of Erika's collecting habits, was Joshua and Geney's room key. That key was found on a table in the condo.

There was also the implication that only a novice shooter could have shot that .357 and missed, which a bullet found in the grout of the tile floor proved. Thus, looking at it from the perspective of BJ being the mastermind, the main shooter, how could a navy SEAL, who was an expert marksman, miss a shot at such close range? Todd asked. No, only an inexperienced shooter could have done that—which meant, *yes,* ladies and gentlemen, Erika Sifrit had fired that round.

Which made her a murderer.

Todd next focused on the 911 call Erika had made from the Rainbow at 3:01 A.M., after she and BJ met Geney and Joshua, explaining to the jury, "The state would submit . . . that a reasonable inference in the facts in this case is that at the time this call was made, Joshua and Geney were already dead."

Then it was on to the dragon ring. Erika had photographed Joshua wearing the ring at Seacrets; film developed from her own camera proved this.

But then Todd projected a photograph taken by the ME of Joshua's dismembered arm sitting on a metal table. "That's Josh's left hand . . . and it didn't have a ring on it on that table, but there's the ring there, at Seacrets nightclub, just an hour or so before he was killed."

It was powerful imagery.

Todd talked about all the evidence collected from the Jeep Cherokee.

Then he talked about all the blood—much of it mixed—found in the Rainbow bathroom.

Then Todd recounted how his medical examiner testified that the bodies were chopped up with a serrated knife—the same knife recovered from Erika's front pocket on the night she was arrested.

The state's attorney talked about the photographs taken of Erika after the murders, asking the jury, "Have you seen [a photo] yet where she's *not* smiling, where she's *not* having a good time?"

Regarding Karen Wilson and Todd Wright, Todd wanted to know how a person could be totally innocent of the two murders a few days before and still invite Todd and Karen up to the condo—*knowing* what her husband was supposedly capable of doing?

It was a fair judgment.

After describing the charges against Erika, one by one, Joel Todd concluded with a final thought: "The defendant and Benjamin Sifrit are a team. Hooters burglary was teamwork. Each had knives. Each had ski masks. Remember, there were two ski masks, not just one! The flex cuffs. Each had guns. . . . They were in this *together.* They were working *together.* The defendant is *guilty* of all the charges against her."

He paused.

"Please find her so. Thank you."

101

Circumstances

After a lunch break, at 1:53 P.M., Arcky Tuminelli got right to work on what he believed to be Joel Todd's ridiculous theories, which Tuminelli thought relied heavily on speculation and jumping to conclusions, but was light on actual hard evidence.

Facts.

Wearing his trademark shiny, double-breasted, expensive-looking suit, Tuminelli stood and walked toward the jury, thanking each of them for their astute attention and determination to sit, listen, and watch the proceedings, and for taking "copious notes." It was good to see that people still cared about justice, he suggested.

"Something . . . happened that's very odd in the last two months," Tuminelli began, "and what happened was the state—Mr. Collins and Mr. Todd—somehow forgot"—he looked over toward both men—"about four witnesses. This case, as you know, was tried in Montgomery County approximately sixty days ago, and between Montgomery

County and this courtroom—this week—they forgot about [Charles Atwood] and they forgot about [Karen Wilson]. . . . You have never heard of any of those people until Mr. Ceraso got up and mentioned to you that we were compelled, because they wouldn't present these witnesses to you, and you have to ask yourself . . . exactly what is going on here, because . . . the truth is the truth is the truth. They knew what the truth was sixty days ago, but somehow those witnesses who were—"

Joel Todd stood and objected.

It was a good thing, too, because jurors looked to be bored and confused by the comments.

The judge sustained the objection.

When Tuminelli continued along the same path, Todd asked if he could approach.

When he began again a few moments later, Tuminelli kept his focus on what the state had left out of the trial more than what he and Ceraso had presented as evidence to exculpate Erika. Sure, on paper, the defense didn't need to prove innocence and the state needed to prove guilt; but in the reality of jurors and what they want to hear and see, Tuminelli and Ceraso could offer little evidence to prove Erika was not involved in those two murders. In fact, the available evidence—albeit most of which was circumstantial—pointed to the contrary.

Still, Arcky Tuminelli did his best with what he had, continuing along the metaphoric lines of talking in parables, saying, "Now, it's sort of like a jigsaw puzzle. If you know what the picture is on the front, it's a lot easier to assimilate the pieces and know where you're going. But if you don't have a picture, as we did, then it's a little harder, so it's our opportunity to get up and talk about the evidence, and what we believe the evidence proved."

It sure sounded good.

But also confusing.

Collins and Todd listened, smiled, and, at times, took notes. Trials can sometimes be a war of words, and Tuminelli was getting into that aspect of his closing.

"I need to address the evidence in this case," he said after apologizing to jurors if his closing was going on too long, "and what it showed because we're talking about this"—and he pointed to Erika, who sat stoic, motionless, and emotionless—"young lady's life. Now, I know that Mr. Todd doesn't want to hear that, because to him she is 'Little Miss Scrapbook,' and I submit to Mr. Todd that these proceedings are much too serious to be so flip. She's a lot more than 'Little Miss Scrapbook.'"

Tuminelli's main point was that the state was trying to have it both ways. You couldn't "pin the crime" on BJ during his trial, and then turn around and pin it on Erika during hers because you wanted a double conviction.

The law didn't work that way.

"The state blames Erika Sifrit every bit as much as it had Benjamin Sifrit, even though the state knows Benjamin Sifrit was the killer," Tuminelli raged.

Then he added that Erika was nothing more than a "fragile, psychologically weak young woman" who assisted BJ in this gruesome horror, "only because she craved his affection."

Lulling the jury into what could only be described as a meditative coma, Arcky Tuminelli broke into a long and tedious discussion regarding the charges, breaking them down into lawyer speak he believed the average Joe could comprehend. It got so monotonous and repetitive that by the end there was no way to tell one charge from the other.

After that, Arcky Tuminelli went through every situation Todd had brought up during trial and explained it away as if Erika had simply gotten mixed up with the wrong guy. And yet, looking at the case in retrospect, what did Tuminelli truly have to defend? What did the guy have at his disposal to go to the jury with? Erika had not only made things difficult for her lawyers, but in her hubristic sense of self, she kept things back that might have even *helped* her cause.

The judge gave the jury instructions after Joel Todd's rebuttal.

Then the jury was off to deliberate the rest of Erika Grace Sifrit's life.

102

Judgment Day

In the scope of high-profile murder trials, four days of testimony is not a lot. But that's what Erika's trial had amounted to, when all was said and done. On June 10, the jury indicated it had reached a verdict. After what had happened during BJ's trial, many family members of the victims were nervous that "Miss Scrapbook" might also walk away with a slap on the wrist and a few decades behind bars.

Saving family members of Joshua and Geney from any more anguish and trauma than they had already gone through, and would forever have to deal with, the jury found Erika guilty of second-degree murder in the death of Geney and first-degree murder in the death of Joshua. She was found innocent—some consolation—of all the other charges against her. What swayed many jurors was the fact that there were scores of photographs of Erika after the murders living it up on the boardwalk and eating chicken wings at Hooters and drinking beers and playing miniature golf. How could a woman be shattered by such horrible crimes one day, scared for her life, living under the violent reign of a controlling whack job, but then run around town having fun, too?

"It was hard to get around that," one person close to Erika later said.

103

The Butcher

With Erika's case out of the way, BJ was cleared to be brought back into court for sentencing. It was July 7, 2003. What would the judge do? some wondered. How would the judge react to what the jury found in BJ's case? Essentially, the jury had collectively said with its verdict that BJ had little to do with the actual murders—and it would appear that the jury in Erika's case backed this up, placing the burden of the blame on her.

BJ sat with a sullen look about his pale face as the judge cleared his throat and started proceedings. It was obvious in the judge's tone that it wasn't going to be a good morning for the former SEAL.

Joel Todd spoke first. "Mr. Sifrit is a wicked, evil, rotten human being." There was some movement in the room. Many who knew him expected no less from Joel Todd.

Montgomery County circuit judge Paul Weinstein was firm, suggesting that he wanted to give BJ *more* prison time than the maximum, but he was confined by the laws of the state and the jury's recommendations.

"This was nothing more than a thrill killing that you and your wife committed," the judge said sternly, sounding frustrated and a bit uncomfortable that he had to stay within the sentencing guidelines set before him—and even a little upset by the jury's decision.

Long sighs could be heard throughout the room as the judge continued to speak. There was a bit of redemption in this case. After all, with a second-degree murder charge, and no prior criminal record, BJ could be walking the streets in as little as a decade if the judge was lenient.

To that, Judge Weinstein added, "This is one of the few instances in my twenty years in which I have disagreed with the jury's verdict in a case." He shook his head, looking up from the paperwork in front of him.

Then, staring directly at BJ, Weinstein lashed out, comparing the dismemberment of Geney and Joshua that BJ admittedly took part in to the Holocaust. "You're a butcher—a *butcher*!" Weinstein shouted. "You cut these people up for no reason. . . . If not for the masterful job by your defense team of William Brennan and Burton Anderson, you would probably be facing a life sentence."

When Weinstein laid down the thirty-eight years (the maximum he could give), BJ looked up at him without emotion and seemed unmoved. Giving BJ the maximum made it impossible for BJ to sit in front of the parole board for at least nineteen years. Then he added that if he's still alive when BJ is up for parole, he wanted to be notified, so he could walk in and tell the board how cruel and vicious these crimes were.

"Would you like to make a statement?" Weinstein asked.

BJ shook his head, indicating no.

104

The End of
Her Humanity

A little over a month later, Erika and her team were back in court to face sentencing. Erika was looking at some serious time. Luckily for her, Arcky Tuminelli had gotten the death penalty taken off the table that first night he had met her. The most Erika could receive was life.

Before sentencing, several of the victims' family members stood and spoke. It was emotional and gut-wrenching to sit and listen to the pain and loss in the words of family members who had gone through hell over the past year, and here they all were back once again for more of the same.

Would it ever end?

After Joel Todd introduced her as being "raised almost as a sister to him," Joshua Ford's cousin spoke first.

"Josh was more than a cousin to me," the woman said, her voice broken and lethargic with pain. "He was my very best friend. We shared all of our hopes and dreams together. We had many plans for our future. We even used to talk about retiring together. I think of him constantly. Every day. Every hour. When I heard he was missing, I was terrified. When I heard he was murdered, I thought I would stop breathing." The death had been so tough on Joshua's cousin that, she added, "for the first nine months after losing [him], I had to pretend he was still alive because I couldn't face the truth."

Then she told a story of having to drive to her daughter's school on the day she heard the terrible news, pull the poor child out of class, and explain what had happened to her godfather.

There was not a dry eye in the room.

Joshua's sister spoke next.

Then Geney's stepdaughter: "I called her 'Mom.'"

Next, Geney's "little sister," Anita Flickenger, stood and spoke her piece. She talked about the media wanting quotes and she being the least quotable person in the room. "But I would like to be quoted on this," she said patronizingly, looking around, pausing for a brief moment, having a terrible time looking Erika in the face. "The fact that justice has been served in this action is due to the professionalism and the dedication of the lead detective, Scott Bernal, to that of Joel Todd and Scott Collins, the members of their staff, and to the twelve men, tried and true, the jurors of Frederick County, who saw the truth and rendered a *just* verdict."

Erika sat without saying or doing anything.

"We owe each of you a debt, which can never be repaid," Anita continued. "'Thank you' is so inadequate, but I say to each of you, thank you."

Later in her statement, Anita went straight at Erika, making a point of what perhaps many were feeling on that day, but no one had yet vocalized: "I believe that when Erika and her husband butchered Geney and Josh and placed their bodies in the Dumpster to find their way to the Hard Scrabble Dump, she completed the process she began in that awful [rest]room. It was not just Geney and Josh's body you threw away, it was the last shred of your humanity."

Anita had struggled with the loss of her sister, as any sibling would. It was back during that week when Joshua and Geney went missing that Anita's pain, Detective Scott Bernal later said, began to pull on the detective's heartstrings. Anita had called one night shortly after the OCPD had found Geney's car. Anita was certain Geney and Joshua were in the trunk of the car. She called the OCPD and asked if they could just bust it open and take a look. It was one of the hardest things Bernal said he had ever done: approaching that trunk and popping it open.

The most vexing words of the day, spanking of a streetwise toughness that growing up in South Boston had likely played a hand in, came from Joshua's brother, Mark Ford. Mark was angry, sure. He was in a state of total disbelief, having buried both a daughter and brother to murder in the span of eight months. But he was also, on this day, ready to point out for Erika what she could expect from life behind bars. In a certain way, although he probably didn't plan it, Mark Ford made a case for abolishing the death penalty in lieu of allowing heinous criminals to suffer for the rest of their lives.

"It is judgment day," Mark said after introducing himself and calling Erika a murderer. "It is time for you to pay the consequences. Erika, today is the day that this honorable court holds you accountable for your murderous acts. Erika, today is the first day of your lifetime walk down Jessup Prison's memory lane. You're going to have lots and lots of quality cell time. In prison, you will experience the inner panic and terror of loneliness and isolation. Erika, you are twenty-five years old with a life expectancy of another fifty years, of which you are going to have plenty of time to think about what you did to Josh and Geney."

Erika sat and looked away, shaking her head slightly. She was incensed. It was clear from the twisted expression on her face. One courtroom watcher later said that Erika seemed to be seething at the core of her being. This was one situation well beyond anything Erika could control, and she was livid at the notion that people were allowed to say such things about her.

Mark continued: "Erika, here's some reality. Benjamin won't be your cellmate at Jessup, and your backup death row husband (Jimmy) won't be stopping by for visits, either. . . . You're going to be locked up in a five-by-nine cell, hopefully painted purple, without a tanning booth and with no beach to sunbathe on, and you cannot bring your three pet snakes with you. . . . I don't think they will be serving crabs and cold beer. . . . Erika, your special treatment time is over." Erika was looking down and away. She didn't want to acknowledge Mark's comments by staring at him and showing any emotional reaction. As she did that, Mark said loudly, "Please look at me! . . . Please take a *long* look at me. Shortly you will hear Josh and Geney's message to you, it's judgment time. Thank you, Your Honor."

Mark walked back to his seat. There was total silence in the room. Some of Joshua's relatives sitting there had worn vials of his ashes around their necks in solidarity and support and love. In some ways, this plain gesture of honoring the dead was a subtle reminder to the judge—although none was surely needed—of what was left of Joshua's and Geney's bodies.

Cookie Grace stepped forward after the victims' families had their chance to speak. With pure and dramatic tears, which were certainly genuine and heartfelt,

Cookie said how sorry she was to the families of Geney and Joshua—and she meant it. She expressed her sympathies, then said, "I love my daughter and I wouldn't trade her for anyone in the world."

Erika was sentenced to life in prison, plus twenty years. Judge G. Edward Dwyer called Erika a "Jekyll and Hyde" after steadfastly denying a request by Erika that she be placed in a mental hospital.

"State prison," the judge chided.

Gavel.

Epilogue

Mitch Grace told me that he speaks with Erika by phone just about every day.

"I leave my phone line open between nine and ten-thirty A.M. during the week, in case Erika calls," he said.

Throughout this project, I asked Mitch questions based on information I had uncovered, with the implication that he would talk it over with Erika during those phone calls. I never received a straight answer to anything important I had ever asked. Most of Mitch's responses pertinent to the case—and what he wanted to share—are in this book.

Can we blame Mitch, however, for not wanting to ruin his daughter's chances on appeal?

Near the end of the project, I asked Mitch one last time to talk to Erika on my behalf. "Explain to her that I am offering her a voice in this book if she wants it. But time is running out."

Mitch said he would, but that Erika's lawyers would likely advise her to keep quiet.

Which she did.

I respect that.

In light of this offer, Mitch asked if he could extend it to several of Erika's fellow (and former) inmates.

"Sure," I said. "Like to hear from them."

And so . . . in came the letters. One batch of five. All of them had an "Erika is a loving and caring person" type of tone—that Erika was, more or less, nothing more than a "victim of love." That she had hooked up with an abusive, controlling, manipulative man, who had fundamentally stolen her emotional identity and then convinced her to do the unthinkable for (and with) him. He baited her, so to speak, and then set her up to take the fall for those crimes.

The evidence, of course, points to a far different scenario. Erika's own recollection of that night in the condo with Joshua and Geney, as she explained it to Secret Service SA Carri Campbell, telling her that she had told BJ to "just fucking do it," is, in and of itself, an entire contradiction to the story she would later refuse to let go of.

I do, however, respect the loyalty, love, and friendship these women, who *truly* believe in Erika, showed by writing to me. Many of them displayed an eternal devotion to Erika. There's a "you don't know the *real* Erika Sifrit" sense to these letters.

I cannot help but think that those of us who use the facts as our guide have been blinded somehow by our own ignorance. Is there a convicted criminal serving time for a crime—no matter what that crime is—who would ever condone the actions of a jury?

I have not yet met him or her.

One woman who wrote to me on Erika's behalf, Leslie Johnson, articulated her thoughts about Erika in a way that touched me. I feel for women like Leslie and, believe it or not, all the others who wrote to me. Many of these women are doing time in prison solely because the men they loved either abused them or dragged them down into an abyss of criminal activity, for which they saw no way out. Many of these women have children on the outside who are being taken care of by their mothers, friends, and relatives. Many of these women committed crimes to protect their children, to feed their children, and to give their children a chance in life. I've met women like this throughout my career. They get mixed up with a criminal, have his kids, and end up taking the fall with (or for) the guy when the ride is over. It's a sad American story played out in towns and cities across this nation, which usually involves the abuse of drugs and/or alcohol.

Still, this is a separate issue when we begin talking about Erika Grace Sifrit. Despite the role she now plays in prison when housed with these same women, Erika doesn't fit into this subsection of the criminal justice system.

Erika is a convicted murderer. She was not abused by her husband in this same way.

Leslie Johnson wrote, *I'm sure you have heard many horrible things about Erika because of the nature of her crime, but she is not a horrible person to me.*

Emphasis on *"to me."*

Those are the two words that truly belong in the context of these letters.

Erika Sifrit can be whatever and whoever she wants to be in prison: it is her domain now, her world. A place in which she is, essentially, preaching to a choir of women who will sympathize with her.

I'm not saying she is 100% innocent in this matter, Leslie continued, *but what she did was out of love and loyalty for her husband. . . . Some people, like myself, don't know who they are and need a man in our lives to define ourselves. So why is everyone so hard on Erika?*

Erika Sifrit was not codependent. She wants us now to believe she was, but that is not the truth of the matter, at least according to all of the available *evidence.*

* * *

I wrote to BJ Sifrit twice. I received a two-word response from him:

Not interested.

Mitch Grace and I went back and forth and spoke at length about his daughter's case, Erika's life before and after her arrest, his son-in-law, and a father's desperate love for his only child—a daughter beyond the reach of his comforting arms. There is a pain in Mitch's voice as he speaks—one that words on a page cannot convey. There is a part of his nature that screams of a father constantly questioning himself. Constantly wondering what tomorrow will bring. Constantly hoping that by some swipe of a magic wand, he will wake up one day and be told that his life for the past six-plus years has been a terrible nightmare.

Mitch asked me once, "What if this happened to your daughter, Mr. Phelps? Would you be doing anything different?"

I could not answer no.

During one conversation, I asked Mitch to please consider the idea that his daughter could be responsible for these heinous crimes, of which there is no plausible explanation. No *why*. No purpose.

I raised this person? I don't know this person. Who are you?

Although he steadfastly believes that BJ is fully responsible, and Erika was set up (but not totally innocent, either), Mitch Grace told me it wouldn't matter if Erika committed these crimes. She is all that he and Cookie have, and they will stand behind her until they leave this planet.

Erika should count her blessings that she has parents as loving and caring as Mitch and Cookie. She needs to stop lying to these people who raised her and tell them the truth so they can all move on from this and begin to heal.

They have time. Why waste it in a chasm of lies?

Mitch and Cookie deserve the truth.

Mitch has had a lawyer "on my payroll," he said half jokingly, for the past six years. As expected, Erika is exhausting every possible appeal and opportunity at her disposal to get out of prison. The Maryland Supreme Court rejected a 2005 appeal of her conviction and sentence.

As of this writing, Erika awaits a court date on a hearing regarding that seemingly open-ended agreement she signed with the state's attorney's office, and the possibility that she had inadequate counsel, which also includes a filing that she couldn't live without BJ and was abused by him and felt trapped into doing what he said—or else. Erika is claiming now that BJ had total control over her actions (the wizard behind the curtain). I'm told that the argument Erika will present in court is that she cannot be held "criminally responsible" for the murders and was incapable of conforming her own conduct because of the power BJ wielded—i.e., routine and constant spousal abuse.

When I called one of Erika's former supporters and told him about this development, he said, "You're kidding, right? This is a joke! Has to be."

It is clear in the information I uncovered and presented in this book that the polar opposite of that very weak argument is true.

Erika has new lawyers. Tom Ceraso and Arcky Tuminelli are out.

In November 2007, BJ and his lawyers requested a new trial. When I heard this, I thought, *Does this guy really want to roll the dice again with a jury?* Seems to me, he hit the jackpot last time around and should maybe just let sleeping dogs lie.

As Joel Todd told reporters back when BJ filed a motion for a new trial, this case is ongoing and seems to have no end. Just when you think you've learned something new about it, another bombshell regarding what happened is dropped.

Then, in September 2008, BJ and his camp made another move. BJ dropped his bid for a new trial and asked a federal court to throw out his conviction. The argument, legal experts note, is a pretty good one. BJ's new claim is that the state "violated his right to a fair trial by presenting a contradictory theory of how the crime occurred when it prosecuted his wife for the same slaying."

During BJ's trial, in other words, the state argued that he was the primary killer, the man with the gun in his hand. At Erika's trial, the same state prosecutors proposed the idea that Erika was the principal killer, bearing full responsibility for both deaths. In legal mumbo jumbo they call this a "federal habeas corpus petition." On the street, however, we call it a smart way to kick out the back door and find an easier way out of prison.

We shall see.

Law enforcement close to this case that I spoke to are convinced BJ and/or Erika are responsible for a murder outside Ocean City with certain earmarks and signatures shared by the two of them, but another man now serves prison time for that crime—maybe wrongly so. I was never given a name, state, town, or any details about the case that would help me begin to look into it myself.

I also spoke to one person who believes Erika and BJ could have killed in other states.

Who knows?

Once someone is convicted of a crime this evil, this gruesome, and this monstrous, the floodgates open and cold cases become hot.

What remains clear to me is that the horror Erika and BJ perpetrated against two wonderful, kind, caring, and loving human beings in Ocean City on that Saturday night before Memorial Day is, at its core, an immorality of such gargantuan proportions that the true nature behind these crimes can *never* be fully explained, understood, or accessed emotionally. It's hard to really wrap our minds around what happened in that bathroom after Geney and Joshua were so viciously murdered and, equally important, during the subsequent days when Erika and BJ were running around Ocean City seemingly celebrating what they had done.

Erika has her supporters. Indeed, they will always be there to cheer her on. They stand behind her. Friends and inmates she's met in prison. They claim the "real" Erika would never do something this despicable. That it "had to be" all BJ's doing. That he brainwashed her. That he abused her. That he put so much fear into her, she would do anything for him—including murder and dismemberment. I heard Stockholm syndrome mentioned. Patty Hearst.

But it must be understood that this is the story Erika promulgates behind those prison walls. I won't deny her the right to survive that environment the way in which she sees fit.

But it doesn't make any of it true.

The evidence, on the other hand, if *truly* looked at objectively, points directly to Erika's culpability, responsibility, and involvement. And if you look really hard, staying in between the lines of reality, you might even take a stab—no pun intended—at saying Erika could have played a larger role in this entire crime than BJ, and that two juries returned just verdicts.

Lastly, lives were ruined over this case. That much is a fact. But I want to point out that for the detectives involved—one of whom, entirely because of this case, no longer works for the OCPD detective squad—this case had an emotional impact on them the likes of which they will never be able to comprehend.

In closing, I'd like to speak directly to my readers. This is my tenth true crime book. I am entirely grateful for your support throughout the years, along with the opportunity you've given me to write these books. I want all of you to know that I read *every* e-mail and letter I receive. Even if I cannot answer each correspondence personally, I am indebted to have such wonderful, intelligent, dedicated readers.

I listen to your advice. I take into account the cases you suggest. And I always take the time to consider your thoughts.

I am a lucky author to have such dedicated, loyal fans. I never take any of this for granted.

If anyone wishes to contact me, please visit my Web site, *www.mwilliamphelps.com*, or write me at:

PO BOX 3215
Vernon, CT 06066

GREAT BOOKS,
GREAT SAVINGS!

When You Visit Our Website:
www.kensingtonbooks.com
You Can Save Money Off The Retail Price
Of Any Book You Purchase!

- **All Your Favorite Kensington Authors**
- **New Releases & Timeless Classics**
- **Overnight Shipping Available**
- **eBooks Available For Many Titles**
- **All Major Credit Cards Accepted**

Visit Us Today To Start Saving!
www.kensingtonbooks.com

All Orders Are Subject To Availability.
Shipping and Handling Charges Apply.
Offers and Prices Subject To Change Without Notice.